Public
Values,
Private
Lands

Public

Farmland

Values,

Preservation Policy,

Private

1933–1985

Lands

Tim Lehman

The University of North Carolina Press

Chapel Hill and London

© 1995 The University of North
Carolina Press
All rights reserved

Manufactured in the United States of
America

The paper in this book meets the
guidelines for permanence and dura-
bility of the Committee on Production Guidelines for Book Longevity of
the Council on Library Resources.

Tim Lehman is associate professor of
history at Rocky Mountain College.

Library of Congress Cataloging-in-
Publication Data
Lehman, Tim.
    Public values, private lands :
farmland preservation policy,
1933–1985 / by Tim Lehman.
        p.   cm.
    Includes bibliographical refer-
ences and index.
    ISBN 0-8078-2177-2 (cloth : alk.
paper). — ISBN 0-8078-4491-8
(pbk. : alk. paper)
    1. Land use, Rural—Government
policy—United States—History—
20th century.   2. Agricultural
conservation—Government policy—United States—History—20th
century.   I. Title.
HD256.L44   1995
338.76′16′0973—dc20   94-19636
                              CIP

99   98   97   96   95
5   4   3   2   1

For Kate,

Tom, and

Topher

Contents

Acknowledgments

Many people have helped to make this book possible. Otis Graham nurtured the project along from an early stage and has provided enormous inspiration and insight throughout. He believed in the manuscript when I lost faith, and he showed me how it could be better when I thought it was already good enough. It is no exaggeration to say that this book would not exist without his guidance. Many others have helped at crucial stages. William Leuchtenburg, Richard Andrews, Robert Healy, and Peter Coclanis read an earlier version of the manuscript carefully and saved me from many errors in writing and thinking. Douglas Helms and Wayne Rasmussen at USDA helped me to locate some invaluable sources. Many people were generous with their time and allowed me to interview them. They are listed in the bibliography; my thanks to all of them. In addition, Rupert Cutler, Senator James Jeffords, Charles Little, Neil Sampson, Howard Tankersly, and Warren Zitzmann allowed me to read through their personal papers on farmland preservation. This kindness gave me access to written documents that compensated in part for the relative scarcity of archival materials on so recent a historical topic. My thanks also to the editors of *Agricultural History* and *Environmental History* for allowing me to use material which first appeared in these journals. Paul Betz, Lewis Bateman, and Christi Stanforth, my editors at UNC Press, were helpful and patient in encouraging this project into its final form. Together these people have taught me that scholarship can be humane and collegial, and for that I am grateful.

Abbreviations

AAA	Agricultural Adjustment Administration
AFT	American Farmland Trust
BAE	Bureau of Agricultural Economics
CEQ	Council on Environmental Quality
CRP	Conservation Reserve Program
CRS	Congressional Research Service
EPA	Environmental Protection Agency
ERS	Economic Research Service
FSA	Farm Security Administration
GAO	General Accounting Office
NACD	National Association of Conservation Districts
NALS	National Agricultural Lands Study
NRB	National Resources Board
NRI	National Resources Inventory

Public

Values,

Private

Lands

Introduction

In 1960, as incoming president John F. Kennedy assembled his staff, he had this instruction for Harvard economist John Kenneth Galbraith: "I don't want to hear about agriculture from anyone but you, Ken, and I don't want to hear about it from you either." When Kennedy ordered his staff to prepare reports on all major policy problems facing the nation, agriculture was not among the topics.[1] The urbane president had little taste for agricultural problems, and the urban nation paid little attention to farmers or farmland. Agriculture was distinctly out of fashion among policymakers and historians alike. To the liberals of the sixties, farm problems were an anachronism and farmers were politically retrograde. Intellectual energies were turned toward more modern problems.

This perception changed during the seventies as a variety of interlocking crises focused attention again (for the first time since the thirties) on agriculture as a legitimate issue for a progressive political agenda and as a serious subject for historical inquiry. The new agriculture was a changed topic from the one which Kennedy had so easily dismissed. Environmental concerns about land use and chemical pollution, questions about world food scarcities, renewed concern about soil erosion and water shortages, and a revival of interest in small farming all challenged the postwar consensus that farm problems could be solved chiefly by restraining production. One issue in particular—the preservation of agricultural lands—proved strong enough to resist the conservative swing of the 1980 election. When President Reagan's choice for secretary of agriculture, John Block, announced his support for federal policies to protect prime agricultural lands, he provoked the pious secretary of the interior, James Watt, to utter what some say were his only profane words; they were edited for publication as "Holy cow!"[2]

During the 1970s, concern for the supply of farmland was only part of a larger challenge to the complacency of the agricultural establishment. The mainstream view for a generation had been that agriculture was remarkably successful in producing abundant food at low cost for an increasing percentage of the world's population. One commonly recited statistic was that one American farmer raised enough to feed fifty or more of the world's hungry people.[3] Problems arose only when food was not distributed fairly among the poorer nations and when the inevitable social adjustment off of the land proved difficult for small farmers. But these were accepted as technical problems or perhaps political problems—certainly not as fundamental flaws in an overwhelmingly successful food-producing system. The Department of Agriculture provided institutional support for these ideas, major commodity organizations organized political support, and the discipline of agricultural economics marshaled intellectual backing.

During the seventies a competing view emerged that saw agriculture not as a success story but as a social and ecological failure. In its single-minded preoccupation with food production, the agricultural establishment had become a lopsided creature that ignored ecological or social complexity. Agriculture, critics charged, dumped chemicals into the soil and water; produced chemically tainted and nutritionally inadequate foods; mined nonrenewable soil, water, and energy resources; depended dangerously on a monoculture that rested on a slender genetic reservoir and vulnerable technology; and mistreated the rural poor and farm workers. This critique began with an indictment of federal agricultural policy, agricultural research, and corporate farming. Ultimately, the search for causes of the crisis led to capitalist agriculture, scientific hubris, and the deeply embedded cultural ethos that encouraged humankind's domination of nature.[4] Advocating a new kind of farming that was variously termed organic, sustainable, or renewable, these critics argued for an agriculture more sensitive to natural limits and less disruptive of natural ecosystems. Implicit in this critique was a sense that agriculture's most basic resource—land—was itself in limited supply.

This mixture of concerns within this movement to preserve agricultural land naturally led to some confusion as to the movement's definition and goals. Farmland preservation might mean efforts to preserve the family farm by encouraging agricultural units to be small and family-owned. Farmland preservation also could be linked to the quality of the soil—that is, to soil conservation. This study is concerned more with the quantity of farmland acres—specifically, the protection of agricultural land from conversion to urban and related uses. Different constituencies might give a different twist to these meanings; for example, some farmers wanted to "preserve family farms and farmland" but were generally less interested in rural land use planning or other remedies proposed by conservationists. While these issues blur together in places, my interest is primarily in the history of the unfulfilled hopes for agricultural land use planning.

The movement to preserve agricultural land, so defined, should find its place among land use history and, more broadly, environmental history. The traditional subject for historians concerned with land has been the public domain, first as it was rapidly parceled into private hands during the nineteenth century and then as various conservationists attempted to reclaim a public interest in these private land parcels during the twentieth century. The history of the American land has often been synonymous with the history of the public domain;[5] this study, on the other hand, is a part of the history of the attempt to attach public values to that portion of the American land— approximately two-thirds—that lies in the private domain. In that sense this study is an attempt to follow the advice of eminent public land historian Paul W. Gates, who in 1976 concluded an essay on public land policy with this assertion: "[W]hile the management of our remaining public domain is still a most serious and important problem, the management of that portion of our territory that has become private property is a more serious problem. In fact, the old distinction between public and private is losing its sharpness, or is being eroded away, and for the sake of later generations it should be. Has a man a right to destroy good, irreplaceable agricultural land by covering it up with cement or stripmining it?"[6]

Gates's question gets at a fundamental issue of this study. If private land has inherent public values, how is it to be governed in a society that resists regulatory controls? In particular, in a society that views the farmer as the paragon of individual freedom, how is farmland to be governed for the sake of long-term environmental and social benefits? And how can the federal government protect the national interest in private land when land use has traditionally been a policy arena for state and local governments? In their attempts to answer these questions, the soil conservation movement of the 1930s and the environmental movement of the 1970s ran squarely against the profound American hostility toward centralized regulatory controls. Scholars in recent years have begun to draw a picture of the state in America as structurally fragmented and profoundly decentralized in comparison with its European counterparts.[7] Conservationists in the 1930s and 1970s challenged these characteristics by calling for coordinated policy planning and federal recognition of a national interest in private lands. Recent scholars have also noted that the modern American state has grown up together with social science expertise, which, despite its promise of providing value-free guidance, has exerted a profound and frequently unexpected influence on the making of social and environmental policy. Farmland preservation, like many social and environmental issues, involved the competing claims of social science experts. At that level the question was not one of popular appeal but of technical expertise, and the demand for certainty of information worked against reform. The themes here thus make up part of the larger fabric of twentieth-century American political history; they illustrate how the antistatist political culture of the United States, combined with the workings of scientific expertise, helped to create the conditions for reform, shaped the contours of reform, and ultimately provided the resistance to reform.

The Rise and Fall of New Deal Agricultural Land Use Planning

Roots of the Conservation Movement

"The soil must be governed," wrote Russell Lord in 1938, at a time when concern for the public protection of private agricultural land was strong.[1] There have been only two serious attempts in our history to regulate agricultural land use at the national level as a response to anticipated shortage and resource abuse—one during the New Deal and a second during the 1970s. Although the circumstances were in many ways different, the mere fact that the problem reappeared suggests that the first attempt at controlling land use was not completely successful. In many ways the rise and fall of the land use issue during the New Deal brings to mind Paul Conkin's observation that "the story of the New Deal is a sad story, the ever recurring story of what might have been."[2] While this statement may not stand as a comprehensive judgment on the New Deal, it holds some truth for the more experimental reforms of the decade. This sense of missed opportunity does not mean that New Deal land use reform lacked vision or ran out of ideas. The sadness comes not from the internal inadequacies of the reform ideas but from the external obstacles to change. This is not the story of a reform that failed; rather, it is the story of another reform that was never fully tried.

New Deal land use reform was a natural, perhaps even inevitable, reaction to the historical pattern of land abuse in the United States. Until the twentieth century this pattern of soil exploitation, what Lord called a "soil rush," was conditioned by the abundance of land. Farmland was traditionally cultivated for as long as it was fertile, and when the topsoil washed away or became exhausted, the farmer would find new lands to the west. Predictably, the earliest concerns for better land use grew up in the agriculturally declining areas left behind. In New England soil reformers such as Jared Eliot and Isaac Hill urged better care of the land, while in the Old South John Tyler and later Edmund Ruffin linked soil conservation to the future of southern civilization. These early soil conservationists are usually remembered for their technical refinements—Ruffin's experiments with marl for fertilizer, for example—but they also called for better land management practices, such as crop rotation, smaller and more intensively cultivated farms, and the retirement of hilly and other highly erodible lands. In keeping with the dominant ideas of their time, however, they did not advocate government action and instead relied solely on private initiative.[3]

The period of greatest soil exploitation up to the New Deal era came in the last half of the nineteenth century. Between 1850 and 1930 the amount of land in farms more than tripled, rising from 239 million acres to 987 million acres. The most rapid period of expansion came in the last two decades of the nineteenth century, when over 300 million acres of new land were opened to cultivation. Even though most of the best lands were claimed by 1890, settlement continued to expand into environmentally sensitive lands, especially on the Great Plains.[4] This agricultural expansion came just as agriculture was increasingly being incorporated into national and international markets. This more thoroughly commercialized agriculture gave farmers an economic incentive to cultivate marginal lands and to ignore erosion for the sake of maximum production. Federal land policies assisted the pattern of abuse, because they opened vast amounts of land to agriculture with no apparent regard to environmental costs.[5]

This rush to farm the unexploited lands of the Great Plains did not go without protest. In 1878 John Wesley Powell, fresh from his explorations of the Colorado River, issued his *Report on the Lands of the Arid Regions,* a call for land classification and planned settlement in the arid West. He believed that western lands should be divided into three "great classes"—irrigation, timber, and pasture—according to their "physical conditions" of temperature, soil, and rainfall. Classification would become the basis for "comprehensive plans" that would be necessary for the "redemption of these lands."[6] Powell's environmentalism and his collectivism made his plan twice damned in the nineteenth century but provided a precedent for the conservation efforts of the twentieth.

The most sustained criticism of nineteenth century land use practices, however, came from George Perkins Marsh, who in 1864 published his classic *Man and Nature.* Marsh, a Vermonter, took a global view of a full range of environmental problems. He challenged the prevailing notion that resources were inexhaustible and argued instead that "the ravages committed by man subvert the relations and destroy the balance which nature has established." Although he concentrated on problems of deforestation, given his holistic view Marsh could not ignore agriculture's potential for disturbing nature's balance. He complained that "the slovenly husbandry of the border settler soon exhausts the luxuriance of his first fields, and compels him to remove his household gods to a fresher soil." Marsh also believed that farming had "felled enough trees everywhere" and insisted that there should be a "fixed ratio" between "wood land and plow land" in order to restore nature's equilibrium. Yet Marsh had no confidence in the "action of local or general legislatures" because "public property is not sufficiently respected in the United States." Rather, he trusted "the diffusion of general intelligence on the subject, and . . . enlightened self-interest."[7]

Other late-nineteenth-century critics worried that destructive farming practices resembled the "cut and run" habits of loggers and that the better-publicized fear of a "timber famine" had its parallel in an impending "soil famine." Thomas Magee, a western writer, warned that American farmers had "reduced a soil from virgin richness to utter barrenness" and admonished the country to be "land-killers . . .

no longer." John Strong of California fingered monoculture for blame: "The constant and changeless cultivation of any plant will exhaust the earth. . . . The history of grain culture . . . is a complete illustration of the folly, if not iniquity, of man's violation of this inexorable and immutable law of nature." This concern was echoed in the East; one Vermont writer noted that many hill farms in New England were "played out" when the farmers moved west.[8]

Early in the twentieth century these concerns reached a crescendo in the conservation movement led by President Theodore Roosevelt and his chief forester, Gifford Pinchot. Issues of public forested lands dominated this movement, both because the legal rationale was clearer for controls on public than on private lands and because the intellectual rationale, based on the ideas of Marsh and the worries about a timber famine, viewed deforestation as the primary environmental threat. Yet the same logic that guided the national forests—the logic of planned use according to nature's dictates—could also apply to private agricultural lands.[9] This land use planning concept appeared in the three-volume inventory of forest, land, and mineral resources released by Roosevelt's National Conservation Commission in 1909. The report made explicit the connection between population, soil exhaustion, and the supply of agricultural land. "Our population will increase steadily," the commission reported, "but there is a definite limit to our cultivated acreage." With the best farmland already in cultivation and the best topsoil already mined, the necessary increases in food production would have to come from higher productivity per acre. This meant that "our mode of farming," which "neither conserves the soil nor secures full crop returns," would have to change. Combining Progressivism's moralism and its emphasis on efficient use of resources, the conservation commission pronounced erosion both wasteful and an "evil" to be "remedied without delay." In a creative and still untried use of liability law, the report called for communities and states to consider soil erosion "a public nuisance"; accordingly, the report maintained that the landowner "should be held liable for resulting damages to neighboring lands and streams."[10]

Some observers echoed these themes in more explicit language. Railroad magnate James J. Hill, the eccentric plutocrat who became converted to Malthusian ideas, thought that "the proper utilization of the soil" was "the first and most necessary item of conservation." In a series of lectures later published in book form, he complained that "the exhaustion of virgin fertility" had proceeded so rapidly that natural soil productivity had in a few decades "already deteriorated more than it should have in five centuries of use." This wastefulness was especially dangerous, Hill concluded, because anticipated population increases meant that "an army of another hundred million people" were "marching in plain sight toward us, and expecting and demanding that they shall be fed."[11] Although most Department of Agriculture scientists considered Hill an extremist, one of USDA's leading soil chemists and most flamboyant personalities, Harvey W. Wiley, went even further in condemning America's land use habits. The "agricultural rapist," Wiley wrote, had exhausted in less than a century the abundance of thousands of years of stored soil fertility. With "virgin fertility" exhausted and virtually no land still available for "new conquests," conservation and restoration of the soil were essential. American agricultural history was, for Wiley, "the history of bad farming."[12]

Another source of concern about land during the early part of the century was expressed in the Country Life movement. This loosely connected movement shared many of the same ideas and some of the same personalities as the conservation movement. It focused on improving the quality of rural life in America, in part through a more efficient agriculture. The first report of the Commission on Country Life, issued in 1908, expressed worry about the "lessening productiveness of the land" due to the "mining of virgin fertility." The Country Life movement, more than the conservation movement, emphasized the relation between land and society. "The social condition of any agricultural community," the report stated, "is closely related to the available fertility of the soil." This relationship was especially crucial now that available new lands were limited, thus forcing a "certain class of the population" to move to "poor lands, becoming a handicap to the community and constituting a very difficult social problem." The report warned that continued "soil deterioration" could lead to farmers' becoming a "dependent class," as southern sharecroppers already had. Thus in the Country Life movement a Malthusian concern about agricultural inefficiency blended with a social emphasis on rural poverty—two problems that both stemmed from "a lack of appreciation of our responsibility to society to protect and save the land."[13]

L. C. Gray and New Theories of Land Use Policy

A direct link from the first conservation movement to the New Deal came in the person of Lewis Cecil Gray, who extended the logic of conservation to agricultural lands. Gray was steeped in the ethos of progressive conservation at the University of Wisconsin; he began his graduate education there in 1908, at the vibrant center of reform ideas in terms of both place and time. He matured in an intellectual climate heavily influenced by the Turner thesis, by the progressive notion that government had a positive role to play in regulating the economy and especially in managing natural resources, and by a firm belief in the duty of the professional to serve the public interest. It should come as no surprise that Gray accepted the idea of land scarcity; thought that government planning of natural resources should replace the laissez-faire approach; and served his career, Paul W. Gates later remembered, as a "lovable, gentle, and thoughtful" government official who inspired his staff to work extra hours in pursuit of high ideals.[14] Gray maintained that whereas the first conservation movement challenged "the assumption of . . . abundance in regards to forest, mineral and water resources," his efforts involved applying the same ideas to agricultural lands. The focus on publicly owned land had now shifted, Gray thought, because "the land problems of the future have to do mainly with the utilization of lands in private ownership."[15]

Just as the first conservation movement was based in part on the emerging science of forestry, so the land utilization movement of the 1920s sprang from the new academic discipline of rural land economics. L. C. Gray's mentor at Wisconsin, Richard T. Ely, played a signal role in the development of this new profession. Ely was educated in Germany, where he became immersed in ideas of scientific forestry, interventionist economics, and the positive role of government in society. He came to believe that the state was, as he later wrote, "a guardian of the permanent interests of society," especially of society's natural resources.[16] Contrary to the laissez-faire tradition, Ely held that government could improve society and that social scientists had a professional obligation to join academic research with the public interest. Ely was thus part of that emerging managerial class of which Gifford Pinchot was the best-known member.

At the University of Wisconsin Ely developed a curriculum in the economics of resource conservation as early as 1892 and began to train graduate students to conduct research in this new field. In 1919 Ely and some of his former students convinced Secretary of Agriculture David Houston, himself an agricultural economist, to start a Division of Land Economics, headed by L. C. Gray, in the Department of Agriculture. In 1922 Gray's division was incorporated into the new Bureau of Agricultural Economics (BAE); it became the focus for land use research throughout the twenties and thirties. Also during 1922, at the National Agricultural Conference called by President Harding, Ely called for a new national land policy. He contended that land policy should not be tailored to the agricultural depression then beginning but must be "fundamental and far-reaching" so as to make "this and succeeding emergencies . . . less acute." Noting that "satisfactory land settlement presupposes quality classification," Ely defined land policy as "a conscious program of social control with respect to the acquisition, ownership, conservation, and uses of the land." Convinced that "the era of free, accessible land of good quality is past," the conference committee on land recommended that "a deliberate and unified plan of national land utilization is imperative."[17]

The best look into the intellectual mindset of the early land use thinkers can be found in the report of the Committee on Land Utilization appointed in 1921 by Secretary Wallace and chaired by L. C. Gray.[18] Published in the 1923 *Yearbook of Agriculture,* this analysis of land use problems was the most comprehensive to date and in many ways anticipated the work of the National Resources Board (NRB) a decade later. One agricultural economist called the 1923 report "a significant turning point in land policy thinking" and considered it more authoritative because it was backed by the research of the new academic discipline of rural land economics.[19] Gray's analysis marked an interesting midpoint between the conservation movements of the Progressive and New Deal eras as it echoed themes of the older movement and anticipated ideas that reached fuller form in the 1930s. He noted the deterioration of soil resources, which in some ways paralleled the decline of forest resources, and worried not so much about a timber famine as about actual food shortages in the future. Gray's report deplored waste, sought more efficient land use patterns, and habitually spoke in terms of conserving resources for future generations. Later in the century conservation goals often would be held in conflict with economic efficiency, but for Gray the two concepts were intertwined: conservation meant long-term, efficient production. Gray found the culprit for soil exploitation in the nineteenth-century policies that hurried the transfer of the public domain into private hands. Past land policies and an unregulated market economy shared the blame for "the fact that our forests have been wastefully sacrificed, our soils needlessly impaired, and the entire fabric of our rural civilization has come to manifest serious depreciation." Gray concluded that "the let alone policy of the past few decades has been a source of enormous economic waste and social misery."[20]

Gray's thinking was heavily influenced by the turn-of-the-century sense of limits on the amount of available land. Having witnessed the closing of the frontier, Gray and other land use reformers tended toward the Malthusian notion that continued population growth eventually would press upon the supply of agricultural land. Although the population growth rate had slowed from 35 percent per decade in the 1850s to only 15 percent in the 1910s, Gray anticipated a national population of about 150 million by midcentury. This analysis of past population growth showed that the nation had "reached an apogee of agricultural land supply in proportion to population about three decades ago, and . . . we have entered a period which will necessarily be marked by a continually increasing scarcity of land." The problem was not an absolute shortage of land; rather, it was that forest, grazing, and crop uses of the same land competed against each other and that, as a result, there was "practically no important reserve area for the expansion of any one of these three uses except at the expense of the others." Even a midcentury population of 150 million would force either economies in production or reductions in per capita consumption. "Consequently," Gray continued, "the growth of our population has resulted in an ever-increasing scarcity of our land area."[21]

This Malthusianism, still present in 1923, receded to the distant background by the 1930s. Continued farm surpluses and declining birth rates in Europe and America led land use reformers to worry more about overexpansion of agriculture than eventual shortages. Some demographic projections looked for the nation's population to decline after reaching its projected midcentury peak of 150 million. Stationary populations in some European nations, falling fertility rates in the United States, and lower enrollments in elementary schools seemed to confirm that the United States was following Europe in this "demographic transition" to a mature society.[22] In 1932 Gray wrote confidently that "in the present century at least," only half of the nation's land would be needed for crops, leaving the rest for forest, wildlife, or other environmental uses.[23] This meant that in the short term, at least, Gray favored a contraction in the amount of land in farms and in the number of farmers. This temporary decrease, or "adjustment," would promote the long-term prosperity of commercial farmers as well as more efficient, conservation-oriented land use patterns. This long-term adjustment could only be accomplished, Gray reasoned, with "a policy of unified and systematic direction to land settlement." Even if the "extreme physical limits" of food production were never reached, Gray maintained, it was helpful to know what they were. Although Gray was not an ecologist, he wrote of physical limits as an ecologist would of carrying capacity, with a constant awareness of land as an actual or potential limiting factor in population growth.[24]

The logical first step in this process of rationalizing land use patterns was to reconcile the contradictory land use activities of the federal government. Initially this effort called not for an increase in federal authority but for a coordination of existing authority. According to Gray, "the essential need is for a unification in the future development of national land policies. Unfortunately during the past hundred years the different functions connected with land policy have been distributed among various government agencies." Yet these functions, although scattered throughout the federal bureaucracy, were "vitally interrelated, requiring unification in administration." In particular, Gray hoped to rein in the growing irrigation empire of Elwood Mead in the Interior Department's Bureau of Reclamation. Reclamation, Gray wrote, was "carried out with little attempt to relate the rate of reclamation to the nation's needs for farm land" and was a "sectional rather than a national" policy that encouraged settlement in areas not well adapted to permanent agriculture. Expansion of irrigation without regard to demand for additional farm crops added to already depressed farm markets and exacerbated the problems of existing farmers. In 1926 Gray proposed that the Department of Agriculture create a central agency to unify the department's land policies.[25] This modest proposal came to life briefly during the later years of the New Deal, but it did not last. Even if it had, it would have coordinated only one department and left the Bureau of Reclamation to pursue its own empire of irrigation. Ironically, the New Deal created new agencies, each charged with a special purpose, and so made Gray's goal—to have the government recognize the economic and ecological interrelationship of all land uses—even more elusive.

Central to Gray's vision for a new national land policy were land use classification, land planning according to its best use, and the extension of conservation measures from public to private lands. Gray argued in 1929 for a "program of land classification and regional planning based on a careful study of the physical and economic characteristics of the region."[26] Classification included both economic and ecological considerations. Soil surveys, "natural science" studies of vegetative cover, and agronomist studies of soil yields and erosion rates would be combined with economic studies such as the size and location of markets and available transportation to determine what use was best for different areas of the country. Aside from John Wesley Powell's survey of arid lands, classification had little precedent in this country. The idea rested on the new realization that not all vacant land is suitable for farmland, as nineteenth-century land policies had assumed, and on the assumption that government policy should encourage and perhaps require classified lands—whether public or private—to be used for their designated purpose. Here the Progressive notions of efficient use and sustained yield were taken from timber to soil and from public lands to private. Land classification would become the basis for federal conservation policy on all of the nation's lands.

The most urgent need for classification as a prelude to ending destructive land uses was on the Great Plains, where, as Richard T. Ely had stated in 1922, "land suitable for grazing only has been plowed up," causing such erosion that "a hundred years would not be sufficient to repair the damage." In fact, a dozen years before the dust storms of the 1930s, Ely added that "the good elements in the land have blown away." But the Great Plains area was only the starting point. "Gradually," Gray hoped, "the program of classifying the land, formulating a program of utilization, and replanning community life would be extended to areas where economic distress and disorganization are less acute."[27]

Classification of lands also formed the basis for differentiation of farmlands. Some soils and some regions were better adapted to certain crops by virtue of soil type, climate, or available markets. This idea of regional specialization became the focus of a bill offered to Congress in 1930. Developed by Howard Tolley and M. L. Wilson, the bill was known by the name of its congressional sponsor, Victor Christgau of Minnesota. The Christgau bill divided the country into distinct agricultural regions, each with its own planning board composed of farmers and specialists who would provide information on the best crops and latest techniques to make the most of each region's comparative advantage. Supporters of the bill hoped that no coercion would be necessary, that farmers would voluntarily cooperate in achieving the desired changes in land use. According to Christgau, this decentralized planning structure would not only plan with nature, it would maintain farm incomes by providing a "scientific adjustment of production."[28] The Christgau bill reflected the economists' perception that land use maladaptations were a central cause of the agricultural depression and therefore that a solution to the problem of farm income must begin with more efficient patterns of land use. Russell Lord later wrote that the principal purpose of the bill was "not simply to raise farm income" but that the bill was meant "primarily as a device for national planning" in agricultural land use.[29]

When the Christgau bill became stalled in a congressional committee, land use reformers turned to the executive branch for support. Gray convinced BAE chief Nils Olsen of the need for a national conference on land utilization to build support for the issue among farm organizations. Secretary of Agriculture Arthur Hyde went along with the idea in part because it would be a way for his department to claim leadership on land issues and thereby get ahead of the newly created Federal Farm Board and the older Bureau of Reclamation. Also, a conference might help calm the cries for more action to alleviate the plight of farmers. The reformers' agenda came together with these political and bureaucratic needs to convince Hyde to call such a national meeting. Sponsored by the Department of Agriculture in conjunction with the Association of Land Grant Colleges and Universities, the National Conference on Land Utilization met in Chicago on 19–21 November 1931. Attended by over 350 people representing various government agencies, land grant schools, farm groups, conservationists, and business groups, this conference marked the culmination of pre–New Deal thinking about agricultural land use.[30]

The conference gave widespread support to the conclusions that L. C. Gray had reached nearly a decade earlier. In the opening address Secretary Hyde announced that the "epic of land settlement" had been completed. It was now time, Hyde continued, to "write a new epic" that would limit agricultural production, check erosion, and "conserve our land inheritance."[31] Other speakers agreed that chaotic land policies had contributed to farmers' distress; they emphasized the need for a "proper land policy" that would control surpluses by keeping marginal land out of production. Soil conservationists, concerned with "the permanency of American agriculture," stressed that "the time will come when we will need every acre of productive land." Different reasoning led participants to the same conclusions: classification of private lands; increased regulation of the public domain for watershed, rangeland, and timber production; public acquisition of marginal lands; and further restrictions on the expansionary tendencies of federal reclamation projects or private land settlement projects. Richard T. Ely took personal pleasure from the conference because so many of its participants were his former students, and its results made him feel "in sight of the promised land."[32]

Two committees—the National Land-Use Planning Committee and the National Advisory and Legislative Committee on Land Use—were created to carry on the work of the conference. The first was a technical committee composed of representatives from the land grant colleges and from federal agencies dealing with rural land, such as the Department of Agriculture, the Department of the Interior, and the Federal Farm Board. The second, a political committee, was composed of representatives from the major farm organizations, conservation and business groups, and the farm press. Guiding both committees was the executive secretary of the Planning Committee, L. C. Gray. For two years these committees were the focus of the increasing interest in land use. With support coming from such diverse sources as the Farm Bureau, social workers, conservationists, the *Saturday Evening Post,* and the *New Republic,* Gray thought that land use ideas had spread beyond the experts and had "come to have significance for the average citizen."[33]

A second, distinct movement for better land use also developed during the 1920s; this one focused not on economics but on soil erosion and was led by Hugh Hammond Bennett. Raised on a family farm in North Carolina, Bennett had been active in the Division of Soil Erosion since nearly the turn of the century. In 1928 he sounded the alarm with *Soil Erosion—A National Menace,* in which he warned that "the evil process [of soil erosion] is gaining momentum" and could be stopped only by "a tremendous national awakening."[34] Bennett's personal style earned him the reputation of a "professional" alarmist among his critics but also inspired a large and loyal following. For Bennett, soil erosion was an affront to both morality and economy, and his conservation efforts combined the fervor of a religious crusade with the technical expertise of the social scientist. From the beginning Bennett emphasized a comprehensive approach to erosion control using a variety of techniques and based on the premise that soil should be used according to its natural characteristics. For instance, hillsides, thin soils, or other erodible lands should not be cropped intensively but rather should be put to such uses as grazing or timber. Physical factors determined the land's best use, and erosion control was inseparable from land use control.[35] At Bennett's urging, in 1929 Congress appropriated $160,000 to the Department of Agriculture for erosion control; that year Bennett also helped to establish the nation's first agricultural experiment station, at Guthrie, Oklahoma, to study and demonstrate ways of holding the soil. Two years later Congress doubled the funding, and the department set up nine other research stations. Despite this activity, on the eve of the New Deal the Department of Agriculture had neither a coherent policy nor a coordinated program concerning soil erosion.

The New Deal's First Land Policies

By the 1932 presidential campaign, talk of land use was building in both parties. Republican secretary of agriculture Hyde persuaded his party to accept a platform plank calling for the retirement of submarginal lands, and President Herbert Hoover called for the Department of Agriculture to be reorganized into a Department of Agriculture, Land Use, and Conservation and for government to begin leasing submarginal farmland in order to retire it to other uses. In keeping with his principles, however, Hoover supported land use reforms that could be made in the name of efficiency but stopped short of any federal initiative that might be construed as coercive.[36]

The Democratic Party's support for land use was much stronger. Candidate Franklin Roosevelt was governor of New York, the state to which the 1931 Conference on Land Utilization looked for a model on the retirement of marginal farmland.[37] At the 1931 Conference of Governors Roosevelt delivered a speech entitled "Acres Fit and Unfit," in which he advocated withdrawing the nation's submarginal land from farming. In his major farm policy speech, delivered the next summer in Topeka, Roosevelt spoke in favor of "a definite policy looking to the planned use of the land."[38] Roosevelt's instinctive receptiveness to land use ideas was backed by Rexford Tugwell, who advised Roosevelt on farm issues. Tugwell had written in 1929 that land abuse had "no single danger to compare with it in ultimate consequence" and that conservation was therefore at the heart of the farm problem. He reasoned that a national land use program should regulate public lands and "control the private use of the areas held by individuals to whatever extent is necessary for maintaining continuous productivity."[39] M. L. Wilson, who taught at Montana State College and became another of Roosevelt's advisers, believed that "[t]he whole conservation idea leads easily and naturally to the idea of planning." When M. L. Wilson presented candidate Roosevelt with a proposal for government purchase of submarginal lands and agricultural planning based on local, regional, and national planning committees, Roosevelt responded, "See here, Mr. Wilson, is this your plan or my plan?"[40]

Although land use concerns had dominated the thinking of many land economists during the decade prior to the New Deal, the urgency of the Great Depression meant that the New Deal's first major agricultural legislation, the Agricultural Adjustment Act of 1933, did not deal with land use concerns. In fact, some of Roosevelt's advisers were cool to the domestic allotment scheme precisely because, as Rexford Tugwell advised, "It adjusts the supply to the moment's market, but it neither conserves the land nor makes provisions for permanently bettering farmers' lives."[41] Wilson worried that a general acreage contraction would not necessarily move production away from marginal lands or concentrate farming on lands that had comparative advantages. Nevertheless, he supported the domestic allotment idea because it would "stimulate a great lot of discussion and talk about planning" and could "act as a cat's paw which will at least drag into discussion the principles of the Christgau bill and a new land policy bill."[42] Although the planners preferred the land use approach of the Christgau bill, they supported the Agricultural Adjustment Act because they hoped it would inject a measure of government planning into agriculture and become the beginning of a more satisfactory approach.

Resource issues did, however, become a central part of the thinking of the New Deal's planning agency, which went by several names. Created in 1933 as the National Planning Board, it became the National Resources Board in 1934, then the National Resources Committee in 1935; finally, in 1939, it received its best-remembered name—the National Resources Planning Board. In 1934 the NRB issued a comprehensive survey of the nation's natural resources, the land use section of which synthesized the work of Gray and others and gave more authority to the land utilization ideas that had been building for a decade. The quality of analysis surpassed anything previous to it; the report reads remarkably well even today. It anticipated many of the concerns of the 1970s environmental movement and suggested solutions that remain untried and scarcely considered half a century later. Contradicting the received tradition, the report asserted the primacy of public interest over private property rights. "Heedless and unplanned land exploitation" that served "merely private advantage" should give way, the report argued, to federal land policies geared to the "general welfare." Most of the serious land problems, the report reasoned, grew from the "virtually unlimited powers of use and abuse which we have permitted in our system of private property in land." Although the government had hastened land into private hands throughout the nineteenth century, considerations of the public welfare should convince governments—especially state governments, which had the clearest constitutional claim—to assume their "reserved rights in land."[43] The Land Committee of the Board considered itself to be on the verge of a new historical era in which public stewardship would overtake private interests in land. The history of the next fifty years proved this hope to be far too optimistic.

The Land Committee's report weighed carefully the future supply and demand for agricultural land. While the report acknowledged the crucial role of population growth in projecting demand for agricultural products, it was heavily influenced by the decline in birth rates during the depression and followed other demographic projections that population would stabilize by 1960 at just over 140 million and perhaps decline after that. The report went beyond conventional analysis in considering the uncertain pace of industrial recovery as an influence on the demand for agricultural land. A full recovery might mean labor-saving machinery and thus a reduction in the farm population by one-third to one-half, the report calculated, while an incomplete recovery would mean more "crude, self-sufficing" farms, which required more land and had a "lower standard of living than is desirable." Thus the demand for agricultural land would increase at an uncertain rate, while yield per acre, the Land Committee and all other analysts projected, would see no significant increases. In retrospect, this miscalculation is glaring, particularly in light of the fact that Secretary of Agriculture Henry A. Wallace perhaps knew as much about the productive potential of corn hybrids as almost anyone in the country. Wallace had experimented with corn hybrids while in college and in 1924 had developed the first hybrid seed corn for actual use. During his tenure as secretary of agriculture he delighted in discussing the scientific details of hybrids with USDA scientists and predicted in 1933 that corn yields could rise 20 percent in ten years, thus releasing corn acreage for other uses.[44]

The Land Committee, however, was less impressed by hybrid potential and more impressed by long-term soil exhaustion. The foreseeable advances in hybrid seed varieties and fertilizers, the committee reasoned, would be offset by the lower yields achieved as farmers moved onto the arid Great Plains and as the long-term loss of fertility from soil erosion became more acute. Together with the overgrazing of western rangelands and the depletion of forests, the evidence led the committee to conclude that "the agricultural resources of the nation as a whole are declining." Wallace concurred that "unfettered individualism" had led to a national tradition of soil exploitation that had damaged the productive potential of tens of millions of acres and threatened to "destroy the physical foundations of national longevity."[45]

The Land Committee's serious underestimation of productivity was matched by its projections for early population stabilization. In one sense these two trends have compensated for each other, leaving the nation in a roughly analogous situation in the 1970s as the 1930s. The matter of which of these two forces, population or productivity, has the most independent momentum was and is the most important determinant of the seriousness of impending land scarcity. The best evidence of the 1930s led analysts to underestimate both. As a result, the report foresaw the need for nearly 30 million acres of new cropland by 1960 plus another 25 million acres to compensate for lands withdrawn from production. This long-range forecast of scarcity in the face of New Deal policies to reduce farm acreage might seem "strange," the report admitted, but the apparent contradiction made sense if one understood the difference between emergency measures to ease farmers through the 1930s and 1940s and permanent policy to protect long-term land resources.[46]

Against this backdrop in overall supply and demand for agricultural land, the Land Committee gave special attention to several critical problems in land use. One problem area that was forcing its way onto the land use agenda was soil erosion. Although this concern originated more from the crusading work of Hugh Bennett than from the land use movement of the 1920s, it fit perfectly with Gray's emphasis on land use according to classification, since erosion control depended on proper use of the land. The NRB report was based on the nation's first-ever soil survey. This hastily completed reconnaissance of soil erosion in every county in the nation was completed in two months of fieldwork involving 115 erosion specialists; it provided the knowledge basis for all subsequent discussions of erosion in the United States. This Soil Erosion Service survey found that 50 million acres had been "destroyed" by erosion, 125 million acres had had most of their topsoil stripped by erosion, and another 100 million acres were on the way to becoming "soil-stripped." In addition, the report estimated that erosion cost the nation $400 million annually because of reduced crop yields, siltation of reservoirs, and damage to water supplies.[47]

Naming soil erosion as one of agriculture's most "acute" problems, the Land Committee called for a coordination of all erosion control efforts and emphasized that erosion control was primarily a matter of farming in accord with the dictates of the land. Such techniques as contour plowing or crop rotation could reduce erosion on many soils, but the committee insisted that some lands were not suitable for cropping and should be retired from agriculture. Erosion control was not simply a matter of the voluntary application of new techniques, of applying the proper technology to the land resource. Rather, it meant adjusting the pattern of resource use to conform to the capabilities of the land. This might require "public assistance" to compensate farmers for the expense of installing conservation measures and could potentially mean government controls to protect the government's investment. Since land use adjustments, not technical improvements, were the ultimate cure for soil erosion, the Land Committee also reasoned that public controls might be necessary if farmers could not be convinced to farm the land according to the classification of its physical characteristics.[48]

Erosion was only one manifestation of the general maladaptation of land uses, according to the Land Committee. The problems of settlement on "submarginal lands"—a phrase that usually meant the arid Great Plains—had dominated the land use discussions of the twenties, and the dust storms of the thirties provided dramatic new evidence of land abuse. Here environmental themes meshed with social considerations. Settlement on poor land not only resulted in soil degradation; it also led to rural "slums" where poor land kept farm incomes low and, in return, farmers, trying desperately to make a living, drained the soil of its fertility. Although submarginal lands were concentrated in the "problem areas" of the Great Plains, the "cut-over" regions of the Great Lakes states, and the southern Appalachians, the Land Committee's state land planning consultants identified submarginal lands in each of the forty-eight states. Nationwide, 20 million acres of cropland, 20 million acres of woodland, and 35 million acres of pastureland, or a total of 75 million acres, were judged to be unsuitable for farming.[49]

This analysis provided an agenda for land reform for the rest of the decade. Soil classification, erosion control, governmental coordination, rural land use planning, and the retirement of submarginal land all gathered momentum. In order to reach the admittedly ambitious goal of retiring 75 million acres from production, the Land Committee proposed that the current emergency land acquisition program be continued at the rate of five million acres per year for fifteen years at an estimated cost of $45 million each year. But even if 75 million acres could be taken out of production (and only 11 million acres were), this would only repair the damage already done and would be futile unless accompanied by other land use policy changes to prevent the pattern from recurring. Thus the report applauded the recently passed Taylor Grazing Act, which withdrew the remaining public domain from homesteading, as Gray had advocated a decade earlier. Similarly, it urged federal and state governments to utilize a range of land use policies to guide future settlement away from poor land. The committee optimistically declared that rural land use planning, which was being tested in several states, "will ultimately become just as effective a tool in that field as it has in city planning." The committee also urged such novel ideas as the conditioning of federal credit and relief payments on cooperation with land use plans; long-term contracts between the federal government and property owners to "exclude unwarranted settlement" or to control erosion; and permanent restrictive covenants which the government might buy from landowners and which would stipulate allowable uses of the land.[50] These proposals represented a creative way around the obstacle that whereas some land use problems are national in scope, land use controls constitutionally belong to the state and traditionally are exercised, if at all, by cities and counties. Here was a reform package designed to give the federal government leadership in planning for better land use. Aside from several brief experiments in the 1930s, that package remains largely unopened.

The 1934 report was recognized at the time as a "landmark" in natural resource history and still sets a high standard for land use policy analysis. Its immediate political impact was less clear. M. L. Wilson, who chaired the Land Committee, claimed that it fulfilled the promise of the "Roosevelt-Pinchot conservation movement" and helped to create a "broader national consciousness of land as a national asset . . . to be preserved . . . for the public welfare." Roosevelt submitted the report to Congress in early 1935 with the hope that Congress would provide for "a permanent policy of orderly development in every part of the U.S." The Land Committee followed up on its 1934 report with eleven supplementary reports detailing the broad themes of the initial report. From then on the focus of land use activity shifted to the Department of Agriculture, as L. C. Gray led nearly his entire staff with him first to the Land Policy Section of the BAE and then, in 1935, to the Land Use Planning Section of the Resettlement Administration. In keeping with the recommendation that the government coordinate all land use efforts, a small staff stayed behind to record federal land purchases in an attempt to avoid agency overlap.[51] Even this minimal function fell short of the ideals expressed in the 1934 report. Insofar as land use planning meant generating ideas, the Land Report succeeded in that it set the agenda for the rest of the decade and beyond. A second purpose of planning—the central coordination of governmental agencies—remained more elusive, for the NRB and its successors never were able to rein in the various land-related agencies.

Federal Acquisition of Submarginal Lands

Even before the NRB issued its report in December 1934, Gray had begun to implement his ideas on government acquisitions of submarginal land. From his office in the newly established Land Policy Section of the Agricultural Adjustment Administration (AAA), Gray supervised the selection of lands for purchase by the federal government. Initially the project was funded at $25 million, a sum he recognized as far from adequate to meet his goal of retiring 75 million acres. Still, he was excited that this beginning, in his words, "marks a definite entrance of the administration on a land program of far reaching scope." Land use reformers emphasized that federal land acquisition was only part of a broader land use program. The goal was not public land ownership for its own sake but the use of publicly owned land as a catalyst for multiple social and environmental purposes. Changes in land use patterns were essential for limiting erosion, restoring soil productivity, controlling floods, and alleviating rural poverty. This might mean contour plowing, switching to soil-conserving crops such as legumes or alfalfa, or converting plowed land back into grassland or forest. In combination with other programs such as soil conservation districts, grazing districts, rural zoning, and federal rehabilitation loans, federal land purchase would become "the key that unlocks the door to reconstruction of much larger areas and to the rehabilitation of a much larger number of families" than those acres or farmers directly involved.[52]

This land reform program was thus vitally connected with social reform. Tugwell, Gray, and other social scientists believed that rural poverty was caused in part by inefficient use of land. Gray was especially concerned with the poor conditions associated with southern tenant farming; he thought that cotton monoculture on thin and erosive soils had contributed to much social misery. The land reformers' solution was for the government to buy submarginal land, restore it to environmentally appropriate uses, and move people to cities, suburban homesteads, or other places where they might find an adequate living. Thus in 1935, by executive order, Roosevelt created the Resettlement Administration; he provided funding from the Federal Emergency Relief Administration, placed Tugwell in charge, and gave the agency a mandate for land reform, resettlement of farm families, the construction of model resettlement communities, and rural rehabilitation in the form of grants and loans to marginal farmers. Gray brought almost his entire staff from the Land Policy Section of the AAA to the new agency, and for a time the Resettlement Administration was the focus for New Deal land purchase programs. Tugwell, Gray, and others favored resettlement to rehabilitation in place because they believed that the farm population was too large, that many marginal farmers had no realistic chance of becoming successful, and that much marginal farmland, only barely able to support farming, could be put to more environmentally sound uses. By the autumn of 1935, fears of government regimentation and the alleged "collectivizing" of agricultural lands forced the Resettlement Administration to shift emphasis from resettlement to rehabilitation. In 1937 the Bankhead-Jones Farm Tenant Act officially recognized this change by rechartering the Resettlement Administration, with additional funding, as the Farm Security Administration (FSA). The FSA had some success with rural rehabilitation and some fascinating resettlement projects, but the land reform agenda, which Tugwell had seen as fundamental for long-term solutions to the problem of farm poverty, was no longer a priority.[53]

Even so, the land acquisition program had some success stories. On some portions of the Great Plains, government land purchases reduced the population of dry land farmers, most of whom were willing to move, and established a less dense range economy using cooperative grazing districts and government contracts on leased land to control the carrying capacity of the range. By combining in this way with other land use controls, one purchase in Montana was able to protect over one million acres of range in a cooperative grazing district through the purchase of a crucial 260,000 acres of scattered small farms within the area. In total the National Resources Planning Board estimated that the acquisition of 6.5 million acres of select land in the arid West had "facilitated adjustment to a more stable economy" and protected the land on about 23 million acres. Yet by 1940 only 11 million acres had actually been purchased, at a cost of $46 million, far short of the original 75 million acres and even farther from the Soil Conservation Service's revised calculation that 86 million acres of land in farms should be purchased.[54]

Although the land acquisition program had many advocates in the Roosevelt administration, especially Rexford Tugwell and M. L. Wilson, it nevertheless ran into opposition from both inside and outside the administration. Roosevelt himself was interested in the program but not personally involved. In 1934 he inquired of Secretary of Agriculture Wallace: "What is the status of the land acquisition policy about which we have so often talked?"[55] Wilson lamented the fact that FDR was kept too busy to give land acquisition more personal attention, yet he was pleased that FDR had a "genuine interest in this subject" and thought it fortunate that "we have a president with a deep knowledge of land problems who had the experience of pioneering a land policy in a great state with intricate land problems of its own."[56]

Despite this knowledge, Roosevelt and his Secretary of Agriculture Henry Wallace, also sympathetic to public land use controls, backed down from pushing a politically liable land use program too hard. In part this was because Roosevelt's director of the budget opposed land acquisition on the grounds that it would obligate the government to "a long-time land policy, the scope and annual cost of which is wholly indeterminate" and because it was "directly in conflict with the administration's financial program." In an argument that would gather greater force in the 1970s, the budget office objected to further spending "until the important and costly experiments now under way . . . begin to prove something."[57] This insistence that more research should precede action was thus part of the conservative attack on federal land planning and suggests that social science, though it is usually seen as having a liberal influence on policymaking, could have its methods turned to conservative ends as well. The land acquisition program also suffered from the fact that relocation of farm families, which Gray accepted as the government's responsibility, lagged behind the purchases so that relief officials worried that acquisition was adding to their burden. Outside of Washington the program had the support of some farm leaders, but many newspapers and businessmen opposed the program because they perceived it to be radical or because they worried that it might depopulate their region and leave local businesses without customers and local governments without taxpayers.[58]

The land purchase program faded away during the 1940s as one of the New Deal's more controversial and costly programs. Of the 11 million acres purchased, about 50 percent were in the Northern Plains, 20 percent were in the South, and another 15 percent were in the Southwest, with the rest scattered throughout the country. These lands went to a variety of purposes. The Soil Conservation Service (SCS) managed seven million acres as demonstration projects, dam sites, or rangelands reseeded and leased to grazing associations. In 1954 nearly nine million acres, including all of the SCS lands, were transferred to the Forest Service. During the 1950s these acres were either designated as national grasslands, taken over by the Bureau of Land Management, added to Indian reservations, turned into wildlife reservations, or given to state and local governments for use as parkland. Thus the program had some value in a small-scale way as a demonstration of valuable alternative uses of poor farmland, but its ultimate success, according to one later analyst, "depended largely upon the extent to which it was supplemented by other programs."[59] Judged on this basis, the land acquisition program was hemmed in by inadequate funding and by the failure of planning to take hold in the countryside.

The Creation of Soil Conservation Districts

M. L. Wilson once wrote that each land acquisition project should act "as a leaven for future planning."[60] He hoped that land acquisition would boost the scattered bits of rural zoning that were just starting in several states. County land use zoning, as distinct from urban zoning, began in the late 1920s in an upper Wisconsin county that wanted to reduce local expenditures for roads and schools by restricting farm settlement in a sparsely settled area. Zoning land into different uses like agriculture, forestry, and recreation fit perfectly with the land economists' notion of land use according to classification and was hailed in the 1934 NRB *Report* as a promising development. By 1940 rural zoning had spread to twenty-five "cut-over" counties in Wisconsin and enabling acts had been passed in several other states, including Michigan, California, Washington, and Colorado.[61] This growth led some land economists to believe that rural zoning was analogous to urban zoning, only twenty years slower in coming—that, as one New Deal planner wrote in 1937, "the rural zoning ball is rolling and gathering momentum."[62] This view proved to be overly optimistic, for rural zoning faded from consciousness during the production-oriented 1940s. Moreover, as some conservationists noted at the time, zoning was overrated as a measure for land use protection, because it could prevent certain broad categories of use but could do nothing about existing problems, especially those "within the fence-lines," such as soil erosion. Despite what many considered to be its promise, a more appropriate conclusion about zoning came from F. F. Elliot: "Zoning has never been considered, nor has it yet demonstrated, that it is a particularly effective instrument of control in our major farming and ranching areas, where, obviously the problem of land use is of greatest concern."[63]

An innovation that many reformers considered to have more promise than rural zoning was the soil conservation district, an idea that came from Hugh Bennett's stream of conservationist activity. Bennett's emphasis on proper land use as a means of erosion control fit nicely with the New Deal; so in 1933, when the BAE proposed an erosion control program under its control based on building terraces, Bennett quickly responded with a program of his own. He argued that "mechanical means of erosion control can never be as effective as vegetative methods," that a comprehensive approach would be superior to one based solely on terraces. With help from Rexford Tugwell and Interior Secretary Harold Ickes, the Soil Erosion Service (SES) began in 1933 as an agency of the Interior Department under Bennett's direction. But the SES relied on demonstration projects, which Bennett began to think were inadequate because they did not reach enough farmers and, more important, because they relied on farmers to understand and then to voluntarily undertake complicated and sometimes expensive conservation improvements. By 1935, when Congress moved SES to the Department of Agriculture and gave it permanent status as the Soil Conservation Service, Bennett was ready with a more ambitious plan.[64]

Bennett thought the severity of erosion called for a strong federal response. Systematic information about erosion was barely beginning to accumulate, and the measurement of erosion rates over time, which was at the heart of Bennett's contention that agricultural erosion was greater than natural geologic erosion, was a very inexact science.[65] The Dust Bowl, however, provided dramatic evidence that something was wrong even if the exact dimensions were not yet known. This doubt, fed by incomplete information, quickly gave way to a sense of urgency about the erosion control project.[66] The recently completed SCS soil erosion survey provided the first systematic nationwide measure of the magnitude of soil erosion and allowed Bennett to testify before Congress in 1935 that it was impossible to "maintain permanent prosperity over large areas of the United States if the present rapid destruction" of agricultural land was not arrested. "The remedial step that inevitably must be taken is the application of a coordinated land-use and land-protection program in accordance with the specific needs and adaptabilities of all types of valuable land needing treatment." A federal initiative was needed because erosion control was a complex matter, because watersheds crossed political boundaries, and because flooding and silting of reservoirs affected public dams and waterways. Bennett wanted "conservancy districts" established in every watershed according to the natural boundaries of the watershed. The original plan was to reorganize the nation's landscape into seventy-six natural drainage basins, each constituting a soil conservation district. Bennett backed off from this idea because he was not sure that Congress would grant such sweeping new authority for land use regulations. He hoped, however, that watershed-sized districts within the states would formulate land use plans for each watershed and that these plans would in turn become the basis for national agricultural land planning.[67]

Bennett's case for soil conservation was thus grounded firmly in the New Deal idea that there was a national interest in private land use and that there should thus be federal controls. This idea had broad support and was at the core of New Deal land use reform. President Roosevelt, with his characteristic interest in land use, expressed his view to Wallace: "The nub of the whole question is this: if a farmer in upstate New York or Georgia or Nebraska or Oregon, through bad use of his land, allows his land to erode, does he have the inalienable right as owner to do this, or has the community, i.e., some form of governmental agency, the right to stop him?"[68] This theme echoed loud in the Department of Agriculture, where M. L. Wilson explained the connections between individual and society:

The assumption is that society has an interest in the privately owned farm, forest and grazing lands of the nation which is at least equal to the interest of the owner himself. That is to say, the land-owner does not really own his land with an absolute and unlimited title, but, instead, owns his land in partnership with society. If this be a correct assumption, then the partnership throws upon society the obligation to assist the landowner to make the best use of his lands and it throws upon the landowner the duty so to use his lands to conserve the soil and its fertility that the future generations, whose interest society seeks to protect, will inherit fertile fields and forests rather than eroded slopes and barren plains.[69]

Paul Appleby, a land reformer in USDA, thought that although there was a "clear line of demarcation" between public and private lands, it was nevertheless true that "almost everyone but the Supreme Court seems willing to admit that private lands do have public significance."[70]

Bennett's legal counsel acknowledged "very definite" limits on the power of the federal government to regulate private land but still favored the "growing legal theory" that challenged the common law doctrine of unlimited landowner rights and insisted instead that "a landowner, from the point of view of the nation, is no more than a life tenant." Bennett gave favorable mention to a 1928 Italian erosion control law that made cooperation mandatory for private landowners but helped with the cost of installing erosion control measures. The reciprocal relationship between landowner and society made it fair for the government to defray the expense of conservation on an "equitable cost-sharing basis," and in exchange the federal government would have the authority to "provide the technical direction and supervision and would establish regulations protecting any erosion control measures which might be installed." W. C. Lowdermilk, Bennett's assistant, added that federal funds spent on erosion control were wasted without prior planning for the "adequate regulation" of land use.[71] Secretary of Agriculture Henry Wallace provided official support for these ideas; he argued that without an ongoing program of land use controls, "I do not see how the federal government can justify the expenditure of additional federal funds" for erosion control on private lands.[72] These conservationists thus anticipated the concept that in the 1980s became known as conservation compliance, the idea that federal funds were contingent upon landowners' adopting acceptable conservation practices. Their idea was that the public interest in private lands called for both subsidy and control.

Acting on these ideas and working closely with Assistant Secretary of Agriculture M. L. Wilson and the Land Planning Committee of the NRB, in 1935 Bennett directed his staff to draft enabling legislation allowing states to create soil conservation districts. Philip Glick, a young lawyer with the SCS, actually drafted the model legislation, and debate persists over who should receive the credit for the district idea. Regardless of who hit upon the exact form of the conservation district, the general approach reflected the converging environmental ideas of the different strands of land use thought. As Assistant Secretary J. D. LeCron explained, "a genuine attack on erosion" required more than individual application of technical measures such as terraces or dams. Instead, "practically all the lands in particular watersheds must be brought under uniform control. Arbitrary boundary lines should be ignored, and programs formulated over naturally bounded areas." These land use plans might be quite detailed for individual farmers and could, for example, regulate "engineering operations, changes in the methods of cultivation, the growing of vegetation, and changes in use of land—on all lands within the district, whether public or privately owned."[73]

Soil conservationists argued that voluntary efforts alone could not control erosion: the efforts of isolated farmers would be negligible because large numbers of other farmers would continue erosive farming practices. In addition, the reformers argued, federal investments in the form of conservation improvements (terracing, labor from CCC camps, or technical expertise) deserved to be protected with federal regulations. President Roosevelt summarized these themes and personally endorsed the district concept in a letter to all state governors:

> The nation that destroys its soil destroys itself. . . . [T]he failure to control erosion on some lands, particularly if such eroding lands are situated strategically at the heads of valleys or watersheds, can cause a washing and blowing of soil onto other lands, and make the control of erosion anywhere in the valley or watershed all the more difficult. We are confronted with the fact that, for the problem to be adequately dealt with, the erodible land in every watershed must be brought under some form of control. . . . Unless state legislation provides such a mechanism by which farmers can organize themselves for cooperative action, to apply on their lands the lessons in erosion and flood control which they learn from federal programs, the full benefits of the federal expenditures and cooperation cannot be realized.[74]

Yet no one in the New Deal thought it wise to force an unpopular program on reluctant farmers, and they knew that the success of the program depended on avoiding that "regimented" feeling among farmers. Fearing that "an attempt to impose regulation from above may make the [conservation district] statute as unenforceable as was the prohibition legislation," Wilson called first for farmers to be "educated to cooperate voluntarily."[75] The enabling legislation provided for districts to be created by a popular referendum in order to ensure broad support, and Wilson, Wallace, and others consistently emphasized the importance of democratic organization and the "local acceptance of responsibility" for erosion control. Land use controls, enacted "if and when the farmers so desire," required a two-thirds vote of the district membership. The hope was first that education would lead to broad support for better land use practices, and second that an informed majority would, if necessary, coerce a "recalcitrant minority" into compliance with regulations.[76]

These New Deal reformers were struggling with one of the central dilemmas in twentieth-century American political history. Land use regulations were vital to the success of their program, so much so that one scholar has concluded that their "central objective" was to manage the soil conservation program "through a unit of government possessing the power to make and enforce land use regulations."[77] Yet they knew that success depended on avoiding a coercive administrative apparatus for enforcement. Wilson suggested that land use controls should be "democratic"—that is, locally written and enforced—rather than "bureaucratic," or federally administered. Historians Ellis Hawley and Barry Karl have described this tension in other aspects of the New Deal. Farmers personified the autonomous individualism at the core of the American identity, whereas planners valued order, rationality, and conservation as the keys to greater democracy. Thus New Dealers in a variety of policy areas tried to reconcile their hopes for regulatory reform with what Hawley calls "the anti-bureaucratic tradition" in American politics. In soil conservation, as Hawley has found elsewhere in the 1930s, there was a desire for increased management of private property for public purposes, combined with an "overlay of anti-statist rhetoric attuned to the anti-bureaucratic symbols and traditions long embedded in our political culture." In Karl's view, the result has been an "uneasy state" that brokers interest groups and competing bureaucracies but that lacks the capacity for general planning or overall coordination. Hawley calls this a state with a "hollow core."[78] In soil conservation, this same tension between an anti-statist political culture and increased public regulations led to the creation of a new unit of government—the soil conservation district—in the hope that local controls might successfully reconcile this tension. Ultimately, the regulatory capacity of the districts was abandoned, with the unintended result that the New Deal system for agricultural conservation came to provide subsidies but not controls.

Originally, however, the New Dealers placed great hope in the soil conservation districts. There were other reasons besides the fear of bureaucratic regimentation for favoring the creation of a new administrative unit. Constitutionally, land use regulations had to originate from state governments or from smaller units, such as cities or counties. Yet most land use reformers wanted to keep the program out of the hands of what Tugwell referred to as the "courthouse gang," both because counties were conservative politically and because they lacked the expertise and inclination to initiate a land use plan.[79] The most important reason for the new unit of government was the environmental necessity of attacking erosion along natural boundaries rather than along political boundaries. The concept of watershed protection was central to a variety of New Deal land programs, from reforestation to flood control, so it was natural for the district idea to be linked to the concept of watershed boundaries. Eroded dirt had such downstream effects as increased flooding and silted dams, and this interrelatedness of land and water made the watershed a logical and an ecological unit for government. As originally conceived, these districts along natural boundaries might evolve into full-fledged, locally run "departments of natural resources and conservation," a rival local governmental structure for land issues.

This larger mandate for soil conservation districts had the support of the secretary of agriculture. Wallace thought that a "genuine attack" on erosion would "require considerable modification" of current farming practices and would, contingent upon majority approval, require "the police power of the state" to force a "recalcitrant minority" to conform so that "virtually all lands in particular watersheds" would be farmed according to conservation practices.[80] Near the end of 1937 Secretary Wallace gave these instructions to Bennett:

> It seems to me that these districts in the future may be found to present an opportunity to the department to unify a number of the different action programs which the department is now authorized

to carry on. Through the local soil conservation districts the department should be able to assist farmers in formulating and executing comprehensive plans for bringing about wise land use. I think it is important, therefore, that the districts should not come to be looked upon as having significance only for the program of the Soil Conservation Service, but that they should be seen as local governmental units, organized democratically, functioning over properly bounded areas, and possessing the necessary governmental power to enable them to carry on well-rounded agricultural programs.[81]

These instructions were circulated to all agency chiefs in the department, and Bennett seized upon this "greatly broadened" role for the SCS. In his view, "what was formerly an agency concerned primarily with the conservation of soil and water resources is now an agency concerned with promoting adjustments to achieve better land use and permanent systems of farming."[82] This broadened mandate implied changes in the SCS's relation to other agencies and carried with it the unspecified promise of making the conservation district system *the* New Deal agency for agricultural land. Secretary Wallace was supporting a fundamental intellectual and bureaucratic change in USDA operations. This "revolutionary change in agricultural administration," as one scholar described it, would have absorbed the AAA and other departmental activities within the SCS and the district structure. The shift in intellectual orientation would have meant that conservation—the building of what Bennett called a "permanent agriculture"—would take priority over other goals, such as supply management or income enhancement.[83] M. L. Wilson saw soil conservation districts as the "most significant of all" New Deal land planning activities and thought that these districts might fulfill the cooperative promise of the New Deal. But this larger potential of the district-enabling legislation was rarely understood and never fully realized.[84]

During the first five years of soil conservation districts this potential for land use planning was partially achieved. As states began to pass versions of the standard enabling act, local districts were formed at a rapid rate. The first district was chartered in 1937 and included Bennett's home in North Carolina. Two years later there were 113 districts in twenty-five states, and by 1942 there were 771 districts in forty-one states, covering nearly 452 million acres and over two million farms. By 1950 there were 2,164 districts, covering every major farm region in the country.[85] However, the growth in numbers concealed the fact that nearly all of these districts were formed along county boundaries, so that the original hope of watershed resource planning was lost. As Wallace admitted in 1937, "We doubt that appropriate procedures can be developed with conservation districts limited strictly to county basis."[86] Still, the SCS took land use seriously in the early years. Bennett, concerned with farmers' opposition to land use regulation, wanted to introduce regulations "gradually" over the "next two or three years." The extra time would also allow the SCS a better chance to gather more technical information and so provide a firmer scientific basis for realistic erosion control standards. Thus the SCS developed a three-layered system of support for the new districts. The twelve states that included land use regulations in their enabling laws qualified for full SCS technical and financial assistance. The second category gave only technical aid to those states whose district legislation allowed for marginal land use provisions. The third layer of states received no SCS assistance and included states whose enabling legislation omitted the provision for land use regulation.[87]

These categories lasted only until 1942, but during their short existence they encouraged districts to pass land use controls. Several state legislatures amended their enabling legislation to give districts broader land use powers. Colorado featured thirteen districts with land use ordinances that regulated grazing districts, restricted plowing on certain lands, and established "blow land" provisions to control wind erosion. Other Great Plains states such as New Mexico adopted rangeland and farmland zones to restrict grazing and plowing to the lands best suited to each use. By 1951, thirty-three states gave districts the authority to regulate land use, but by 1967 only a few districts in Colorado and one each in North Dakota and Oregon had actually used that latent authority.[88] Elsewhere the land use potential of the districts lay dormant.

The demise of the planning function of the SCS can be attributed to several factors. The general deadlock of the New Deal made any reform initiative more difficult, and some observers suggest that land use regulations were relaxed because they were a handicap in Roosevelt's 1940 reelection bid.[89] Philip Glick, author of the standard district enabling legislation, thought land planning suffered because of the excessive demands placed upon the SCS field personnel, who spent nearly all of their time answering requests for assistance, so that they had no time and little inclination to initiate land use regulations.[90] Implementation was similarly weakened, according to Bennett, by the "tendency on the part of the field organization in some sections to compromise with individual farmers."[91] D. Harper Sims, author of the standard history of the SCS, argues quite rightly that land use regulations were politically damaging in some rural areas. Sims adds somewhat improbably that regulations were practically unnecessary because districts "found persuasion and the force of local sentiment more effective."[92]

Perhaps the most significant reason for the failure of the districts to realize their planning potential was the number of institutional obstacles working against land use reform. From their beginning, soil conservation districts threatened the land grant college/extension service complex as a rival organization for delivering services to farmers at the local level. Opposition was so great that extension agents generally refused to tell farmers of the services offered by the SCS and in some instances worked against the creation of soil conservation districts. Wallace noted that "improper location of district boundaries" and "inadequate public discussion," by which he meant opposition from the extension service, might "give the whole project a serious setback." He specifically accused the Texas Extension Service of being a source of "opposition and misinformation."[93] The extension service complained repeatedly in the late 1930s that SCS requirements for districts were burdensome, a charge to which Secretary Wallace answered that the agency had "the responsibility of seeking permanent results from the expenditure of federal funds for erosion control." In addition, extension's ally, the Farm Bureau, urged Congress in 1942 to cut funds for the fledgling SCS.[94] Under these pressures the beleaguered SCS naturally jettisoned the most controversial part of its program. The pared-down SCS provided erosion control assistance to farmers who asked for it, but by the early 1940s the agency had already become something less than its founders had envisioned.

The Mount Weather Planning Process

As the New Deal ran its course, the initial optimism of the land use reformers faded, especially since general land use planning for agriculture remained elusive. Erosion control and marginal land acquisition proceeded, even if at a slower pace than hoped. Tugwell was enthusiastic about the progress already made but still had a warning:

"The states and nation are now unleashing the greatest broadside attack on land use problems of our history. If this task is completed, our national heritage will be secure. If not, we shall go the way of Mesopotamia, Egypt, and China, and part with our collective birthright for a mess of individualistic pottage."[95] Gray, who had been fighting in the trenches since the early twenties, was even more sure that the new age was here: "The future historian of land policy will surely regard this past five years as revolutionary. It marks an almost complete break with the traditional policies of America."[96] Others within the department were less sanguine. One inside analysis claimed: "With an almost maniac vigor we have destroyed or wounded a considerable part of our common basic wealth in this country. . . . We have made much of our country ugly. . . . Despite the remarkable progress made in recent years, we must in all frankness admit that we have not yet stemmed the tide of soil and fertility losses. As to soil, we are not yet even on a maintenance basis."[97] In 1936 the National Resources Committee reported that "the general feeling of the committee is one of encouragement" and that the progress of the previous years was "satisfactory—provided no reaction to previous conditions of irresponsibility occurs."[98] Two years later the committee saw continued progress but worried that "the land use program has not always moved as rapidly" as desired and that the movement was "uneven," with "important gaps."[99]

Among these gaps was the often-cited need for bureaucratic coordination of the land-related agencies in the Department of Agriculture. The proliferation of action agencies inside the Department of Agriculture had led to overlapping and even conflicting implementation in the field. The older extension service competed with the newly created agencies, such as the SCS or the AAA. Meanwhile, Secretary Wallace jealously guarded his turf from the schemes of Secretary of the Interior Harold Ickes, who wanted to consolidate all conservation agencies, including the Forest Service and the SCS, into a new Department of Conservation. To deal with these external and internal pressures, Wallace created the Land Policy Committee in 1935 and the Committee of Departmental Coordination in 1936, both chaired by M. L. Wilson. In 1937 both were replaced by the Office of Land-Use Coordination, chaired by Milton Eisenhower. This move did not solve the problems, however; the land grant colleges and their extension allies continued to complain that they were being bypassed as the new agencies established direct links with farmers.

This problem of bureaucratic infighting presented an opportunity to implement land use planning as a basis for bureaucratic coordination. This was the idea behind the Mount Weather agreement, the name of a new working relationship between federal agencies and the state land grant colleges; the parties had started this relationship at a conference held on 7 and 8 July 1938 at the Virginia mountain resort of Mount Weather. The agreement was based on a proposal drafted by Wilson and Eisenhower that stated: "[T]he principal solution to the present federal-state relations problem lies in devising a method which will result in the formulation of sound county, state and national land-use plans, on the basis of which all land-use programs may be brought into united action toward common objectives. . . . [P]lanning is the key to coordination."[100] This proposal continued to spell out a new structure for decentralized land use planning for the nation. Each county would eventually set up a land use committee composed of ten or more farmers and the county extension agent. These committees would classify land according to its actual and its desired use, study soil classification maps, and prepare land use plans for the county. These county committees would coordinate their activities with a state land use planning committee headed by the state director of extension services and including farmers and representatives of the various federal agencies.

At the national level Wallace elevated the BAE, headed by Howard Tolley, to shape general planning goals for all of the land use committees. Enforcement of these plans remained somewhat elusive, since there was no power to coerce landowners to cooperate. Federal agencies, on the other hand, were expected to conform their activities to local land use plans unless they could show that local plans contradicted the national interest.[101] Thus local land use planning would provide the means and the rationale for coordinating action agencies at the federal level; as Wallace noted, "Action programs cannot deal with one segment out of relation to other parts of the program. Out on the watershed and on the farm, where our real job lies, we are dealing with a complex of interrelated factors." Local planning committees, he believed, "would give farm people an effective voice in formulating, correlating, and localizing public agricultural programs." Wallace hoped this "significant and far reaching" experiment would be a "renaissance of democracy" that would bring "new democratic patterns in farm life and in the rural community."[102] Another social scientist in the department saw the Mount Weather agreement as an "epoch-making" step in the effort to construct the "machinery for doing the land use adjustment job as it needs to be done."[103] What was most remarkable about the Mount Weather agreement was that the search for bureaucratic efficiency led straight to comprehensive land use planning.

Agricultural planning under the Mount Weather agreement spread rapidly. Forty-five states signed the memorandum of agreement during 1939, and by June 1941 every state except Pennsylvania participated. Nearly 1,900 counties—about two-thirds of all agricultural counties—established land use committees, involving some 200,000 participants.[104] This quick response was due partly to the structure of the planning process. County extension agents took an active role in setting up most committees and often personally selected the farm members for the county committees. This arrangement made for ease in organizing committees but also meant that most committees were dominated by the commercial farmers of the Farm Bureau, who were the usual clients of extension. The leadership of the Department of Agriculture, including Wallace, Wilson, and Tolley, wanted elected committees, while some sociologists in the BAE wanted proportional representation.[105] These issues were never resolved in the few years that the committees existed, which meant that although the committees covered a lot of ground, they were not rooted very solidly.

During their short lives the land use committees engaged in a wide range of planning activities. The basic task of each committee was to prepare a map based on soil classifications of all agricultural land uses in the county and then to compare this map with actual or projected uses. Within each county this soil classification map became the basis for advising farmers on needed changes in crop selection and soil conservation and for bringing the different federal agencies into conformity with each other and with local conditions. What started as a way to coordinate competing federal agencies quickly extended to include a host of local matters, such as designating lands for public purchase, locating roads, revising tax assessment, establishing wildlife areas, selecting school sites, and even planning school bus routes. Naturally, under such a decentralized process, local variation was great. One committee in the state of Washington found that, based on soil and climate, larger farms were necessary for a stable farm income; this group thus appealed to the FSA for loans to enlarge their farms. A New Hampshire county arrived at a ten-year plan for improving overgrazed pastureland, while many committees assisted in organizing soil conservation districts. The committee in Culpeper County, Virginia, helped subsistence farmers on poor soils to find seasonal off-farm jobs, and in several cases the committees even arranged for cooperative equipment buying and crop marketing.[106] The most often cited success story came in Teton County, Montana, where the local committee, as the *New Republic* glowingly reported, "decided that 20,000 acres of low-grade plow-land should be returned to grass. The AAA agreed not to permit any of those acres to enter its program as cropland. The FSA agreed to make no loans for farming them." This "democratic planning," the *New Republic* concluded, "may quietly become a major factor in shaping a new pattern of farm life" and "point the way to voluntary coordination of private and public action."[107]

Despite all of this apparent success, the Mount Weather planning process had many problems. At the local level much of the planning was "quite superficial," as one might expect from a committee with little or no training for the task.[108] County agents who were schooled in the ways of increasing productivity had no expertise in and sometimes no inclination for land use planning. Farmers, who composed the majority of the membership, were being asked to do for a county what many of them had never done for their farms. Thus L. C. Gray argued for the role of specialists who would fuse "expert knowledge" with the farmers' "practical experience" in an educational process that would lead farmers into an acceptance of planning.[109] Given time this plan might have worked, but time was one thing the committees did not have.

At the national level the coordination of land-related programs never came about. The BAE was placed in charge of "general land-use planning" and oversaw the work of the state and local planning committees. Yet the BAE itself was not an action agency with a field staff; it was restricted to collecting information and generating ideas. The action agencies, especially the SCS and AAA, resented plans formulated by intellectuals who lacked a farm background, and they especially distrusted Tolley, whom they judged to be both too intellectual and too ambitious. They often saw the county committees as a potential rival organization and viewed the BAE/state/county planning structure as a competitor rather than as an overall coordinator. Meanwhile, Milton Eisenhower's Office of Land-Use Coordination had the task of "operational planning," but his powers were not specified, and he was reluctant to force his will onto the other agencies.[110] The result was that the potential for coordination among agencies with seemingly similar conservation goals based on land use plans never really materialized.

This seed of land use planning might have been able to overcome these problems had it been given a chance to mature. This chance never came, for a variety of reasons. Planning in the Agriculture Department lost a key supporter in 1940 when Secretary Wallace left to become vice president. The new secretary, Claude Wickard, had risen through the ranks of the AAA and had little sympathy for Tolley, for the BAE, or for planning in general. In the 1940s the Farm Bureau, which after its early interest had grown hostile toward planning, began looking for a way to end the Mount Weather program. The bureau saw the county planning structure as a rival for power in rural America and so lobbied successfully in Congress for reducing BAE's funding. When the Department of Agriculture began to coordinate the wartime production effort in 1942, Secretary Wickard organized county war boards under the direction of the AAA, and the land use planning committees fell by the wayside. Friends of planning argued that the war boards should logically be placed under the county land use planning committees, but Secretary Wickard felt more comfortable with the established AAA and wanted to waste no time in mobilizing a comparatively new organization.[111] Deprived of support from the secretary's office, viewed as an unwelcome competitor by other federal agencies, and actively opposed by the nation's strongest farm group, the county land use planning committees faded under pressure from the war. With their death the idea of land use, which only a decade before had been one of the brightest new ideas on the agricultural agenda, disappeared from sight for three decades.

Historians have come to different conclusions about the significance of the Mount Weather agreement. Sidney Baldwin, writing from the perspective of the rural poor, saw it at the local level as simply another tool of the county agent system and at the federal level as "little more than a piece of paper."[112] Richard Kirkendall, from the perspective of the social scientists, saw the arrangement as a significant if temporary elevation of the power of the land economists in the BAE. Both writers, however, consider the crucial issue to be the bureaucratic power struggle that was then taking place in Washington. A third historian, whose subject is land use planning on the Great Plains, concludes rather that the planning committees marked "an important stage in the story of regionalized land-use planning."[113] From the point of view of land use reform, the Mount Weather agreement had the potential to develop into an effective system, but that opportunity only existed for a few years. The demand for maximum production during World War II closed the door on land use reforms and soured the Department of Agriculture on this controversial idea. What survived the New Deal instead was the program of agricultural subsidies that had begun as an emergency measure in 1933. The temporary program became permanent, while the goal of a "permanent agriculture" based on land use planning proved to be temporary.

Even as land use was falling into such disfavor, there were hints of changes that would give the issue a different flavor in the decades to come. Government planners were beginning to ask the question, "When city problems move to the country, what happens to the country?"[114] The Land Committee of the National Resources Planning Board gave this question increasing attention during the latter years of the New Deal and worried that the pattern of scattered urban growth would be a "devastating intrusion" into "the beauty of the unspoiled countryside" and would lead to vacant land, unfair tax burdens on farmers, and "the slow undermining of the economic stability of the farms." The Land Committee urged a series of studies on the problems associated with the urban-rural fringe and specifically suggested that local governments were not capable of planning for this variety of emerging problems. They were not yet considering the loss of agricultural land to urban and suburban uses as a resource issue, but they did have a clear sense that "rural life and institutions" were in jeopardy.[115] The stillbirth of New Deal agricultural land use planning meant, among other things, that the nation lost the capacity to anticipate the urban demand for agricultural lands. Not only did the land problems of the 1930s remain only partially solved; the nation was also deprived of its chance to foresee the land abuses that the next generation of urbanization would bring.

The Reemergence of Agricultural Conservation

The Declining Importance of Farmland

For three decades following the New Deal, the idea of food shortage lay buried beneath mountains of surpluses, while agricultural land use planning was ignored by conservatives and liberals alike. However, these decades saw momentous changes that drastically altered the context for agricultural policy in the 1970s. Agriculture became agribusiness; farms grew dramatically in size and decreased significantly in number; a unitary farm bloc in Congress was fractured from within and dragged off its Jeffersonian pedestal to become just another special interest group competing to make farm and food policy; population grew at surprisingly strong rates, and these increasing numbers were spread across the countryside in new patterns; and an environmental movement emerged to challenge some of the basic assumptions of American agriculture. Changes that went largely unnoticed during the 1950s and 1960s became the center of controversy during the 1970s as agricultural surpluses gave way, at least temporarily, to relative scarcity. The prospect of food shortages emerged in the 1970s at the same time as agriculture's physical constraints—fossil fuel dependence, increased erosion, limits to irrigation—became more obvious. This volatile mixture of political, economic, demographic, and environmental change forms the backdrop for the United States' second attempt to plan for the use of American farmland.[1]

The productivity leap in American agriculture between 1940 and 1970 marked a sharp break from the prevailing pattern and was one of the greatest productivity leaps in history. Analysts described these decades as a "revolution," a sharp and sudden break from the past, and a "wholly different order from all that had gone before."[2] This great transformation had mechanical, biological, and chemical bases, each significant in its own right yet reinforcing the others in overall effect. The switch from human and animal power to gasoline-powered machines was the most obvious change. Tractors numbered 1.6 million in 1940; by 1970 there were over 5 million tractors in use on American farms. Corn pickers, cotton pickers, grain combines, and electric milking machines made it possible for fewer farmers to produce more crops. Complementing these mechanical changes were biological and chemical transformations. Seed hybrids for corn, developed commercially by Henry A. Wallace in the 1920s, became commonplace among corn growers by the 1950s, resulting initially in doubled or even tripled yields per acre. Simultaneously, the use of commercial fertilizer went from under 10 million tons in 1940 to nearly 40 million tons in 1970. The overall result of these changes was that farm production doubled during this thirty-year span, while the cropland acreage remained nearly constant during the 1940s and 1950s and actually declined slightly in the 1960s. Because of this widespread application of new machinery, seed hybrids, and petroleum-based fertilizers and pesticides, yield per acre, which was not significantly higher in 1940 than it had been in 1840, soared by the 1970s to nearly twice its 1930 level. For some crops the productivity increase was much greater than this average. Wheat averaged slightly over 12 bushels per acre from 1870 to 1935, then jumped to nearly 32 bushels per acre by 1970. Corn yields declined from 26 bushels per acre in

1870 to 20 bushels per acre in 1935, then quadrupled by 1970. Cotton rose slightly, from 174 pounds per acre in 1870 to 185 pounds per acre in 1935, then leaped to 436 pounds per acre in 1970.[3] Meanwhile, the number of farms dropped from nearly 7 million in 1935 to 2.7 million in 1970. The number of Americans living on farms went from 30.5 million (23 percent of the population) in 1940 to 9.7 million (4.8 percent of the population) in 1970. During that same time the average farm size more than doubled, from 155 acres to just under 400 acres. Labor requirements declined by 26 percent during the 1940s, 35 percent during the 1950s, and 39 percent during the 1960s.[4] Farm productivity was so great during these decades that the nation's "farm problem" at that time meant the chronic overproduction of farm products and consequent low prices for farmers. U.S. productivity was touted as an "agricultural miracle" that in 1970 allowed one U.S. farmer to feed forty-seven other people and made U.S. agriculture the envy of the world.[5]

The conventional view of this agricultural transformation held that land was an increasingly minor part of the productivity equation. The conservationist ethic that had animated the land economists of the 1930s gave ground to the dominant notion that agricultural land was more a commodity than a resource. The influential agricultural economist Theodore Schultz articulated this new view in 1951 with an article in the *Economic Journal* aptly titled "The Declining Importance of Agricultural Land." Schultz concluded that technology had "relaxed the niggardliness of nature" and that, contrary to what Malthus had predicted, "agricultural land was declining markedly in its importance."[6] This new wisdom became widely accepted within the ranks of Resources for the Future (RFF), the prestigious think tank of the resource economics establishment. RFF began in response to the president's Materials Policy Commission, better known as the Paley Commission after its founder, William Paley. Motivated by the Cold War (resources were "helping beat back from the frontiers of the free world everywhere the threats of force and of a new Dark Age which rise from Communist nations") and committed to the principle of economic growth ("it seems preferable to any opposite, which to us implies stagnation and decay"), the Paley Commission sounded an official alarm over the permanent and pervasive resource shortages that threatened the nation's ability "to sustain its civilization." Even so, the Paley Commission foresaw no serious problems in raising agricultural productivity by increasing both fertilizer use and cropland acreages.[7] Following up on this initial concern, Horace Albright, former director of the National Park Service, and other conservationists secured $3.5 million in grants from the Ford Foundation in order that Resources for the Future might continue this sort of analysis of resource shortages. With ties to government, academia, and corporations, RFF was restricted from recommending policy but tended toward optimistic analyses of resources questions. At the group's inaugural conference, the Mid-Century Conference of Resources for the Future, which supporters likened to Theodore Roosevelt's 1908 conservation conference, analysts noted some concern about "fertile acres" being "lost to agriculture" and questioned whether the best farmland should "grow crops or houses." Another analyst worried about excellent farmland being lost to "premature subdivision" in the "fringe areas between city and rural land."[8]

This concern for limits to agricultural production virtually disappeared from Resources for the Future during the 1950s. At that time the group took a distinctly cornucopian outlook, both because continually rising crop yields made agricultural abundance seem more permanent and because New Dealers became less welcome at RFF as the group became influenced more by Eisenhower conservatism (presidential aide Sherman Adams complained that RFF employed too many New Dealers) and by the business foundations who paid the bill. In 1957 Thomas Nolan, speaking at an RFF conference, argued that material prosperity had so changed the conservation movement that Progressive or New Deal concerns with resource scarcity could safely be ignored: "Research and technologic development have to a large extent eliminated from the conservation movement concern over the adequacy of our resource base."[9] In 1960 a major report on land resources prepared for RFF by Marion Clawson, R. Burnell Held, and Charles Stoddard echoed this conventional view about the fading importance of land. This report concluded that there "existed a large reserve productive capacity in American agriculture" that was "surely a far cry from the dismal outlook of Malthus." In this view, land was "only one of the productive factors" in agriculture and was an increasingly less important one than technology, which acted as a "basic cause" of productivity growth and "greatly reduces the importance of land."[10]

The Green Revolution's Impact on the SCS

In this context of a declining emphasis on agricultural land, the political landscape for soil conservation changed in important ways. The Soil Conservation Service found its institutional existence repeatedly under attack, and it did what was necessary in order to survive. Pressured by political conservatism and continuing crop surpluses, the SCS retreated from its earlier broad purpose as a federal instrument for a more environmentally sound use of public and private land to become an agency that provided very limited technical assistance on private farms. Whereas Bennett had approached conservation as a moral imperative, the SCS of the 1950s came at the problem as a matter of scientific expertise. The emotional temperature of the agency cooled, and its emphasis moved from ethical arguments to economic and soil science analysis. The mission of the agency shifted from protecting the soil from erosion to conserving soil for the sake of enhancing productivity. Efficient production rather than the health of the soil became the rationale, and the idea of public land use controls lost what feeble hold it had had within the agency. The institutional amnesia was so complete that in 1950 one SCS supporter pronounced: "Compulsion or regulation of any kind is against the principles and beliefs of our Soil Conservation districts."[11] Historian and critic Donald Worster argues that early on the SCS became "an agency of engineering" that "came to speak the old, familiar language of the marketplace, of private gain, and of technological solutions to cultural problems."[12]

In many ways the SCS demonstrated in these years the patterns of autonomous activity that Theda Skocpol and others have described as characteristic of modern state bureaucracies.[13] Skocpol identifies arranging for popular support and building a body of technical expertise as two key features of modern managerial states. The SCS did well at both of these efforts. In 1947, in the face of uncertain congressional funding and recurring hostility from the Farm Bureau and its allies in the extension service, the SCS acted to shore up its political support by encouraging the formation of the National Association of Conservation Districts (NACD). This became the national interest group for the SCS and immediately began lobbying in Congress to protect the SCS from being reorganized out of existence.[14] The SCS also continued mapping and measuring soil erosion in order to aid field technicians developing farm "treatment" measures and to guide national policymaking. In 1940 the SCS began a land capability classification system, which divided land into eight categories based on its physical characteristics and value for farming. Classes I–III were considered the best cropland, while class IV land was marginal for use as cropland. The bottom four classes applied to grazing land, with class VIII considered usually unsuitable for grazing. This classification system became widely accepted and later the source of much controversy.[15] Using this system, data from other survey sources (such as the census of agriculture), and observations from its own fieldworkers, the SCS published Conservation Needs Inventories in 1945, 1958, and 1967. These reports reflected the agency's change in emphasis from erosion control to conservation for increased production, for they combined physical measurements of erosion with estimates of conservation "needs" (as defined by soil conservationists). The defining rationale for these needs was "to maintain and improve the country's productive capacity."[16]

This same shift from erosion control to production and income enhancement also shaped other SCS activities in the 1950s. In 1954 Congress authorized the SCS to build dams on the headwaters of frequently flooded rivers in the name of flood control. Because it was a federal cost-sharing program, this small watershed program instantly became popular among farmers. The program conserved soil and reduced flooding, but it also increased commodity production during a time of surplus, raised individual landowners' property values at public expense, and decreased wildlife habitat.[17] Two years later Congress passed the Great Plains Conservation Program, which provided financial assistance to plains farmers who enacted conservation measures to check wind erosion. Often this meant returning plowed land into grassland, but the program also subsidized such production measures as improving irrigation, leveling land, and digging wells for watering livestock.[18]

As the soil conservation mainstream moved in this direction of managing soil for increased production, a minority view persisted, even if its voice was scarcely heard. This view rested on a unique blend of ecology and agrarianism—a belief in the interconnectedness of living things, including the soil, and in the essential virtues of rural living. This soil ethic was common in much of the soil conservation activity of the 1930s and persisted into the decades of surplus.[19] From 1941 until 1954 this minority ethic had a voice in *The Land,* a periodical published by the Friends of the Land. Many veterans of the

New Deal land planning efforts contributed to this publication, including Henry A. Wallace, Rexford Tugwell, and Hugh Bennett. For this small audience of around six thousand readers, Stuart Chase answered the claims of technological progress: "Nature always comes into the equation at base. Science cannot save us this reckoning. Science can help us meet it, only if it recognizes basic realities, and the unified order of enduring life. We are creatures of this earth, and so are a part of all our prairies, mountains, rivers, and clouds. Unless we feel this dependence we may know all the calculus and all the Talmud, but have not learned the first lesson of living on this earth."[20] This "first lesson" was fast disappearing as the land economics of the 1930s, animated by this mystical devotion to the land, evolved into the agricultural economics of the postwar decades, with its view that land was an increasingly less important factor in farm production.

These environmental agrarians of the 1930s who had helped to shape the New Deal now found their notions distinctly at odds with the dominant intellectual and political currents. This transition can be seen clearly in the career of Russell Lord, an agrarian mystic who traveled in New Deal land planning circles, worked for USDA during the 1930s, wrote extensively on agriculture (including *The Wallaces of Iowa* and *Forever the Land*), and edited *The Land*. He maintained that the "temporary overabundance" of the 1950s and 1960s did not alter the long-range threat to society posed by deteriorating soils. The economic yardstick of soil as a productive "input" was not sufficient to measure the true value of soil, Lord believed, because economics was "but one branch of ecology, which deals with relationships as a whole."[21] The starting point, Lord argued, was not economics but a religious reverence for the land: "We must recognize that the thing that binds us in a fellowship is a quiet, deep sentiment—love of the land. All conservation begins with that."[22]

This minority conservation view remained consistent with the land ethic of the thirties and so formed an interesting critique of the SCS as that agency trimmed its broader mission in order to conform to the prevailing devaluation of agricultural conservation. Historian and conservationist Bernard DeVoto complained in his monthly column in *Harper's* about the "sacrifice of conservation values" in the SCS. The focus of DeVoto's ire was the 1955 reorganization of the SCS from a regional to a state basis and the shift of most technical services from the SCS to the land grant colleges and the Extension Service. DeVoto, who in 1946 had established his credentials as a conservationist by opposing the transfer of Forest Service lands to state control, saw a similar theme at work on this issue. He attacked as "propaganda" the portrayal of land use controls as a struggle between the local interest and federal bureaucrats and insisted instead that it was a conflict of "a special interest and the public interest." "In every aspect of this kind of conservation," DeVoto continued, "this kind of 'local control' must inevitably mean local vulnerability, local manipulation, and local intimidation."[23] Similarly, Milton Eisenhower, former USDA land use coordinator, called the failure to implement New Deal land use programs "mortifying" and insisted that "true conservation cannot be achieved by the haphazard application of individual practices." He preferred a farm policy based on what a later generation would call cross-compliance—namely, that "all governmental economic aid to the individual farmer be made conditional upon that farmer's establishing and maintaining a conservation program for his own." Eisenhower warned that "mere example has not been enough" and insisted that a voluntary approach to soil control would not suffice to bring conservation practices to farming. This was all the more urgent, Eisenhower believed, because of the "pincers movement" of continuing soil deterioration and rising population, which put mankind in a "headlong plunge towards disaster."[24]

In many ways this minority conservationist tradition was simply the persistence of the New Deal land ethic into the postwar era, but this mention of rapid population growth injected a dramatic new element into the discussion of agricultural resources. The Malthusian concern for overpopulation, which land planners of the Progressive Era had discarded during the twenties under the influence of declining birth rates in Europe, had been noticeably missing from New Deal thinking about the supply of farmland. World War II changed conservation thinking by drawing attention to diminishing supplies of some renewable resources and especially by exposing conservationists to the burgeoning population of the Third World. Two books, both published in 1948, demonstrated this recognition of the massive population potential in those parts of the world recently unloosed from colonial domination. Fairfield Osborn, in *Our Plundered Planet,* sounded many familiar themes about the necessity of caring for our "good earth" and of cooperating with nature. He warned against "man-applied chemistry," which might raise soil yields but could not halt soil deterioration, and he wrote prophetically of the danger of the pesticide DDT, which might control agricultural pests but was already killing birds and, given the interdependence of nature, would eventually harm humans as well. What was most striking about Osborn's approach, however, was in the book's first sentence: "Yesterday morning more than 175,000 mothers looked down upon the vague and uncomprehending eyes of their newborn babes."[25] If the birth of so many babies was an ambiguous event for Osborn, this kind of population growth was an outright disaster for a second author, William Vogt. Vogt had worked with the Audubon Society during the 1930s and spent World War II working in Latin America, where the combination of population growth, resource depletion, and intractable poverty made him a confirmed Malthusian. His book *Road to Survival* was the largest-selling conservation book prior to Rachel Carson's *Silent Spring*; it influenced the thinking of Bernard DeVoto, who used his literary influence to publicize the book, and Paul Ehrlich, who carried the same theme to a much wider audience two decades later. Vogt's tone was somber, even apocalyptic ("The Day of Judgment is at hand"). He suggested that the United States already had too many people, that the American lifestyle was indulgent and wasteful, and that unrestrained private ownership had damaged the health of the American land. Even his word choice was designed to jolt conventional thinking: "By excessive breeding and abuse of the land mankind has backed itself into an ecological trap. By a lopsided use of applied science it has been living on promissory notes."[26]

This new thinking on the population-resource nexus led naturally to questions about the adequacy of the nation's supply of farmland. Most analysts, including those from the Paley Commission, answered that the supply of good agricultural land was sufficient for the foreseeable future.[27] An interesting exception to this orthodoxy came from Samuel H. Ordway, who in 1953 proposed a somewhat vague theory on the limits to economic growth. Specifically, Ordway countered the Paley Commission's assumption that growth was good and its conclusion that the supply of agricultural land would not restrict food supply. He interpreted U.S. Department of Agriculture data to show that 16 million acres of farmland had been lost to urbanization during the decade from 1935 to 1945, and he suggested that this "serious trend" could more than offset the gains in agricultural productivity brought about by technology. Scarcely more than an extended pamphlet, Ordway's *Resources and the American Dream* was wrong in some particulars and had little influence in challenging the general notion of economic growth or in boosting the specific cause of protecting farms from urban expansion.[28] Yet it was a striking anticipation of the concerns that would reemerge in the early 1970s. This sensitivity toward agricultural land that was contained in the writings of these agrarians, environmentalists, and Malthusians remained a distinct minority voice, so thoroughly discredited by the mainstream that what could have been a bridge from the 1930s to the 1970s was largely forgotten.

Growing Suburbs and Shrinking Farms

The resurgent growth of population and the unprecedented expansion of cities and suburbs into the farm landscape brought wholly unexpected pressures to bear on the agricultural land base. The land planning of the 1930s was based on the conventional demographic assumption that population would continue along its slower growth curve until it reached a stable plateau of 153 million by about 1980. The United States, demographers believed, would follow the pattern of "mature," industrialized countries, in which a decline in fertility rates accompanied the transformation from a rural, agrarian society to an urban, industrial one. The nation's crude birth rate (annual births per 1,000 people) had declined from 55 in 1820 to a low of 18 during the 1930s, a trend which the National Resources Committee calculated had put national reproduction rates "already below that required for permanent population replacement."[29] What actually happened was that fertility rates rose suddenly beginning in 1941 and hovered near 25 births per 1,000 people for each year during the late 1940s and 1950s. Instead of declining, the annual population growth rate increased from 0.7 percent in the 1930s to 1.9 percent during the 1950s before again slowing down in the 1960s and 1970s to around 1.0 percent. This meant that total population passed 200 million in 1970 and possessed enough momentum from the children of the baby boom to continue to grow for another seventy years even if couples had only two children and immigration was restricted. This demographic surprise drastically altered the population-resource balance so that even with the addition of two new states, there were sixteen more people per square mile of land in 1970 than there had been in 1930.[30]

The years of the baby boom were also the years of the most rapid suburban growth in American history. Although suburbs had been draining population away from the central city since the late nineteenth century, as Kenneth T. Jackson has shown, the postwar explosion of the urban periphery was unprecedented. Even with the development of affordable automobiles and decent roads, suburbs grew between 1920 and 1940 at a modest rate, from 17 percent to 20 percent of the total population. By 1960 this percentage had jumped to 33 percent, and by 1977 nearly 40 percent of all Americans lived in the suburbs. This was a greater proportion than lived in either city or country; suburbs had become the nation's dominant place of residence. Another measure of the suddenness of this peripheral growth is single-family housing construction, which averaged nearly 500,000 during the late 1920s, declined during depression and war to a low of 114,000 in 1944, then increased to 1,692,000 in 1950—more than a tenfold increase from the war years, and three times the previous high of the 1920s.[31] Generally, these houses were hastily built on the cheapest available land, which was necessarily far from the urban core. The Model T of suburban housing came from William and Alfred Levitt, who in the late 1940s used mass production techniques and standardized house plans to build over thirty houses per day in developments such as Levittown, Long Island. Although these developments were sometimes criticized for being too crowded, Jackson points out that Levittown was only one-half as dense as the earlier streetcar suburbs.[32] Regions that tried to prevent this sort of mass development could lose even more land to piecemeal suburban development, as critics noted. In one instance, Chester County, Pennsylvania, relied on large lot zoning and "private conscience" to prevent unsightly suburbanization, yet scattered development raised the local tax base, debilitated the farm economy, and left other landowners with little choice but to sell. The result was that as the "inexorable sequence" of development moved into the countryside in a less compact pattern, more land was used to house fewer people.[33]

The causes of this outward movement, like any great migration, cannot always be discerned without ambiguity. What Jackson calls the "anti-urban tradition in American thought" is at least as old as Thomas Jefferson and influenced such diverse personalities as landscape gardener Andrew Jackson Downing ("The love of country is inseparably connected with the love of home"); Frederick Law Olmsted ("No great town can long exist without a great suburb"), who designed New York City's Central Park as an escape; and Henry Ford ("We shall solve the city problem by leaving the city"), who provided the technology for escape.[34] Thus suburbs mushroomed in the postwar decades in part because increasing affluence and more accessible transportation allowed Americans as never before to move close to the country. Yet this was not simply a natural process; rather, it was a slow movement that was greatly speeded up by governmental policies. The New Deal's Federal Housing Authority issued nearly all of its mortgage insurance for houses in suburbia, and together with the Veterans Administration, federal agencies financed nearly half of all suburban homes. Federal income tax regulations making mortgage interest deductible provided a further subsidy for suburban homeowners, while the 1956 Interstate Highway Act, which provided 90 percent federal funding for 42,000 miles of new highway, in Jackson's words, "virtually guaranteed that future urban growth would perpetuate a centerless sprawl."[35] Thus the great postwar exodus onto the agricultural landscape was immeasurably reinforced (albeit indirectly) by government policy, just as the nineteenth-century movement onto western farmlands was aided by government land disposal policies.

Because much of the most fertile farmland was located adjacent to cities, this careless spread of housing developments and highways paved over some of the nation's best farmland with no thought of the permanent loss of the soil resource. The farmer's gently rolling field, well drained and with trees already removed, also happened to be the cheapest land on which to build. For Russell Lord and others the problem was not just the loss of potentially productive soil. More important was that the "age of bulldozers" created "something deeply unsatisfying, feverish, uncertain, and ugly."[36] This combination of aesthetic, ethical, and agricultural concerns prompted Luther Gulick to elaborate on how the growing city violated his sense of "rational land use." He worried that California, Florida, Pennsylvania, and New Jersey were losing "some of the finest and most productive agricultural land on the continent." Irreplaceable productive land, which was also a "wonderful spiritual resource," was being lost to the "degrading operations" of the bulldozer and the developer, all in the name of "progress."[37] In the age of surpluses urbanization posed no threat to overall productive potential. Instead, the issue was framed in terms of the decline of specialty crops and the loss of the agrarian spirit.

The soil conservation movement, now a part of the agricultural establishment, also began to notice how sprawling urban growth changed the conservation equation. The 1957 Conservation Needs Inventory, based on estimates from the agency's field personnel, concluded that 17 million acres of good-quality farmland (Land Use Capability classes I, II, III, IV) had been lost from cultivation between 1942 and 1956. Three-fifths of this 1.1-million-acre annual loss went to private housing, industrial, and commercial uses, while the remaining two-fifths went to public uses such as airports, highways, and defense plants. Don Williams, SCS administrator, attributed this farmland loss to population growth; an expanding industrial economy; the developers' preference for level, arable land; the construction of major highways; and the "snowballing process" of patchy suburbanization, rising property taxes, and declining farm profitability (the combination of factors that became known in the 1970s as the "impermanence syndrome"). Although this loss was concentrated in the rapidly growing states of the Northeast, Midwest, and West Coast and in southern areas near defense establishments, Williams argued that it was a national concern because the surpluses of the 1950s "should not cloud the fact that some day we may need every acre of cultivable land to produce food and fiber."[38] At the 1956 annual convention of the National Association of Soil and Water Conservation, Williams argued that farmland loss intensified other, more traditional, conservation problems. As fertile, level cropland was "buried under steel and concrete," farmers turned to less productive land, thus raising production costs and increasing erosion.[39] Williams's attempt to link the land use problems of urban expansion with accepted soil conservation concerns raised some people's hopes that the districts would broaden their perspective in the direction of their original intent, toward becoming more of a natural resource conservation movement concerned not only with erosion but also with the interrelated problems of water use, recreational lands, urban sprawl, and land use on all privately owned lands. These hopes were fleeting, however, and Williams's efforts in this regard proved inconsequential.

The Department of Agriculture gave slight mention to the connection between farmland loss and sprawling urbanization in its 1958 *Yearbook of Agriculture*. Several authors raised the issue, but none sounded the alarm. Raleigh Barlowe, a land economist at Michigan State University, calculated that conversion of farmland to other uses would "have only a relatively small impact on our total agricultural potential," but he still warned that "[w]ithout a certain amount of overall coordination, the suburbanization movement can very easily lead to wasteful and chaotic conditions." Better land use would come only from deliberate planning, Barlowe concluded. Mason Gaffney cautioned that the development process, especially capital gains tax policy, encouraged a "virtual scorched-earth policy" that idled many acres of productive farmland as land speculation took the place of farming. Urban expansion had a "baleful influence" on the farms because it forced farmers to become land speculators and thus to ignore farm improvements and soil conservation. A third writer, Hugh A. Johnson, took a more panglossian approach. He argued that the fears of the "grasping tentacles of an urban octopus and the specter of a land-starved future" were "exaggerated," that urban expansion did not pose a serious national problem for agriculture. Yet Johnson did admit that "directing nonfarm growth along desirable channels," which could only mean land use planning, was "one of the critical problems facing agriculture today." The overall sense of these authors is that a problem was on the horizon but that prudent planning could easily lead the nation past the danger. Looking back it is hard to find reason for their optimism, for "leapfrogging suburbanization, ill-planned highway networks, and industries scattered hit or miss over the countryside," which Johnson assumed could be avoided, became the rule of the next two decades.[40]

The issue of farmland loss, however, was usually framed in local and state terms, not as a national problem. The best statistical measure of the problem came from the National Inventory of Soil and Water Conservation Needs prepared by the Department of Agriculture, completed in 1958 and updated in 1967. Interpretation of these inventories later became the subject of intense controversy, but from the first it was clear that each year over one million acres of productive agricultural land was being converted to "urban and built-up uses." Almost half of this farmland loss came directly from cropland, with the rest coming from pasture and rangeland.[41] A 1959 survey conducted by the National Association of Soil Conservation Districts showed that over five hundred conservation districts felt that cities posed a major conservation threat.[42] As would be expected, both studies reported that the most acute farmland losses were taking place in the densely populated regions in the Northeast, the Pacific Coast, and the Great Lakes. In the age of farm surpluses this loss of national productive potential was barely noticed; interest in the loss of farm acres was confined to the affected areas.

The first policy responses reflected this regional dimension, for they came from local and state governments along each coast. Maryland, a state whose farmlands were fast being lost to suburbia, in 1956 passed a state tax law allowing farmers to pay property taxes at only the use value of their land, not at its higher value for development. This move was intended to make it easier for farmers to remain in farming and thereby to keep some green space between the developing towns. By 1970 over forty other states had passed some form of preferential tax assessment for farmland, sometimes for the sake of farmers but also for the benefit of city dwellers who needed a nearby rural escape from the crowded city.[43] In some instances these needs combined with worry about the loss of a local agricultural economy based on specialty crops. Thus citrus crops in California and truck farms near New York City were the focus of much attention and even state legislation, but only as local or regional matters. The national interest was nowhere in sight.[44]

The Growing Need to Feed the World

This situation changed dramatically in the early 1970s, however, as circumstances changed suddenly and brought new attention to agricultural land. Beginning in the 1960s and building into the 1970s was a new level of concern about world population pressures. Worries that a growing population would challenge a limited land and food supply go back at least to Thomas Malthus in the late eighteenth century and were present in this country, as we have seen, in both the Progressive and New Deal conservation movements. During the 1950s population problems faded from public consciousness as petrochemical farming produced surpluses that seemed to outstrip population growth. In the 1960s a greater awareness of exponential world population growth challenged this confidence. The world's population reached its first billion in 1850; by 1930 another billion was added; it took only thirty years for the third billion; and a fourth billion was expected (and arrived) by 1975. To put it another way, the time required for world population to double had decreased from a historic rate of 1;500 years (a rate that held steady from 8000 B.C. to 1650 A.D.) to a modern rate of scarcely thirty-six years (calculated in 1975). Moreover, the youthful age structure and high fertility rate of Third World countries gave population growth a certain momentum which meant that population growth could not stabilize at the 1975 level of four billion. Most demographers, including those at the United Nations, projected that world population would double or triple to reach 8 or 12 billion before leveling off.[45] Annual population growth of 70–80 million during the 1960s lent a frightening plausibility to this revival of Malthusian concerns.

The language was sometimes inflated, but the warnings about over-population came from scientific authorities. Georg Bergstrom, professor of food science and geography at Michigan State University and a widely recognized expert on world fisheries, warned in 1965 of the "rising human tidal wave" that "threatens to deprive the human race of its future," that the world's population "long ago exceeded the limits of what the world can feed."[46] Development specialists William and Paul Paddock predicted that a "population-food collision is inevitable," that "the locomotive roaring straight at us is the population explosion."[47] In 1968 prominent population biologist Paul Ehrlich wrote *The Population Bomb,* which sold over three million copies and carried on the apocalyptic tradition of William Vogt's *Road to Survival.* Ehrlich claimed that the world was already overpopulated and destined for resource scarcity, environmental degradation, and mass starvation.[48] Not everyone shared this gloomy analysis—Third World countries and many economists tended to blame unequal distribution of resources more than expanding numbers of people for the food shortages—but the sense of impending crisis was so strong that even a dissenter with a strong faith in American agricultural technology described himself only as "guardedly optimistic."[49] The perception of a population problem, both global and domestic, was so widely shared that in 1969 President Nixon delivered an unprecedented presidential address on population and asked Congress to create a commission on population growth. In early 1972 this commission reported: "At a time when the federal government pays farmers to hold land out of production, it seems absurd to be looking forward to a scarcity of good agricultural land and rising food prices. Yet these are the prospects indicated by our analysis of what rapid United States population growth implies."[50]

Events conspired in a rather dramatic way in the early 1970s to fulfill this prospect of a world "food crisis" and bring new attention to American farmland. In 1970 and 1971 the world grain market tightened in response to widespread crop failures. The next year saw major crop failures in Russia and southern Asia, and in 1973 the slide continued as Peru's anchovy production dropped from 12 million to 2 million tons. Drought in the overgrazed Sahel of Africa and crop failures in Bangladesh highlighted the limits of a "green revolution" that even an optimist admitted had "faltered."[51] Initially touted as a miracle cure for hunger in the developing world, by the early 1970s the green revolution proved to be less of a solution than a way to postpone by fifteen years or so the inevitable catching up of population to food supplies. Worse, the green revolution exported American agriculture's thirst for water, petroleum, fertilizer, and indebtedness; it thereby displaced subsistence farmers, forced peasants into greater dependency on multinational chemical companies, polluted water supplies, reduced genetic diversity, and degraded traditional ecosystems.[52] The United Nations' Food and Agriculture Organization suggested, "History records more acute shortages in individual countries, but it is doubtful whether such a critical food situation has ever been so worldwide."[53] In 1974 the United Nations expressed its concern by sponsoring a conference on population in Bucharest and a World Food Conference in Rome. At both of these, especially at the Rome event, the food-producing capacity of the United States was recognized as crucial to feeding the world's expanding population. The "North American breadbasket" emerged as a resource that would be of primary importance in meeting world food shortages.

The U.S. response to this new situation was to plunge into the world food market at record levels. Since 1954, when Congress passed Public Law 480, which authorized the federal government to buy surplus crops and give them to other countries as food aid, U.S. agriculture had relied heavily on foreign exports to soak up surplus supplies. In 1972, for the first time in the postwar era, U.S. agricultural exports increased not as a way to reduce surplus but in response to a sudden increase in demand. President Nixon's 1971 devaluation of the dollar, which made U.S. farm exports cheaper for foreign countries, and the 1972 agreement to export over $1 billion worth of grain to Russia sent U.S. agricultural exports soaring 30 percent between 1972 and 1974. In 1974, for the first time since the New Deal, there were no federal government payments to farmers for idle cropland, and that year world grain reserves reached their lowest level in two decades.[54] The Nixon Administration's free enterprise ideology meshed nicely with an emerging world food crisis, so that farmers' incomes rose even as the U.S. became the generous provider for a hungry world. The overproduction that had characterized U.S. agriculture for decades now disappeared: U.S. grain reserves were cut almost in third, from 74 million metric tons in 1972 to only 28 million metric tons in 1975. This reserve supply, food expert Lester Brown concluded, was enough to satisfy global needs for only twenty-six days, indicating that "the world food supply-demand equation was precariously balanced" and extremely vulnerable to any major crop failure.[55]

This situation provided the perfect opportunity for Nixon's secretary of agriculture, Earl Butz, to implement a policy of raising farm incomes by increasing both farm production and food exports. For Butz, exports were the free market solution to the problems of chronic overproduction, low farm incomes, and expensive government subsidies.[56] Thus Butz championed the Russian grain sale and advised farmers to "plant fencerow to fencerow" as U.S. agriculture cranked up for maximum production, bringing into production land that had been idled during the years of surplus. Farmers planted 25 million more acres in 1974 than they had in 1972, and by 1977 this number had increased by another 20 million acres.[57] Almost ignored was the fact that nearly half of this new land was highly erodible (SCS classes VI and VII) and that this "great plow-out" encouraged farmers to discard soil erosion practices such as crop rotations.[58] This increase in erosion came as the U.S. farm economy became linked to a greater degree than ever before to the world food market. After 1972 U.S. agricultural prosperity depended as never before on such worldwide factors as drought in Africa, the Russian wheat harvest, global weather patterns, and world population growth. Agricultural economists called this leap into the world market, "after the introduction of the tractor, the most important shock affecting the structure of American agriculture in this century."[59] This dependence on the world market made American agriculture more specialized, more intensive, and more vulnerable to market depressions, and it placed new demands on the nation's agricultural land. Exports grew by 9.4 percent annually throughout the 1970s; by the end of the decade one-third of all American farmland was given to export crops, and these agricultural exports composed one-fifth of all U.S. exports.[60] Although Secretary of Agriculture Butz rejected the idea of food as a weapon, discussions persisted of the United States as the world's "food OPEC," and some considered farmland a "strategic resource" for international diplomacy.[61] *Science* magazine reminded its readers that while food exports helped to compensate for the trade imbalance caused by oil imports, this food production came with a high cost of increased erosion. "The bounty of our farms supports and extends the profligacy of our energy consumption," because "for each ton of grain going to Europe or Japan, we export several tons of topsoil to the Gulf of Mexico."[62]

While the plunge into the world food market was immediately obvious, another trend began almost simultaneously that was harder to detect. Farm productivity, after three decades of dramatic increases, began to level off. Yields increased by an annual average of 2.3 percent from 1950 to 1970 but only at 1 percent from 1970 to 1976. Various explanations emerged for the slower growth rates of the seventies. Bad weather hurt some crops in 1973 and again in 1974, causing some to think that reduced yields were a temporary aberration that could be corrected when "normal" weather returned. By 1976, however, evidence pointed strongly to agricultural economist Pierre Crosson's conclusion "that the technology that produced the massive gains in yields and productivity in American agriculture after World War II may have run its course by the early 1970s."[63] A return to favorable weather and higher crop yields in 1979 and 1981 led Earl Heady, an agricultural economist at Iowa State University, to challenge this conclusion. Heady maintained that there was "no firm evidence of yield plateaus" and that the apparent slack in the productivity pace was due more to the combination of bad weather and high fertilizer prices than to the exhaustion of current technologies.[64] However, yields in the 1980s continued to fluctuate dramatically and remained much less predictable than in earlier decades.[65] Crosson has shown that even the high-yield years of 1979 and 1981 fell short of the growth trend of the fifties and sixties, all of which confirmed the notion of a slowdown in productivity growth. As Heady and Crosson both have noted, one major reason for this slowdown was the skyrocketing costs of petroleum-based fertilizers. The price of fertilizers jumped 75 percent between 1972 and 1975, then slowly declined until 1979. The price of diesel fuel followed the same pattern. Thus even if higher yields were possible with more fertilizer, by the end of the seventies it had become too expensive, both environmentally and economically, for farmers to continue to pursue greater productivity through an increased use of petroleum-based technology.[66] Fertilizer use passed 50 million tons in 1977, more than twice its 1960 level and up 10 million tons from its 1970 level. Even when prices edged downward in the late seventies, fertilizer use did not surpass the 1977 level, because farmers found that more fertilizer did not always increase yields correspondingly.[67] Slower gains in yields did not mean that total production slowed during the 1970s but that production increases required more land. Willard Cochrane, a leading agricultural economist, called the seventies a "watershed" period in American agricultural history because "the production response in the 1970s is different from that of the period from 1940–1970. In the earlier period the physical increase in output was generated through rising crop yields on a declining crop acreage. The physical increase in output in the period 1970–1977 was generated on an expanding crop acreage with constant crop yields."[68]

In addition to this leveling of crop yields, another problem that became apparent in the early 1970s was the decrease in the ecological diversity and, with it, the biological stability of modern agriculture. Seed hybrids brought increased genetic uniformity and the possibility for widespread crop failure. By the 1970s, six inbred genetic lines accounted for 43 percent of all corn, and six varieties of soybeans yielded 56 percent of all soybeans grown in the United States. Monoculture's vulnerability was dramatized in 1970 when a leaf blight, a specialized parasite that attacked only one strain of corn, destroyed 15 percent of the nation's corn crop.[69] Genetic uniformity, larger fields increasingly dominated by a few commodity crops, and the greater reliance on chemical herbicides and pesticides combined to create a more vulnerable ecology of agriculture. The diminishing returns of pesticide use provided a graphic illustration of this situation: in 1948, farmers used 50 million pounds of insecticides and lost 7 percent of preharvest crops to insects. In 1980, farmers used 600 million pounds of insecticides and lost 13 percent of preharvest crops to insects.[70]

This ecological vulnerability was perhaps greatest in agriculture's growing dependence, easily overlooked in an era of comparatively cheap and relatively abundant energy, on a finite resource—fossil fuels. Petroleum-based fertilizer consumption went from 1.2 million tons in 1935 to 16 million tons in 1970, nearly a twelvefold increase. During the same years the use of mechanized tractor horsepower increased by five times, while the total number of farm machines skyrocketed from around 2.5 million to over 10 million.[71] This meant that energy substituted for farmland and human labor. From 1940 until 1980, while farm production more than doubled, aggregate energy consumption on farms went up eightfold.[72] Calculating this information another way, in 1950 it took the equivalent of 0.44 barrels of oil to produce one ton of grain, while in 1980 a ton of grain required the equivalent of 1.13 barrels of oil.[73] Thus the technology used to lift production levels carried with it environmental dependencies that were not immediately apparent. From an ecological perspective they could not be missed, as Howard T. Odum warned in 1971:

"[I]ndustrial man no longer eats potatoes made from solar energy; now he eats potatoes partly made of oil." Odum pointed out how the energy flow supporting agriculture began not on the farm but in the city, with the manufacture of tractors, the production of fertilizer, and the development of seed varieties and with the creation and maintenance of markets for buying and selling farm goods. Odum concluded that humans had not "mastered nature" but rather were "overcoming bottlenecks and providing subsidy from fossil fuel."[74]

So long as cheap energy was the rule, agriculture's dependence went unnoticed, but this setup changed suddenly with the 1973 energy crisis. Overall, farms in 1974 used only 3 percent of all energy consumed in the United States, while another 16 percent went to food processing and distribution. Of the energy used on farms, nearly one-third went directly into fertilizers and pesticides.[75] When oil prices jumped from $3 per barrel in 1973 to $12 per barrel in 1974,[76] dependence on energy appeared as a weak link in the U.S. agricultural system. David Pimental led a group of Cornell researchers in a study which calculated that eighty gallons of gasoline were used for each acre of corn produced and that each calorie of food energy (corn) produced required 2.8 calories of energy for production. Over the last thirty years U.S. agriculture had become both more energy-intensive and less energy-efficient as the ratio of calories produced in the form of food to calories consumed in the production process grew steadily higher. According to Pimental, if the entire world of four billion (in 1975) were fed by U.S. technology, and fossil fuel were the only fuel source used, the known world petroleum reserves would be consumed in only twenty-nine years.[77] John S. and Carol E. Steinhart, also working in the immediate aftermath of the 1973 energy crisis, figured that more energy went into U.S. agriculture in the form of petroleum than came out in the form of food.[78] Between 1941 and 1976, fertilizer and pesticide use in U.S. farming increased by more than 500 percent, while horsepower consumption went up more than 400 percent. This increased energy dependence reduced labor requirements, compensated for soil erosion, and made possible the enormous productivity gains of the postwar years. Yet by the 1970s evidence showed that further increases in fertilizer use did not necessarily bring corresponding increases in yields.[79] As American agriculture became more energy-intensive it actually became less energy-efficient.

The seventies saw water join oil as a resource in short supply. Irrigated acreage tripled between 1940 and 1977 and accounted for 14 percent of all cropland and 25 percent of all the value of all crops in 1977. With cheap water coming from federally subsidized reclamation projects or unregulated underground aquifers, irrigation of the arid West played a major role in the production boom of the postwar era. According to one (probably conservative) estimate, the value of crops produced on irrigated lands in 1977 made those irrigated lands equal to 18 million additional acres of cropland.[80] Yet a host of problems emerged in the seventies that exposed fundamental flaws in the growth patterns of irrigated agriculture. Increased competition for surface waters, combined with a spreading disillusionment about federally subsidized water projects, severely restricted new water sources and even put pressures on existing irrigation uses. Mining of groundwater, especially on the Ogallala aquifer of the High Plains, accounted for a significant increase in irrigated acreage from the 1930s through the 1960s, but by the 1970s many acres were returning to dry land farming as this fossil water source was drained dry. In one Arizona county the overdraft of groundwater lowered the water table by 150 feet in ten years.[81] As water levels fell, the energy costs of pumping water to the surface increased to the point that in some places irrigation was abandoned. The only major western exception to this rule was in the Nebraska Sandhills, where a vast underground source close to the surface made possible a surge in center-pivot irrigation that seemed sustainable into the next century. Elsewhere other environmental problems dampened the irrigation picture. The inevitable accumulation of salts on irrigated lands threatened 25 to 35 percent of the irrigated lands in the West, and all western river basins except for the Columbia suffered from high salt levels. One report estimated that in 1979, in the fertile San Joaquin Valley, salination and high water tables from inadequate runoff had hurt productivity on 400,000 acres and threatened another million acres. Although scientists and farmers could report some progress in finding ways to use water more efficiently, notably with drip irrigation, the accumulated environmental problems meant that irrigation could not be counted on for increased farm production in the decades after the seventies as it had been in the decades before.[82]

The new agriculture received its greatest challenge with the rediscovery of soil erosion in the 1970s. After the seemingly successful policy initiatives of the New Deal, soil erosion faded from the public view. Although firm evidence was scarce, policymakers generally viewed soil conservation as a successful example of New Deal policies. The Conservation Needs Inventory of the SCS reported on the numbers of acres that needed conservation treatment but offered no overall measure of progress made. Independent analysts in 1964 reported that "although there is general agreement that progress has been made," there was "simply no clear-cut, well-designed data, especially on a historical scale, . . . adequate to measure the critical questions about soil conservation achievement over the past thirty years or so."[83] Soil conservationists usually pointed to the proliferation of soil conservation districts and to the number of acres for which erosion control plans had been made and assumed that the voluntary approach of the SCS was working.[84] Still, there was no overall measure of actual decreases in erosion, which would prove that plans were in fact being implemented and were effective. That erosion had decreased since the 1930s was generally agreed upon, but whether this decrease came as a direct result of conservation plans or as a result of other changes in agricultural land use was still an open question. As one historical geographer noted, "The fact is that fifty years and $15 billion later, we still do not know the effects of this massive project."[85]

What was certain was that existing conservation policy was not adequate to curb the increased erosion of the 1970s. With the all-out production effort of 1972 to 1975 (the "great plow-out"), farmers ignored conservation practices, plowed up grasslands, cleared shelterbelts, and stopped rotating crops. The result, as a variety of studies showed, was that not only did soil erosion persist in spite of policies designed to alleviate it; it actually worsened. The Corn Belt suffered especially hard: reports showed 70 percent of some Wisconsin lands losing twice the maximum tolerable soil loss, while in Iowa soil losses increased 22 percent in response to the maximum production efforts. Luther Carter summarized much of the new concern in *Science*: "Although nearly $15 billion has been spent on soil conservation since the midthirties, the erosion of croplands . . . remains one of the biggest, most pervasive environmental problems the nation faces."[86]

Carter's conclusions were based on an influential General Accounting Office (GAO) survey that found no significant improvement in soil loss for farmers who participated in government soil conservation programs over those who did not. A survey of available indices of the problem revealed that erosion surpassed tolerable levels on one-third of all croplands, with a total of four billion tons of topsoil lost every year (compared to three billion during the 1930s). The productivity lost from eroded soils equaled $1.2 billion in fertilizer costs, while the washed sediment contributed $163 million annually to water pollution control costs. The GAO study faulted the SCS for taking a "passive" approach in waiting for farmers to request aid rather than seeking out the most severe erosion problems. SCS field staff busied themselves preparing elaborate plans, yet less than half of the farms in the GAO sample actually used these plans. Meanwhile, the cost-sharing program of the Agricultural Conservation Program (administered by the Agricultural Stabilization and Conservation Service), which was designed to subsidize the expense of soil conservation, in fact paid farmers for production-oriented improvements such as installing irrigation and drainage works.[87] Thus government funds that were supposed to enhance conservation were being spent to increase production as the conservation agencies acquiesced in the production mentality of the decade.

The rediscovery of erosion as a national problem moved Congress to pass the Soil and Water Resources Conservation Act (RCA) in 1977. The RCA was a response to a growing awareness of soil erosion and to the need for agency coordination and budgetary justification. The Department of Agriculture was especially embarrassed by the GAO report and its own inability to come up with data proving the effectiveness of its programs. The RCA report noted that water and wind erosion combined to remove 6.4 billion tons of topsoil annually, that 23 percent of the nation's cropland eroded at a greater than tolerable rate, and that nearly 90 percent of all "excessive" erosion occurred on only 10 percent of all cropland. This analysis of the problem became the basis for much policy discussion and, in particular, for a fascination with "targeting" erosion control programs to the 10 percent of lands most heavily eroded. For all of its revealing analysis, the RCA quickly became subject to political pressures, and its policy suggestions were left untried.[88] The continued inability of government policy to deal effectively with soil degradation highlighted modern agriculture's abusive pattern of resource consumption and helped to link the loss of farmland through erosion to the loss of farmland through urban expansion.

Fears of an Impending Farmland Crisis

The environmental movement of the seventies also contributed in several ways to the changed context for thinking about agricultural land.

Many environmentalists tended toward the idea that resource depletion would come suddenly, with catastrophic results. The classic
statement of this view came in 1972 with the publication of *The Limits
to Growth,* written by Donella Meadows and three others and sponsored by the Club of Rome. This group began in 1968 when over thirty
individuals, many of them prominent industrialists, met in Rome to
initiate the Project on the Predicament of Mankind. Funded by a grant
from the Volkswagen Foundation and using a computer model developed by Jay Forrester of the Massachusetts Institute of Technology, researchers examined five factors that could limit global economic growth—population growth, agricultural production, natural
resources, industrial production, and pollution. The conclusion that
limits would be reached within the next one hundred years and that
the result would be "a rather sudden and uncontrollable decline in
both population and industrial capacity" was immediately challenged.[89] More influential than the specific conclusions, which even
the authors were forced to modify, was the premise that resource consumption followed an exponential rather than an incremental curve.
The Limits to Growth made commonplace this old French riddle: "Sup-
pose you own a pond on which a water lily is growing. The lily plant
doubles in size each day. If the lily were allowed to grow unchecked,
it would completely cover the pond in thirty days, choking off the
other forms of life in the water. For a long time the lily plant seems
small, and so you decide not to worry about cutting it back until it
covers half the pond. On what day will that be? On the twenty-ninth
day, of course. You will have one day to save your pond."[90]

The idea that resource consumption as well as population growth
were exponential, which meant that limits would be felt not gradually
but catastrophically, became a staple of the environmental movement.
The parable conveyed the sense of a slowly building but ultimately
uncontrollable crisis. This became the model, sometimes explicit and
sometimes not, for environmentalists' thinking about other resource
issues of the 1970s, whether the "energy crisis" of 1973–74 or the
"farmland crisis" of the late 1970s.

If the "limits to growth" wing of environmentalism contributed a
sense of urgency and even a (perhaps false) sense of crisis to the context for considering agricultural land, what might be called the organic wing of the environmental movement provided a critique of
modern agriculture that placed renewed emphasis on the value of agricultural land. The organic wing was a diverse but recognizable collection of dissidents, ecologists, farmers, and poets who shared a sense

that modern agriculture was not a source of affluence but a cause of ecological and economic distress; in their view, modern agriculture mined resources for today's profit at the expense of both land and people. This group united the economic survival of "rural democracy" with the ecological stability of sustained agriculture.[91] Vermont philosopher Murray Bookchin summarized the movement as an effort "to restore humanity's sense of community: first, by giving full recognition to the soil as an ecosystem, a biotic community; and second, by viewing agriculture as the activity of a natural human community, a human society."[92] The decline of the rural community of people, increasingly obvious throughout the 1950s and 1960s, was equated with the deterioration of the land, a theme of the 1970s. Wendell Berry, farmer, poet, and essayist of the movement, summarized his opposition to the alleged successes of modern agriculture:

> That one American farmer can now feed himself and fifty-six other people may be, within the narrow view of the specialist, a triumph of economics and technology; by no stretch of reason can it be considered a triumph of agriculture or of culture. It has been made possible by the substitution of energy for knowledge, of methodology for care, of technology for morality. This 'accomplishment' is not primarily the work of farmers—who have been, by and large, its victims—but of a collaboration of corporations, university specialists, and government agencies. It is therefore an agricultural development not motivated by agricultural aims or disciplines, but by the ambitions of merchants, industrialists, bureaucrats, and academic careerists. We should not be surprised to find that its effect on both farmland and farm people has been ruinous.[93]

This blend of ecology and agrarianism was not entirely new to the 1970s. Similar themes had surfaced during the New Deal, but these ideas took on renewed poignancy in the changed context of the 1970s.

With all of this new emphasis on agricultural land, it is not surprising that in the 1970s an effort was made to develop a policy to protect farmland. In the new context of the 1970s, the farmland protection effort picked up intensity from a series of isolated, localized reforms to become a national movement. Thus the stage was set for a renewal of an older concern for the creation of federal laws to protect the nation's private agricultural lands.

Farmland

Protection

on the

Federal

Agenda

Initial Efforts to Legislate Land Use

Farmland preservation in the 1970s illustrates several larger themes in recent American political history. As a reform movement, farmland preservation emerged from the larger environmental ferment as an idea with genuine popular support and so can be understood at one level as part of the ebb and flow of reform movements in the post–New Deal system. Conflicts in values were real but in themselves were not sufficient to explain the full dimensions of the land use effort. At times the land use movement reflected the desire of centralizing elites to find rational, orderly procedures for guiding chaotic local land use decisions.[1] At other points the story demonstrates the importance of bureaucratic initiative in defining issues that served institutional needs, a theme that Theda Skocpol and others have emphasized.[2] Finally, farmland preservation efforts highlighted the key role of social science expertise and especially the effects of disagreement among experts. Among other things, the farmland preservation reform illuminates the parallel evolution of state administrative capacity and professional social science into what historian Brian Balogh calls the "prominstrative state."[3]

The issue of farmland preservation emerged from the larger environmental movement of the 1960s and 1970s as a response to conditions of expansive growth and threatening agricultural scarcity. It combined several diverse strands of thought, not all of them related, and this diversity contributed to some confusion and vagueness as to the goals and constituency of this loosely defined movement. Environmentalists' attention in the 1960s generally went to older issues such as wildlands preservation (the Wilderness Act of 1964, the Land and Water Conservation Fund Act of 1965) or to air and water pollution (the Clean Air acts of 1963 and 1967, the Clean Water acts of 1960 and 1965) in an attempt to curb the more grievous transgressions of industrial civilization. This set of priorities was in accord with the "land ethic" expounded in the 1930s and 1940s by Aldo Leopold and with newer fears of chemical contamination of the environment, such as Rachel Carson's 1962 warning about the effects of DDT.[4] As the movement matured in the early 1970s, it moved into new areas in which problems were more complex and solutions more intractable. Historian Samuel P. Hays[5] identifies the 1965–72 period as a transition period from the older thinking about natural resource protection to the newer interest in ecology. Bridging the two decades was the National Environmental Policy Act of 1969, which established an overall federal policy on the environment and a regulatory framework that forced federal agencies to include environmental concerns in their development plans. The act also created the Council on Environmental Quality (CEQ) as a top-level White House advisory agency. The continuity can also be seen in the fact that the Water Resources Council (established in 1965), although never as effective or as comprehensive as some of its congressional backers had hoped, did bring attention to the close connection between water and land resources and left some people in the Washington bureaucracy with the lingering notion that the nation's land resources were being abused and needed federal attention.[6] The environmental movement was so strong that neither party could resist its force, and many of its important achievements came under a conservative Republican president who nevertheless absorbed many environmental ideas. The path of resource protection, which started with public lands and grew to include water quality and quantity, air pollution, and toxic chemicals, led logically to the nation's largest and most visible resource—private rural lands. It was this combination of circumstances that prompted Russell Train, then chair of the CEQ, to write in 1971 about "the urgency we feel with respect to land use as the most important environmental issue remaining substantially unaddressed as a matter of national policy."[7]

The broadest possible context in which to deal with agricultural land protection was that of the national growth policy debate that began in the late 1960s. Inconsistencies arising from the lack of a coordinated federal policy to guide population growth and distribution patterns were becoming more apparent to many critics by the end of the decade. The supposedly natural forces that attracted people from the hinterland to the city and from the city to the suburbs were in fact abetted by a host of conflicting federal programs. The interstate highway system, federally subsidized mortgage insurance, crop subsidies that favored the capitalization of farms, and federal spending for such projects as sewers, airports, and military installations all directly involved the government in deciding where people were going to live. Urban riots, sprawling suburbs, and a depopulated countryside were mounting evidence that something was going wrong. Surprisingly, the first call for a more orderly approach to federal policies affecting population growth patterns came not from urban sources but from Lyndon Johnson's secretary of agriculture, Orville Freeman, and from the rural spaces of Minnesota. Freeman was interested in forging agricultural policies that could prove politically sustainable in a predominantly urban society, and he naturally saw crowded slums and depopulated countrysides as indissolubly linked problems that could be addressed by coherent and deliberate federal policies.

In 1967 Freeman opened the debate by convincing five other departments to join with the Department of Agriculture in sponsoring an Interdepartmental Conference on National Growth and Its Distribution. This conference was followed in 1968 by an Advisory Commission of Intergovernmental Relations (ACIR) Report on Urban and Rural America and in 1970 by the enactment of Title VII of the Housing and Urban Development Act, which required the president to publish four biennial reports on national growth. Thus the discussion about national growth policies began during the last years of a liberal Democratic administration, continued and even advanced under Richard Nixon, moved along in Congress during the Ford interregnum, then faded in the late 1970s despite some support from the Carter administration.[8] This unusual political context suggests that national growth policy was not so much an ideological matter as it was a search for more orderly and rational federal policies, an attempt to overcome what historian Ellis Hawley identifies as the "underdevelopment and incoherence, comparatively speaking, of America's policy planning apparatus in the social sphere."[9]

With the full weight of the American political tradition against the formation of a national policy governing private lands, it is not surprising that the national growth policy discussion remained only that, yet the discussion was informative even if it led to very little change. Equally unsurprising was the fact that the debate over growth policies would lead to worries about the loss of agricultural land. Land use issues naturally flowed from talk of the government's role in deciding where people should live and where factories should locate. At Freeman's 1967 conference Barbara Ward described the English model of protecting rural land as "preservation in perpetuity. . . . When we say 'preserved,' the control goes quite far. It means supervision of all types of development."[10] Following in this vein, the ACIR report the following year stated that "the burdens of sprawl" were "spoiling the dream" and pointed to both local and federal policies that could make a difference.[11] A decade later the same policy critique, with the connection to agricultural land loss made explicit, appeared in the growth report: "Without the more conscious and explicit recognition of the spatial aspect of policy, we are bound to repeat mistakes of the past such as those which have accelerated the decline of central cities and suburban sprawl and the paving over of much prime agricultural land, contrary to the long-term national interest in preserving it for the production of food and fiber."[12] Although the growth reports of the 1970s were widely perceived as inadequate, the discussion they generated did bring attention to agricultural land preservation as a minor but persistent theme. National growth policy advocates approached agricultural land loss not as an isolated resource issue but as evidence of flawed growth patterns. The assumption seemed to be that if overall growth patterns were brought into line, the loss of valuable farmlands to urbanization would be arrested.[13]

There was a lesson here for farmland preservationists—a lesson keenly felt by Senator Daniel Patrick Moynihan, the man who brought national growth policy into the Nixon White House. Moynihan was not much concerned with agricultural land, but he was astutely aware of the "hidden policies" of the federal government, of the fact that federal policy could not do only one thing. Moynihan once proposed that the mark of a competent government official was the ability to see the "interconnections" between specific programs and larger social goals.[14] This should have alerted farmland protection advocates to the fact that success might require more than one program or department to change, that farmland protection approached in isolation would invariably meet resistance from other federal policies with contradictory tendencies. Piecemeal farmland protection might not be any more successful than other single-purpose policies.

One part of the national growth policy with particular concerns for agricultural land was the proposed federal land use planning legislation of the early 1970s. Many of the same problems that pointed to the need for a national growth policy led even more directly to the need for some sort of reform of traditional land use practices. The post-1945 growth spurt seemed to have a momentum of its own, which made it impossible for local governments to control. Between 1950 and 1970 over 35 million people moved to the suburbs, creating expansive new communities built around the shopping mall and the highway but leaving behind stagnant or decaying central cities. This frenetic pace was expected to continue; projections indicated that by the end of the century, new growth in the form of housing, power plants, airports, and strip mines would double the nation's built-up area. Suburbs spread over farmland from Long Island to California's Santa Clara Valley, vacation homes despoiled rural environments from Vermont to Colorado, and new growth threatened water supplies from Florida's Everglades to Arizona's irrigated citrus groves. Deciding where, how, and when this development would take place was difficult for government at any level to control. Local governments, the nation's traditional repository of land use controls, thought mostly of minimizing their own expenses and maximizing their own tax base. They were often overwhelmed by federal projects built according to political considerations or by large developments concerned primarily with returning a profit. Any sense of a larger time and space, of the whole nation's interests over the long haul, was conspicuously absent from the development process.[15]

Support for reform of this fragmented land use planning process came from many sources. *Time* magazine suggested that Americans suffered from a "virulent outbreak" of "land fever" and reported favorably on governmental reforms to manage this "new land rush."[16] Corporations saw land use reform as a way to overcome the fragmentation and unpredictability of local laws,[17] while environmentalists gathered even more evidence of the wastefulness of existing land use patterns. *The Costs of Sprawl,* a study sponsored by the CEQ, found sprawl to be "the most expensive form of residential development in terms of economic costs, environmental costs, natural resource consumption, and many types of personal costs," and the work's authors recommended planning for more efficient development.[18] *The Use of Land,* a report sponsored by the Rockefeller Brothers Fund, described a "new mood in America" that they believed to be nothing less than a fundamental change in the American concept of land—from the perception of land as private property to be exploited at will toward that of land as community resource in need of governmental protection.[19] The *Wall Street Journal* reported, "There may not be any more farmland left in fifty to one hundred years—at least, not enough to feed everybody."[20] Similarly, the *New York Times* editorialized: "The price of planlessness is everywhere apparent in ugly sprawl, blight, choked traffic, misused or wasted resources. If the nation's land and water are to be used in the wisest and most constructive ways, the states can no longer shirk their responsibility to plan their own growth and to reconcile divergent needs."[21] President Richard Nixon merely stated the mainstream consensus when he wrote that the "time has come when we must accept the idea that none of us has a right to abuse the land, and that on the contrary society as a whole has a legitimate interest in proper land use." Nixon not only supported the idea, he called it "the most pressing environmental issue before the nation."[22]

Beginning in 1970 these reform sentiments focused on federal land use legislation, first proposed by Senator Henry Jackson of Washington. As chair of the Senate Interior Committee, Jackson was weary of mediating public lands conflicts between preservationists and developers on a case-by-case basis and wanted to establish a more rational process for resolving disputes. Questions of the siting of major facilities, such as the dispute in the late 1960s over the building of Miami's airport adjacent to the Everglades, broadened Jackson's concern from public to private lands. He worried that the broad national interest was being lost: "In the past, land-use decisions were made too often by those whose interests were selfish, short-term, and private." His original bill was essentially a procedural bill, modeled after and even drafted by some of the same staffers that had written the National Environmental Policy Act during the previous year. Although supported with environmental rhetoric, it was also proposed as a policy-neutral bill. The draft legislation called for improved federal coordination; a better database for land classification; and, most important, federal funds for comprehensive statewide plans. Jackson hoped to elevate planning from the local level, where the willingness and expertise was weak, to a level of government with more capability and greater scope. A rational person with no political instincts might have proposed the creation of new planning units based on regional concepts—perhaps river basins or other discrete ecological areas. The moderate Jackson, however, had good reasons to settle on the states as the appropriate level for planning. States were the constitutional custodians of land use powers and were, politically, the only choice possible. Moreover, the much-discussed "quiet revolution" in land use provided several examples of states that had successfully regulated development.[23]

In 1971 the Nixon administration, led by the CEQ and influenced at key points by John Ehrlichman, a former land use lawyer from Seattle, offered its own national land use legislation. The administration's bill owed its shape to Boyd Gibbons and William Reilly, both of the CEQ. Gibbons's experience was with the Coastal Zone Management law, which had led him to conclude that state regulation might be able to avoid the abuses of local governments, which tended to be preoccupied with local tax rates and dominated by development interests. Reilly reached a similar conclusion by a different route. He had worked with Chicago land use lawyers Richard Babcock and Fred Bosselman, noted critics of local land use practices who had been vital in the writing of the American Law Institute's Model Code, an attempt to reform fundamentally the laws governing land use by, among other things, returning some regulatory authority from the localities to the states. Reilly also had worked with the National Urban Coalition, where he became convinced that most local zoning was exclusionary and that local governments' ways of dealing with regional problems were totally inadequate. Thus both Gibbons and Reilly were persuaded that the key to environmental land reform lay in activating the power of the state to regulate private property. The bill they drafted took a different focus than Jackson's proposal. Whereas Jackson's legislation required states to prepare comprehensive statewide plans, the administration's bill required more selective state planning for special cases: areas of critical environmental concern (which could include farmland), key facilities such as energy sites or airports, facilities of regional benefit (such as waste disposal sites or low-income housing that might otherwise be excluded by local zoning), and large-scale residential or commercial developments. Jackson's approach emphasized program coordination and problem solving, while the administration's focused on environmental protection in critical areas. In 1972 the two approaches were combined into one bill, which went before the Ninety-third Congress with what seemed like a guaranteed passage.[24]

The Land Use Policy and Planning Assistance Act, as the 1973 legislation was dubbed, received widespread support, and farmland protection was central to the thinking of many of its supporters. Jackson opened hearings in 1975 by explaining the need for comprehensive land use planning:

> It is dramatically demonstrated in the growth statistics which indicate that over the next thirty years, an additional 19.7 million acres of undeveloped land will be consumed by urban sprawl—an area equivalent to the states of New Hampshire, Vermont, Massachusetts, and Rhode Island.
>
> Each decade's new growth will absorb an area greater than the entire state of New Jersey.
>
> By the end of the century, five million acres of valuable agricultural land may be lost to public facilities, second home development, and waste control projects, and another seven million may be taken for recreation areas.
>
> The demand for development suggests that between now and the year 2000, we must build again all that we have built before.[25]

Congressman Morris Udall, the House sponsor of similar land use legislation, explained his rationale in a similar way:

> Thousands of acres of our best agricultural land are still being developed for a multitude of other purposes without regard to our future agricultural needs. Our pollution and congestion problems continue and are aggravated, and we continue to waste energy like no other country in the world, in large part due to our land use

patterns and practices. I think it is time we learned from our past mistakes and made a national commitment to develop some sensible land use procedures and policies on the state and local levels—with federal coordination and financial assistance—which can help us to create the decent future society we all want.[26]

Consideration of the bill in the Ninety-third Congress coincided with the changed agricultural context of the early 1970s, in which world food shortages and a record demand for U.S. crops gave rise to a sense that food exports were now our trump card in the game of world trade. With this in mind, Senator Aiken of Vermont spoke on the floor of the Senate on 19 June 1973, linking farm policy, foreign policy, and the protection of agricultural land. Senator Aiken described the world demand for U.S. crops and asserted that "we are in a brand new situation": "never before in history . . . have so many millions been dependent on the American farmer." This new situation, Senator Aiken continued, called for not only a new farm policy and a recognition of new realities in foreign policy but also a reordering of land use priorities. Aiken asked rhetorically, "Has the time come for land use planners and conservationists to add farmland . . . to the list of scarce natural resources that should be protected as a matter of policy in the United States?" This new priority in land use planning, he reasoned, "might actually unite the farmers and the city people" around the "dual objective of containing urban sprawl and conserving farmland." Finally, Aiken was not content to leave this new priority to states and localities. In reference to Jackson's bill, Aiken concluded: "If there is to be a national land use plan, I believe the conservation of farmland should be one of its major objectives."[27]

Given such widespread support for land use legislation, its demise in 1974 came as a real surprise. Although Udall's bill passed easily in the Senate, the House narrowly defeated it. Attempts to revive the bill in 1975 proved fruitless. The causes of this failure reveal much about the genuine difficulty of meaningful reform in this country. Certainly Watergate had much to do with the bill's collapse, both because Nixon withdrew his support in an attempt to consolidate conservative opposition to his impeachment and because Ehrlichman was no longer in the White House to lend his personal understanding to administration land use thinking. The recession that followed the 1973 energy crisis dampened new construction and thus removed some of the development pressure that had made the bill seem so urgent. Suddenly the search for new energy sources took priority over restraining the development process. The ideological resistance mounted over time, and by 1974 the political right, led by the Chamber of Commerce of the United States, mobilized a fierce opposition to federal land use policy.[28] Less obvious in the rhetoric of the debate, but equally important, was the institutional resistance to the centralizing implications of Jackson's brand of federal land use planning. One careful scholar of this episode, Sidney Plotkin, concludes that the initiative was a struggle for the "locus of authority" in the "modernization of the capitalist state"; he thus sees the defeat of federal land use planning as part of the "social resistance to central planning."[29] As with the national growth policy, the decentralized, antibureaucratic, and incoherent tradition of American political culture proved decisive.[30]

Especially significant for agricultural land preservation was the reaction of two different groups, environmentalists and farmers, to the course of the bill. By 1974, as conservative opposition to federal land use planning mounted, environmentalists had already lost much of their earlier enthusiasm for the bill. Although the original legislation was a procedural bill—that is, it mandated a process but not a goal—environmentalists generally assumed that more ecologically sensitive patterns of land use would result from statewide planning. But what if a state came up with environmentally unacceptable plans—say, for the increased strip mining of fragile mountainsides or for the dredging of crucial wetlands? Or what if a state accepted the federal funds and planned according to the new law but then simply ignored the plans? Senator Edmund Muskie of Maine thought that federal funds ought to come with federal goals, so he proposed several amendments to set national standards for protecting farmlands, floodplains, and wetlands. These amendments failed to pass because they roused fears of federal intervention in the planning process. Environmentalists were left with a bill that called for a process of land planning but said nothing about the substance of planning. By 1973, as a later analyst noted, Jackson's bill "amounted to little more than a request by the national government that the states voluntarily review local land-use decisions having a regional impact."[31] Some even feared that the law would provide a convenient centralization of the planning process so that large developments or power plants could be more easily forced on reluctant localities, creating a way, in one lobbyist's words, "for energy producers to rape the land."[32] As reported in *The Nation,* Jackson's bill might "be the first step toward more intelligent land use and environmental protection" because it "could stop the states from allowing the worst uses" of land, yet it might also allow "big developers and their powerful financial backers" to corrupt state officials more efficiently than they had previously been able to corrupt scattered local zoning authorities.[33] Thus many perceived the net effect of the bill to be nearly neutral, perhaps slightly tilted against environment in favor of development, and it is no wonder that environmental groups did not rally when the legislation faltered.

Farm groups, on the other hand, reacted in a different fashion. They initially approached land use reform warily, suspicious of its urban and federal orientation. Norman Berg, who at that time worked for the Soil Conservation Service and in the late 1970s became that agency's chief administrator, recalls of the early land use legislation: "Agriculture was being ignored on this one. It was really an urban view they were cranking into this [land use planning] process."[34] Hearings on the bill brought out a range of agricultural opinion, from the libertarian cattlemen's association, which testified categorically that the government "cannot plan for agriculture," to the liberal National Farmers' Union, which argued for stronger federal guidelines and greater consideration of family farms.[35] The Department of Agriculture reported the most frequently recited fear: "Rural constituents, in particular, have expressed concern that the bill proposed to create a planning process on private lands identical to the process on public lands. To them, that suggests absolute control by a federal agency."[36] Most important for the bill's passage were the positions taken by the American Farm Bureau Federation and the National Association of Conservation Districts. The Farm Bureau predictably opposed the land use initiative as the product of "excessive emotionalism by doomsday zealots" and warned that "the enactment of such legislation would mean a start on the road to moving federal guidelines into federal regulations and the end of that route is often beyond anticipation."[37] Ultimately the Farm Bureau became a part of the conservative coalition, along with the Chamber of Commerce, the National Association of Manufacturers, the National Association of Homebuilders, and the National Association of Realtors, which rallied to defeat the legislation.[38] The NACD, although generally favorably disposed to the land use concerns, shared some of the same reservations as other farm groups. The organization wanted a greater role for the Department of Agriculture and especially objected to the leadership role of the Department of the Interior, where Jackson's bill placed administration of the new program. The NACD also thought that the legislation contained "an excessive concentration on environmental considerations at the expense of economic and social considerations" and argued that farmland should not be included along with other "areas of environmental concern."[39] Thus, the NACD opposed Udall's bill in the House in 1974 and was instrumental in separating out agricultural lands from other areas of environmental concern in the 1975 legislation.[40] The group's hope was to raise the visibility of farmland protection while avoiding troublesome federal guidelines about environmental protection and keeping any agricultural land planning closer to the friendly Department of Agriculture and the pliable states.

The failure of federal land use planning legislation did not mean that the federal government was not involved in planning for land use. The fact that new federal funds would not be available helped to dampen some of the states' earlier enthusiasm for land use planning, and political momentum for land use planning at any governmental level faltered. Still, the early 1970s saw in increase in federal planning activities, although in a fragmented fashion. The Coastal Zone Management Act of 1972 authorized the Commerce Department to give states grants for planning and regulating coastal development; other new laws increased federal regulations for floodplain development and strip mining; and land use considerations were implicit in clean air and water laws, the National Environmental Policy Act's requirement for environmental impact statements, and the Army Corps of Engineers' Section 208 permits, which were required for "dredge and fill" operations on wetlands.[41] In 1975 eminent zoning lawyer Richard Babcock commented that "Congress has passed so many federal land-use regulations that in a few years only a rare development project of any size will get by without two and probably more federal approvals."[42] Yet the defeat of national land use planning meant that this array of federal programs would all proceed piecemeal, according to single interests. The lesson was that a popular policy goal that required land use planning for its implementation—such as clean air or flood protection—might survive the legislative process, but coordinated federal land use planning itself was politically unacceptable. The government's policy planning apparatus would remain comparatively underdeveloped, as Hawley describes it, and subnational units would continue to dominate the federal system. Under such conditions it made sense, as Charles Little later wrote, "to parse the issues of land, to deal with them more or less separately in a legislative sense. That's where the Farmland Protection Policy Act came from—an effort to get some quite specific legislation before the Congress that they could chew on."[43] This approach lost some of the benefits of Jackson's comprehensive plan, especially in the coordination of the many agencies of the federal octopus, yet it offered hope that at least some problems might be better managed. If the land was going to be saved, it would have to happen one parcel at a time, one type of land at a time. The increasing public attention given to the loss of agricultural land made farmland protection a logical place to start.

USDA and the Land Use Turf Battles

Even as land use legislation struggled in Congress, the idea of farmland protection began its second long march through the permanent bureaucracy. The Department of Agriculture had an institutional interest in any problem of agricultural land use, because the department vied with other land-related bureaus for a leadership role. Yet its experience and clientele shaped USDA's response toward cautious and contradictory policies. USDA felt itself bypassed by much of the land use clamor and tried hard to claim land issues as its natural domain, based on its traditional ties to the soil, particularly the SCS. Yet the department moved cautiously when it began to consider land use problems for the first time since the New Deal. As early as 1967 the Department of Agriculture joined the Department of Housing and Urban Development (HUD) in cosponsoring a conference titled *Soil, Water, and Suburbia.* This conference united the traditional agricultural concern for soil erosion with the growing attention to water issues and linked both to land use planning. Secretary of Agriculture Orville Freeman headed his list of grievances against uncontrolled development with this observation: "Every year at least one million acres of farmland are being chewed up by bulldozers and entombed beneath asphalt, concrete, and brick."[44] Concern about the loss of farmland was not limited to the Department of Agriculture. Robert C. Wood, speaking for Housing and Urban Development, noted: "Both our departments are concerned about land-use planning, that the right land is used in the right way for urban expansion and that the right land be retained to support our amazing agricultural production."[45] Although these rumblings of discontent remained muted, the conference did mark official recognition from the secretary of agriculture and undersecretary of HUD that the loss of farmland was a problem worthy of federal attention. The conference also identified an important aspect of the problem: that the federal government, through its subsidies to various sorts of development, was contributing to the loss of farmland. Elsewhere Freeman, in words that recall his involvement in the national growth policy discussion, argued for a "sound land policy" that would stop the federally subsidized loss of "thousands of acres of this prime farmland to subdivisions, highways, airports."[46]

By the early 1970s the Department of Agriculture was on the defensive concerning land use issues. With national land use legislation pending in Congress and the Nixon administration supporting the idea (for a time, at least), USDA appeared to lag behind even its own administration on the issue. Jackson's bill was interpreted within the department as an implicit criticism of its land use activities or, rather, its lack of land use activities. Further, the bill sparked departmental fears of an urban-oriented land use planning that cared little for agricultural areas. From USDA's perspective, the bill subjected rural America to city planners whose maps labeled all farmland simply as "undeveloped."[47] USDA argued that land use legislation should "more fully use existing authority" to deal with problems and should give more consideration to the department's "competence in natural resource conservation and development accumulated over many years and in many programs."[48]

The Department of Agriculture had other reasons to be on the defensive. By 1971 President Nixon, frustrated by seemingly ungovernable bureaucracies, had circulated a reorganization plan designed to make the government more effective—that is, more subject to his command. Reorganization is a recurring theme in Washington, as presidents strive to bend the permanent government to the left or the right. Nixon's administrative reform would have abolished existing departments and replaced them with seven new departments organized around the delivery of services. This plan kindled old memories, for it closely resembled the reorganization scheme of New Deal interior secretary Harold Ickes, who wanted to consolidate in his department all conservation-related agencies. Nixon's plan, like its predecessor, would have stripped USDA of its land-related agencies, including the Forest Service and the SCS, and placed them in a new Department of Natural Resources. This plan was seen by those in USDA as a threat to a good part of its traditional mission, and they feared it would leave the department "stripped down to nothing."[49] USDA was thus battling to protect its bureaucratic turf from this reorganization. Leadership on the land use issue was one way this battle for turf was fought.

The department's fears on the land use issue were heightened by the leadership of the Department of the Interior under its new secretary, Rogers Morton. As the Nixon administration was preparing to present its own alternative to the Jackson bill, Morton took the lead away from George Romney's HUD, which earlier drafts of the bill had made responsible for administration. At a White House strategy meeting, Morton "grabbed" the issue in a bid to make his department the focus of the administration's land use activities. The CEQ, chaired by Russell Train, clearly provided the ideas and the initiative for most administration land use activities, but now Interior was aggressively trying to catch up. With the CEQ active and with Interior perceived within the Nixon administration as *the* land use department, Agriculture felt that it was left out of the land use discussion and worried that it might lose its traditional claim to any land-related activities. This departmental conflict reflected a history of antagonism between the two departments, which only added to the intensity of the rivalry in the early 1970s. The pressure of turf battles and the fear of being out of step with the administration made the early 1970s, in Norman Berg's words, a "sympathetic era for Agriculture to do something about land use."[50]

The Seminar on Prime Lands

USDA began to lay the groundwork for agricultural land protection in 1972 when, with land use legislation pending in Congress and the Department of the Interior seeming ready to run away with the issue, Secretary Earl Butz appointed a small departmental committee, chaired by Norman Berg of the SCS, to examine the issue and to recommend a strategy for the department. (In another sign of the times, 1972 was also when USDA hired its first urban land use planner.) The task of Berg's committee was to assert (or, from Berg's perspective, to reassert) a departmental interest in land use without alienating a conservative constituency generally opposed to any federal land use initiatives. The committee reported back to the secretary in late 1972 with a draft for a departmental land use policy and a prepared slide show and talk demonstrating that USDA had a historic claim to land use concerns "beyond the individual farm."[51] Berg's committee succeeded in convincing Secretary Butz that there was not only precedent but also a strong need for USDA involvement in land use, and with the sympathetic help of Tom Cowden, the assistant secretary for conservation, research, and education and one of Butz's longtime friends, the committee got Secretary Butz to sign two policy memoranda that set the stage for the department's entrance into the land use arena. The first of these memoranda, signed on 26 March 1973, formalized and extended the land use committee in USDA by establishing it as a permanent committee and involving more agencies in its work. This setup reflected Agriculture's inclination to move ahead only as fast as the recalcitrant subunits could be made to agree. The new committee's task was to "coordinate" the department's land-related activities and especially to "give close attention to conservation and best use of productive farmland."[52] Throughout the 1970s this committee remained the center of USDA activity on land use and reflected both the strength and the limits of departmental thinking.

Before long the new Land Use Committee placed before Secretary Butz a departmental policy on land use, which he signed on 26 October 1973. This new policy was a cautious one that emphasized private property rights and local control of land use decisions, but it did include an initiative to "adopt present pertinent programs to help enhance and preserve prime agricultural, range, and forest lands" and specified that the department should "help guide urban growth to preserve prime farmlands."[53] Here, between the reassurances that this was not a threat to private property rights or local control and the promise that implementation would come through existing departmental machinery, was the faint beginning of an interest in preserving agricultural land. From the department's perspective it was a defensive position designed to deflect criticism, protect its turf, and preempt the land use legislation then in Congress. For Berg and other conservationists in the department, it was a "strong position for USDA to take" given the Republican leadership of the department and the traditional conservatism of the department's constituency.[54] The dominant tone of USDA, however, could hardly be called activist. Even conservationists in the department emphasized the adequacy of existing solutions; as Tom Cowden wrote, "Direct federal action would involve complexities of financing and administration which would run counter to our current effort to encourage the state and local governments to take more responsibility in solving the problems of land use and management. . . . State and local governments have the tools to preserve prime agricultural land if they have the will and the skill to use them."[55]

The Land Use Committee was still looking for a way to seize the initiative, to give the general issue of land use its own distinctive focus. It wanted to move away from the land use legislation in Congress, which was not popular with the department's rural constituency, and to provide an alternative to, not a replication of, the leadership of the Interior Department. Any new focus also had to be within the realm of the experience and expertise of USDA. One issue that satisfied these requirements and, according to Berg, "showed promise of becoming an issue of national concern," was that of agricultural land.[56] This focus was chosen by the committee as one that allowed USDA to demonstrate leadership on a land use issue and one that was important to its own agricultural constituency. Yet the need for protecting agricultural land was an issue on which not everyone agreed—certainly not all farmers, and particularly not all agencies within USDA. In an effort to build support for the idea, the Land Use Committee, then chaired by Assistant Secretary Robert Long, began in late 1974 to plan for a conference on the loss of prime farmlands. The committee appointed a special task force to plan the event (including Berg's energetic new assistant, R. Neil Sampson, whose role in the issue would grow larger) and hoped that the conference could reconcile the conflicting opinions in the department. The conference took on a sense of urgency because of the growing unease in the early 1970s about the adequacy of the world food supply. "Is there enough land on earth . . . for future world population?" was the kind of question to put the bureaucracy on edge.[57] So in July 1975, with mixed motives, over eighty participants met for a Seminar on Prime Lands to discuss the validity of concerns about the loss of farmland and to recommend an approach for USDA to take regarding prime farmland. The seminar proved to be a crucial point in the development of USDA thinking on this issue.

The Seminar on Prime Lands marked the emergence in the Washington bureaucracy of the recognition of farmland loss as a national issue. The seminar did not resolve all of the differences within USDA, but it did bring attention to the loss of farmland and to the changing agricultural context that gave the issue much added force. Reflecting a view possible only in the post-1972 agricultural era, the Seminar on Prime Lands concluded that the demand for agricultural and timber products would increase "to the point where the production capability of the nation will be tested." Exports would play an increasingly significant role in this growing demand, and food exports were expected to compensate for energy imports in reducing the nation's trade deficit.[58] The age of agricultural surplus was over, this seminar announced, and agricultural land had become an important resource that, through food exports, could balance the suddenly increased cost of importing oil. The USDA, or at least the participants at this conference, recognized that they were in a new world—a world of actual and potential food scarcity, and one in which the nation's supply of agricultural land was a resource of global significance.

The Seminar on Prime Lands further decided that old approaches, or nonapproaches, were inadequate to the new situation. The economists' solution to the problem of how to allocate land among competing uses—the marketplace—was deemed "not adequate to assure protection and rational utilization of our productive resources over the long run." The market, the seminar reasoned, should be "supplemented" by local, state, and federal policy actions. Finally, in carefully worded understatement, the seminar participants concluded that "USDA should, in light of these conditions, take appropriate action to encourage retention of the remaining acres of prime land."[59] With this cautious language, the seminar indicated that more needed to be done.

The Seminar on Prime Lands had no specific policy recommendations for the Agriculture Department, but its unsettling conclusions and its mention of "appropriate action" provided both the occasion and the rationale for a stronger USDA policy protecting agricultural land. R. Neil Sampson saw the chance to put before Secretary Butz a policy to protect agricultural land, and he wrote a foreword in the secretary's name for the published version of the seminar's background study papers. After some consideration, the Republican secretary of agriculture signed a statement that contained this sentence: "Federal projects that take prime land from production should be initiated only when this action is clearly in the public interest."[60] This was only a slightly stronger statement than in the 1973 policy, but restricting federal monies for development projects in the name of resource conservation was unfamiliar territory for a secretary noted for his free market policies. The weight of circumstances and the urging of conservationists such as Berg and Sampson had pushed Butz to this point, which was probably about as far as a conservative Republican could go in the name of farmland protection.

The USDA Committee on Land Use drafted a similar response to the Seminar on Prime Lands. Seizing on the opportunity presented by the seminar, the committee circulated a supplement to the 1973 policy memorandum on land use. The document, signed by Secretary Butz in 1976, echoed the seminar's concern that the "continued loss of lands" posed a threat to long-term agricultural productive capability and represented a "loss of valuable natural resources." Following the approach already agreed to by Butz, the policy continued: "USDA will urge all agencies to adopt the policy that federal activities that take prime agricultural land should be initiated only when there are no suitable alternative sites and when the action is in response to overriding public need."[61] This formulation of policy was a conservative approach in that it assumed that the federal government, not the private land market, was at fault. It aimed to restrict federal activity, not the marketplace. It was a policy designed to appeal to a free market–oriented department and a constituency fearful of government regulation. In that federally funded projects often did contribute to the loss of farmland, this approach was accurate and needed. Conservatives in the department succeeded in removing the teeth from earlier versions of the policy so that any possibility of actually restricting agency actions was limited. The final version was a bland "wise use policy" that encouraged agencies to consider alternatives but did not force them to do anything. As feeble as the policy was, it was not entirely impotent. Although the statement only "urged" agencies to consider farmland in their actions, as Neil Sampson remembers, a vigorous "urge" sometimes had an effect. That is, the policy was not a general mechanism for moving the bureaucracy, but it did provide ammunition for Sampson and other conservationists to use in specific battles with other agencies in the department.[62]

The momentum generated by the Seminar on Prime Lands spread beyond the Department of Agriculture when the CEQ took up the issue. The council had always had an interest in land use issues, and this was a chance for it to add its voice to the federal support for protecting farmland. On 30 August 1976 CEQ chairman Russell Peterson signed a policy memorandum to all heads of federal agencies instructing them that "prime and unique farmland" was now to be included in their Environmental Impact Statements. The council asserted that the benefits of farmland preservation stemmed from "the capacity of such farmland to produce relatively more food with less erosion and with lower demands for fertilizer, energy, and other resources. In addition, the preservation of farmland provides the benefits of open space, protection of scenery, wildlife habitat and, in some areas, recreation opportunities and controls on urban sprawl."[63] Despite the memorandum's detailed instructions on how to obtain USDA's help in locating valuable farmlands, the effect of the memo was more symbolic than actual. It placed farmland on the nation's list of critical environmental areas and, if it had been followed, might have played an important role in protecting farmland. But as a nonbinding policy directive, the memorandum was widely ignored and had little effect other than giving the issue publicity.

Conservationists vs. Economists

The CEQ memorandum also helped to force a definition of "prime" farmland, an important preliminary step in protecting such land. When the Seminar on Prime Lands met in 1975, it could not agree on a precise definition of its topic. The CEQ memorandum instructed federal agencies to seek USDA assistance in locating and defining prime lands; but the USDA had done neither of these tasks. The first was a matter of technical expertise, of soil surveys and mapping, all of which was familiar to USDA. The second involved competing professional disciplinary perspectives and proved more difficult to resolve. The problem of definition was in part a problem of maintaining a uniform national standard across a large continent with diverse agricultural areas. The definition had to be general enough to include the cranberry bogs of Rhode Island and the irrigated citrus groves in California as well as the thick, level soils of the Midwest. Further, the problem of definition was part of a larger dispute between economists and conservationists, who took very different views as to what constituted "prime" agricultural land. This dispute went on both in and out of the Department of Agriculture and did not cease with the department's publication of the SCS definition of consistent national characteristics of prime agricultural land.

For a few years in the late 1970s different agency needs, conflicting disciplinary perspectives, and divergent value systems regarding governmental controls over the market all came together to make farmland preservation a flash point for institutional, disciplinary, and ideological debate. Although the labels "economists" and "conservationists" obscure individual differences and subtleties of argument, they do suggest the general contours of debate. The dispute, although larger than the Department of Agriculture, was firmly embedded in the bureaucracy of the department and hindered each step of the department's struggle to reach a policy on agricultural land. Within USDA, as within the scholarly community, there were two strong, persistent, and conflicting views on the nature and seriousness of the threat to the nation's supply of agricultural land. These contending views were rooted in the history and structure of the department and were present, if sometimes muted, at all stages of policy development. The strength and persistence of these views makes the agreements at the Seminar on Prime Lands all the more significant. One view, located in the SCS and informed by the principles of resource conservation, provided an argument for public action to protect farmland. The alternate view, centered in the Economic Research Service (ERS) and based on the discipline of economics, responded that government policy was an inefficient interference in the private marketplace.[64] These ideological differences also reflected the different institutional needs of each agency. The ERS was formed in the 1960s as a somewhat politically sanitized successor to the more controversial Bureau of Agricultural Economics. It was specifically divorced from policy advocacy, and its reputation depended upon establishing itself, as it had by the 1970s, as a "reliable, mainstream research organization."[65] The SCS, on the other hand, might claim a more central role in USDA if the problem was judged to be sufficiently serious. Any USDA farmland preservation activities would likely give the SCS new responsibilities and enhanced authority.

The conservation perspective stressed that land was a valuable resource and that high-quality farmland was an irreplaceable one. This idea had its origins in the crusading spirit of Hugh Bennett's original SCS and the land use reform movement of the 1930s. Adherents of this view emphasized the limited supply of high-quality land and its crucial importance in agricultural production. Like their predecessors in the 1930s, they also stressed soil preservation as a key to the social and ecological health of the farm landscape. The Seminar on Prime Lands, with its concern for long-term resource preservation and the protection of prime lands, fell loosely within this tradition. For the conservationists, all land was not equal, and the loss of prime farmland meant not only a loss of agricultural productivity but also that land less suited to farm uses would be farmed. This scenario, according to those from the SCS perspective, would cause greater erosion, require more fertilizer, and make it harder for agriculture to sustain its long-range productivity. Thus the conversion of farmland to urban uses had environmental costs even if new farmland were brought into production so that the total acreage remained the same. Land, especially prime land, was considered not only as an agricultural commodity but also as a resource providing ecological diversity, ample watersheds, natural air filters, and aesthetic qualities. Conservationists valued agricultural land beyond its role in agricultural production and held it, in some senses, to have value beyond the pricing system.[66]

In contrast, the economists viewed land not so much as a resource but as a commodity. This view had its roots in the decades of agricultural surplus and saw land simply as another factor in production, not as the irreplaceable starting point. After three decades of successful substitutions of fertilizer, machinery, and plant hybrids for land, the agricultural economist was inclined to feel that crops could be grown on almost any soil, if only the proper technology could be developed. Three decades of phenomenal increases in production on ever fewer acres of cropland confirmed this view that high-quality land was not particularly essential for agricultural productivity. In the jargon of the specialist, land was just another "input," just as fertilizer and pesticides were inputs. Moreover, given that less than 3 percent of the nation's land area was urbanized, even the projected doubling of the urban area would pose no threat to the supply of agricultural land, because of the overwhelming abundance of rural land for both agricultural and urban development. These aggregate statistics led to the conclusion that "the amount of land preempted by urban growth is trivial."[67] A similar analysis yielded this result: "The amount of agricultural land taken each year for urban uses has had little impact on the total supply of U.S. cropland. In recent years, five or six times the quantity of cropland so taken was shifted to lower-intensity agricultural or forestry uses, or was idled simply because cropping was not profitable. Irrigation, drainage, and clearing add three times as much land annually to the cropland base as urbanization absorbs."[68] Researchers from this view, usually economists but sometimes from other disciplines as well, exemplified what Don Hadwiger has called the "distinctive subculture" of agricultural research. Most agricultural researchers, he reported, "manifest distinctly conservative social and political perspectives" and tend to see government primarily as an "overzealous regulator." Hadwiger noted that one researcher was afraid to attend conservationist meetings for fear of criticism, and some USDA researchers have suggested that farmland protection was a tainted cause because it originated not among farmers but among environmentalists.[69] The agricultural economists tended to regard farmland preservation as an unwelcome intrusion of environmental concerns into the usual policies of land management for production purposes.[70]

The economists' perspective also challenged USDA's uniform definition of prime farmland based on physical characteristics. If crops can be produced on almost any soil, the reasoning went, the definition of prime cannot be based on physical characteristics but must revolve around economic factors. Prime farmland, in this view, moved through space and time as different technologies were applied to different types of land. The definition of prime farmland changed with location (access to markets), ability to respond to new inputs, and the market value of crops; land discarded today may in the future, under new technologies, produce high yields.[71] Technology, not land, was the key variable in this view. The struggle between the SCS and the ERS was in part an argument over whether agriculture in the 1970s more closely resembled the environmentally perilous times of the 1930s or the prosperous years of the postwar decades. As Stanley Schiff noted, "How one sees the future depends to a large extent on how one sees the recent past."[72]

The *Potential Cropland Study*

As Brian Balogh notes in his history of commercial nuclear power, professional specialization and competing bureaucratic agendas virtually guarantee that the experts will disagree on important social and political issues.[73] The presence of two competing views within the Department of Agriculture helps to explain the mass of seemingly contradictory statistics that arose to measure the loss of farmland. More than most issues, the protection of farmland relied on statistics as a measure of the problem. Statistics measuring acres of cropland, rates of conversion from rural to urban uses, and trends in productivity were the ammunition casually tossed around in the battle between the competing perspectives. The numbers changed over the course of the decade, just as the perception of the problem changed. Moreover, people from different perspectives counted different things. SCS and ERS statistics seemed contradictory because they were based on divergent views of what was important. The SCS measured the dwindling supply of prime farmland, while the ERS emphasized the large supply of vacant rural land.

There are two basic statistics that measure the adequacy of the supply of cropland: the total amount of cropland and the rate at which that land is being converted to other uses. Actual cropland acreage can be counted, although estimates of potential cropland still vary. More elusive is the rate of conversion, a figure on which there has always been considerable disagreement. During the 1950s and 1960s estimates of annual farmland loss ranged from 372,000 to 1.1 million acres.[74] Using data from the Census Bureau, Robert C. Otte of the ERS calculated that between 1960 and 1970 there were 730,000 acres of agricultural land converted annually to urban uses. He concluded that this rate of urbanization did not pose a threat to U.S. agricultural productivity, that "in the aggregate there is probably enough land of appropriate capability for major categories of use projected into the next century."[75] This relatively low conversion rate (compared to the one-million-acre figure generally used by the conservationists) and the sanguine attitude that flowed from it found widespread acceptance during the early 1970s as the authoritative reading of farmland loss.

An economic perspective also dominated the derivation and meaning of the other crucial statistic, the amount of total farmland available, for the first half of the decade. The ERS's often-quoted summary series titled *Major Uses of Land in the United States* reported in 1974 that nearly half of the nation's land was used for agricultural production (including crops and grazing). There was, the survey noted, still a large amount of land available for cropland if it was needed.[76] The most commonly quoted statistic on cropland availability before 1976 was 385 million acres of cropland in use with 266 million acres of potential cropland in ready reserve. This statistic was based on the Department of Agriculture's Conservation Needs Inventory, conducted first in 1957 and again in 1967. This inventory originated in the department's attempt to monitor its conservation efforts and the lands with continuing conservation needs. Its figure of 266 million acres of potential cropland was thus a by-product of a survey intended for other purposes. There were those in the department who suspected that it was too high,[77] but for a time it was the only measure available. In 1975 Robert Otte and Thomas Frey of the ERS reported that despite the sudden jump in cropland requirements for the post-1972 export boom there were still "substantial acreages" of potential cropland available. The source of their confidence was the Conservation Needs Inventory's figure of 266 million acres.[78] Two years later, Melvin Cotner of the ERS rebutted fears that the nation was "running out of farmland" with the assurance that "there are as many as 266 million tillable acres" available for use as cropland.[79]

This easy confidence in a vast cropland reserve with urbanization only nibbling at the edges was jolted by the publication in 1977 of the SCS's *Potential Cropland Study*.[80] This study was initiated at Secretary Earl Butz's request in response to an international conference on the world food supply, held in Rome in 1974.[81] At this conference there was much international pressure for the United States to contribute more to eliminating world hunger. Butz returned to the nation aware that farm acreage, in response to market demand and his injunction to "plant fencerow to fencerow," had increased by 30 million acres in the previous two years. Virtually all cropland that had been set aside by federal supply management programs had already been returned to production. In order to find out how much more U.S. agricultural production could expand, Butz instructed the SCS to check the Conservation Needs Inventory in order to determine how much cropland was actually available. The results of this SCS study opened a new phase in the farmland protection debate.

The *Potential Cropland Study* confirmed the suspicions of those who believed that the reserve capacity of American agriculture was smaller than believed and provided reason to conclude that farmland was disappearing at a much faster rate than previous data had indicated. The study rated the 266 million acres of potential cropland identified in the Conservation Needs Inventory as having a high, medium, low, or zero potential for actual development as cropland. Only 111 million acres were found to have a high or medium potential, and of these, 76 million acres carried a high economic or environmental cost in their development as cropland. These results suggested that U.S. farm acreage was much closer to its realistic limit than previously believed. *Potential Cropland Study* data also gave a new and more pessimistic rate of conversion of agricultural lands to other uses. The study's spot checks showed that between 1967 and 1975, 2.1 million acres of land were lost every year to urbanization. Another 800,000 acres were lost annually to water uses, primarily reservoirs. Of this nearly 3 million acres of agricultural land lost annually, 30 percent came directly from cropland, as distinct from grazing, timber, or other agricultural lands. This measure marked a tripling of historic rates of conversion of rural land to urban uses and set off the years between 1967 and 1975 as a new period in which Americans used significantly more land than in previous years. Thus, the *Potential Cropland Study* challenged both measures of the supply of farmland and forced a rearrangement of conventional thinking: a 266-million-acre cropland cushion disappearing at less than a million acres each year was not a problem, but a 111-million-acre reservoir being depleted by 3 million acres annually called for serious attention. Reactions to this news depended on one's perspective. Critics called it a "quickie job" because of its alleged sloppy sampling techniques and waited for the more authoritative and comprehensive National Resources Inventory, due in 1982.[82] This criticism eventually proved partially correct (see chapter 5), and the 3-million-acre annual conversion rate remained a focus of controversy until the early 1980s. The *Potential Cropland Study*'s other finding—that the reserve capacity of agricultural land in this country is limited to slightly over 100 million acres—has gone unchallenged. Cropland conservationists found in the new numbers a catalyst for action and made the *Potential Cropland Study* the basis of their case for new federal policy.[83]

During the late 1970s, acceptance of three million acres as the proper measure of farmland loss became the litmus test for farmland preservationists. The entire dispute between conflicting perspectives on resource conservation seemed to hinge on this one statistic: three million acres was a crisis, one million acres was insignificant. This approach on both sides of the issue was not only shallow, it was also ahistorical, in that it looked for a fixed number to predict the future confidently without examining the historical circumstances of the years from which the number came. The *Potential Cropland Study* conversion figure came from the years 1967 to 1975, years of strong development pressure. To call this an annual conversion rate and project it blindly into the future was a careless use of statistics, for it ignored the fact that development pressures might be different in the future than in the years from which the conversion rate was calculated. Better thinking than this occurred on both sides of the issue, but it was not always apparent on the surface of the discussion. The search for numerical certainty may not have been the best way to describe the dimensions of the problem, yet the frustrations of trying to move an inert bureaucracy led conservationists to try to make ethical statements about the value of agricultural land in terms of farmland acreages.

The focus on an annual conversion rate also masked some important demographic changes which hinted that past conversion rates might be an understatement of the future problem. Until 1975 there was no reason to believe that the centuries-long movement of people from the country to the city would not continue. Yet that year a government demographer, Calvin Beale, reported that this trend had reversed—that population migration into the rural countryside was greater than that into the cities. According to Beale, rural areas grew by over 4 percent during the first three years of the decade, while metropolitan areas grew at less than 3 percent. Significantly, this "decentralization trend" was "not confined to urban sprawl," since rural areas in outlying counties grew almost as fast as those adjacent to cities.[84] Reporting on the 1980 census, Beale noticed that the most remote counties grew almost as fast (14 percent) as counties adjacent to cities (17 percent), and both grew significantly faster than metropolitan counties. Although this unprecedented reversal of the direction of population movement was strongest in the South and West, migration to rural counties increased in every area of the country. The rural revival was truly a national phenomenon.[85] Other studies confirmed this rural revival and documented the reasons why even sparsely populated areas in all regions of the country were growing as never before. The decentralization of industry provided more manufacturing jobs in rural areas, but even more important were the spread into the countryside of retirement and recreation communities; the growth of state colleges and universities; and the growing preference for the rural lifestyles now made easier by transportation improvements (especially interstate highways) and new communication technologies.[86] All of these factors created what one analyst called the "countrified city," defined as "low-density urban conditions in a rural setting," which meant that the costs of suburban sprawl of the 1950s and 1960s were recurring in the 1970s spread across the countryside.[87]

Sprawl in any decade fell disproportionately on prime farmland, as new growth favored the best land. Development projects naturally sought out the land with the best soils—the level, well-drained field not far from the highway. One geographer found that although urbanization accounted for only 3 percent of all land uses, there was a "noticeable bias" for urban development to occur on the most fertile farmland.[88] A federal study of fifty-three fast-growth counties found that on the average, 35 percent of urban land came from cropland, which would indicate that urban land did not disproportionately prefer cropland. Yet there was tremendous regional variation in that proportion, ranging from 6 percent in Florida to 70 percent in the Santa

Cruz and Santa Clara valleys of California, where cropland made up only 16 percent of all land.[89] Robert Coughlin of the Regional Science Research Institute noted that small amounts of rural land converted to urban uses had disproportionate effects on the countryside. Because land conversion concentrated on the best lands, even a modest overall rate of farmland loss could "drastically alter the appearance of the landscape, making former rural areas neither truly rural nor truly urban."[90] Simply put, developers and farmers coveted the same land. As the nation's agricultural base was being diminished, the best land was going the fastest.

With the new patterns of development, new terminology emerged to describe its effects on rural land. "Urban sprawl" was replaced by the more accurate "buckshot urbanization," meaning that the built-up area no longer had a center; instead, small patches of development were scattered throughout a rural area in a seemingly random fashion. This pattern of development resulted in the dramatic spread of an "impermanence syndrome," the sense of transition and instability that dominated the development fringe. Slow-moving farm vehicles, farm odors, and pesticide and fertilizer runoff combined to make the farm an annoyance to new rural residents, who in some instances sought local "nuisance" legislation to limit farm activities. Farmers in turn were subject to the newcomers' trespasses on croplands and the rising property taxes made necessary by the municipal services required for new development. Rising land values often meant that farmers could not afford to rent new lands or pass farms on to their children. All of this led one Connecticut farmer to complain, "Young people have no respect—moral decay is upon us."[91] The very real economic transformation brought on by "buckshot urbanization" was better explained by a California farmer: "Where we once had—within a few miles of each other—homes, orchards, farms, dairies, and a variety of industries, we now have homes, fewer kinds of industries (with the number decreasing), more 'service' operations, and fewer (if any) farms, dairies, orchards, etc. A certain richness to living has been lost; a tapestry has been replaced with vinyl flooring."[92] Analysts talked of agriculture's loss of "critical mass," of how the infrastructure of agricultural businesses and industries that support the farm declined and eventually disappeared in some localities. In this climate of uncertainty many farmers were reluctant to make needed long-term capital improvements and began to plan more for building subdivisions than for growing crops. The result was a premature loss of many productive acres, estimated by Little to be as high as one acre lost to "buckshot urbanization" and to the accompanying "impermanence syndrome" for each acre actually lost to urbanization.[93] This in effect doubled the amount of land lost to agriculture and added an often-unnoticed demographic dimension to the problem. These new demographic patterns should have served notice that any purely statistical measure could not adequately describe the dimensions of the problem—that the total problem was greater than the aggregate sum of lost acres.

State and Local Farmland Protection Efforts

If the federal government would not respond, perhaps state and local governments could preserve farmland. In the absence of a national growth policy, of a national land use policy, or even of a coherent, effective policy from the Department of Agriculture, state and local governments were left on their own. As far as USDA was concerned, this was as it should be. Published opinions emphasized state and local governments as the traditional arenas for land use management and exuded confidence that local protection efforts were adequate to the situation. Privately, USDA officials argued that "state and local governments have the tools to preserve prime agricultural land if they have the will and skill to use them" and even suggested that "the department has very little to offer."[94] Yet the mounting evidence that farmland loss was more serious than previously believed was accompanied by an emerging sense that state and local governments had not yet found an effective response.

The most common state policy for preserving farmland was the differential assessment of farmland. The idea was to provide an incentive for farmers not to develop their lands by taxing farmland at only its use value, not at its potential development value. The promise of differential assessment was that it would preserve open space while it enhanced the profitability of the family farm; thus, the idea appealed to both urban planners and agriculturalists. A lower tax rate, these groups reasoned, would lower the cost of farming in the face of development pressure. Differential assessment is generally categorized in three forms, which reflect the chronological development of these laws. Pure preferential assessment, the first type to emerge, allowed owners of farmland to pay taxes at the lower use-value rate. Many states, uneasy with giving farmland owners such a tax break without requiring anything in return, added a rollback provision that required landowners who developed their property to pay back some or all of the foregone taxes of the last several years (from two or three years in most states to ten in California). A third type of preferential assessment was the restrictive agreement in which the state and the landowner contracted for use-value taxation in exchange for the landowner's promise not to develop for at least ten years. These laws came about with surprising speed. Maryland passed the first preferential assessment law in 1956, nine other states followed in the next decade, and thirty-eight more states enacted some variety of differential assessment in the decade between 1967 and 1976.[95] The rapid spread of this tax incentive during the late 1960s and early 1970s came about because governments were eager to do something to help the family farm and preserve open space. At face value, differential assessment was a painless way to do both.

The reality was that preferential assessment never proved to be successful at slowing the pace of development or even at doing much to aid family farmers. As early as 1968, even as the frenzy for differential assessment was at its height, William Whyte warned that the new tax laws would only create an illusion of open space, that differential assessment might buy time but would never permanently alter development patterns. Moreover, Whyte argued, the lost tax revenues shifted an unfair tax burden to other property owners.[96] Later analyses echoed these same concerns. Thomas Hady, an economist for USDA, surveyed existing programs in 1974 and concluded that it was "doubtful" whether differential assessment could have any effect on changing land uses. Only as "one of a rather large kit of tools for guiding development" could differential assessment be justified.[97] The 1976 study *Untaxing Open Space,* prepared for the CEQ, summarized the consensus of research: "Except for a few specific situations, . . . differential assessment is not likely to be effective in achieving land use objectives." Further, by creating "special tax shelters" for land speculators who owned farmland, "differential assessment programs which are not part of a comprehensive land development regulation system are counterproductive in terms of the broader goals of urban development."[98] This was essentially the same criticism that had been leveled three years earlier in the Rockefeller Brothers Fund Task Force Report, *The Use of Land,* which had stated, "Measures that grant partial relief from real estate taxes on farms in urbanizing areas, but provide no protection, can be worse than nothing at all. . . . The practical effect of such measures can be merely to reduce speculators' holding costs while the development opportunity ripens."[99] Thus the verdict was unanimous from all shades of observers. Differential assessment was more useful to land speculators than to farmers, did little to save open space, and shifted the tax burden unfairly to other property owners. Thus the states held out an illusion of farmland protection that was politically popular but might have done more harm than good in the long run. Instead of providing a tax break to some landowners, states might have faced the problem more directly by spending that same tax revenue to buy land, as William Whyte suggested.

Two states, New York and California, deserve special mention because of their widely publicized attempts to use differential assessment in the context of a more comprehensive program. California, the most populous of all the states and the most agriculturally productive in terms of the cash value of its crops, passed the Land Conservation Act (known as the Williamson Act) in 1965 as a way to protect prime agricultural land from sprawling urban development. The act drew support from conservationists interested in open space preservation and from farm groups looking for a way to protect successful, middling farmers from tax increases and other adverse effects of urban encroachment without infringing upon property rights. The legislation enabled local governments to create "agricultural preserves" and to contract with landowners in those preserves not to develop their land for ten years. In return for accepting this restrictive agreement the landowner would pay taxes only at use value. Despite the attempt to link differential assessment with a contractual restriction on land use, the program was generally recognized as a failure. Contracts were easily broken, even after amendments in the early 1970s to raise the penalty for premature development. Loss of tax revenues was a problem in some counties, which prompted amendments in 1971 and 1972 providing for state funds to ease the counties' load in the redistribution of property taxes. In 1974–75 the state distributed $24 million to local jurisdictions, and counties still had to absorb most of the expense of the program. Although the original intent of the law had been to help small farmers, the tax benefits of differential assessment went disproportionately to California's large landowners, who owned most of the eligible lands. Thus the program unintentionally borrowed from the public treasury to reinforce the state's traditionally concentrated landowning pattern.[100] Moreover, the Williamson Act was unsuccessful at its stated purpose of preserving agricultural land. Early drafts of the bill specified prime agricultural land for protection, but the National Cattlemen's Association succeeded in forcing an amendment to make any agricultural land eligible. In 1970 only 30 percent of the land enrolled under the Williamson Act was prime farmland, while large land, timber, and oil companies received tax subsidies for not developing marginally productive farm- and rangeland. Most of the land enrolled in the act during its first decade was discontiguous and remote from urban areas. This scattered pattern of participation offered no protection for farmland adjacent to cities, where development pressure was greatest, and may have encouraged unsystematic urban growth, in that agricultural reserves could act as a magnet for new development.[101] A similar approach was New York's agricultural districts legislation, passed in 1971 in response to the rapid growth of the New York metropolitan region into traditional farm areas. Under this law, farmers who joined together to form districts of at least five hundred acres were given the benefits of use-value assessment and protection from some aspects of the "impermanence syndrome" (local ordinances may not restrict normal farm activities, public funds cannot encourage development). As in California, participation was widespread (encompassing one-quarter of the state's farmland in 1977) but limited to predominantly rural areas.[102] Even in this more elaborate form, differential assessment as an incentive for farmland protection proved the least effective where it was most needed. In the record of the mid-1970s there was nothing to suggest that voluntary approaches could be successful at saving farmlands.

Mandatory controls had not compiled a significantly better record. Traditionally, land use controls meant zoning, which was an entirely local matter unconcerned with rural environmental protection. The only exception to this rule was the 1930s land use planners' long-forgotten foray into the rural landscape (described in chapter 1). Zoning was largely untested in the countryside, and even regarding its use in the city, there was "a pervasive feeling that local control of land use . . . has been a failure," according to one authoritative analysis.[103] Large lot zoning, often used by suburbs to preserve open space (and sometimes to exclude poor people), generally delayed but did not prevent development and thus was not well suited to preserving agricultural land. In the early 1970s some counties began zoning exclusively for agriculture, with the idea that these agricultural zones would be a permanent designation, not just a transitional zone await-

100

Farmland

Protection

on the

Federal

Agenda

ing later development.[104] Yet there was ample reason to be skeptical of the effectiveness of these new programs. Experience provided too many examples of agricultural zones broken by the high market price of land. As cities approached, farmers found the selling price irresistible and influenced local governments to dismantle the exclusive agricultural zone.[105] What the market did not destroy, the court system might. Despite the claims of environmentalists that courts were beginning to recognize public claims over private property,[106] the Fifth Amendment prohibition on taking private property cast a cloud of uncertainty over exclusive zoning ordinances. In addition, most counties were clearly not up to the task. Although this situation began to change rapidly in the early 1970s, as late as 1968 only 42 percent of municipal and county governments outside urban areas had any form of zoning.[107]

101

Farmland
Protection
on the
Federal
Agenda

The only policy tool with demonstrated success at preserving agricultural lands was the purchase of development rights (PDR) program. Pioneered in Long Island's Suffolk County in 1974, this approach rested on the simple premise that the development right to a property could be separated from the right to use the property in much the same way that mineral rights can be separated from surface-use rights. The municipality then bought the development right, which was determined by the difference between the land's market value and its use value, and created an exclusive use district. More effective than voluntary incentives and more acceptable than zoning, PDR was tried in densely crowded regions along the East Coast and in King County, Washington (near Seattle). The great limitation to PDR programs was that their cost was so great as to be politically prohibitive in all but a few urban areas. Insufficient funding forced Suffolk County to scale back its program and forced local governments to look to the federal government for the necessary finances.[108]

By 1977, then, state and local governments had not yet found a way to slow the movement of people onto agricultural land. Existing techniques were ineffective, politically unpalatable, or too expensive. All of the evidence suggested that farmland preservation could not be effected by any single measure but would have to come from a multiplicity of coordinated policies. Part of the solution would have to be more research on policy options, and indeed, the next several years saw an explosion of interest in innovative local policies.[109] Wisconsin experimented with linking tax relief and agricultural zoning; Oregon placed greater emphasis on farmland preservation in its state land use plan; and Maryland tried a complex transfer of development rights program that would use the private market to aid the government in paying to preserve farmland.[110] Yet the underlying problem was not just that local and state governments did not know how to save farmland but that they were in some ways incapable of doing so in the absence of national decisions. As Philip Raup pointed out,

102

Farmland
Protection
on the
Federal
Agenda

> Land law is state law. The implementation of land use decisions has been jealously guarded as a primary responsibility of local government. But the criteria by which choices among land uses should be guided must of necessity be national in scope. If we refer to the inventory . . . of ways in which we have promoted urban sprawl, it is clear that it is national policies and not local policies that have generated urban threats to rural lands. It is wishful thinking to believe that corrective action can be taken at local government levels, in the absence of clear-cut national guidelines.[111]

Thus the inherent inadequacies of state and local policies focused attention again on Washington for national guidelines, for technical and financial assistance, and for help in controlling national patterns of growth. Local governments were too small, too poor, too low on expertise, and powerless in the face of larger trends. If farmland was to be preserved, the federal government would have to be enlisted in the cause.

4

Farmland

Protection

in Congress

Gathering Momentum for the Jeffords Bill

Nineteen seventy-seven should have been a good year for farmland protection legislation. Between 1973 and 1977 the number of states either passing or considering state farmland protection policies grew to include New Jersey, Connecticut, Maryland, Maine, Oregon, Wisconsin, and Illinois.[1] Local governments too were joining the struggle to preserve farmland, most notably on Long Island's Suffolk County. As the most valuable agricultural county in New York and the second most populous, Suffolk County felt the population land squeeze more acutely than most and in 1977 began spending $21 million to buy development rights on remaining farmland.[2] This state and local activity took on a greater sense of urgency as data filtering out of USDA from the yet unpublished *Potential Cropland Study* showed the loss of farmland to be nearly three times higher than previous figures had indicated. According to Lester Brown of Worldwatch Institute, the problem of vanishing farmlands transcended national boundaries and was truly a global threat.[3] Farmland protection had arrived as an issue on the environmental agenda at all levels of government; even the number of constituent letters calling for farmland protection—letters to both Congress and the Department of Agriculture—was increasing.[4] The federal response thus far was minimal, as the Department of Agriculture's statement on the issue was not well publicized and was even less well enforced. Moreover, the USDA statement was modest enough that it could not be expected to deal with the full scope of the problem. Bureaucratic action was not up to the task of protecting agricultural land, some began to feel, and this meant that a legislative initiative was needed to advance the issue. The mood of a new Democratic presidency contributed to hopes for a more vigorous policy to protect agricultural lands. Perhaps most important, the post-1972 agricultural context of a high demand for exports and a leveling off of productivity began to be seen as a continuing situation, not just a fluke response to a unique set of unconnected trends. Together these reasons motivated a small but growing number of land use planners, environmentalists, and soil conservationists to propose legislation designed to protect the long-term adequacy of the nation's agricultural resource base.

Legislative movement began with the gathering of a network of staffers who were concerned about agricultural land and worked in various places in the bureaucracy. In the Environment and Natural Resources Policy Division of the Congressional Research Service (CRS), analyst W. Wendell Fletcher learned of the results of the Seminar on Prime Lands and thought it was time for legislative action. This idea was confirmed for him by the fact that he was responding (for members of Congress) to an increasing number of constituent requests concerning the protection of farmland. He began to call this issue to the attention of the head of his division, Charles Little, who was hearing about the issue from another source as well. William Haffert, the executive vice president of Garden State Publishing Company (which published agricultural trade journals) and an activist in New Jersey's farmland protection efforts, approached Little about getting federal help in financing state protection programs because New Jersey's program had proved more costly than expected. Little responded to the problem with interest and began to feel that Congress might be ripe for action. Quite by accident, Little soon met Robert Gray, an administrative aide to Vermont representative James Jeffords, and George Dunsmore, a minority staff member of the House Agriculture Committee. While riding a commuter train from Maryland to his Washington office, Little overheard Gray and Dunsmore discussing what could be done to preserve agricultural land from urbanization. This coincidence initiated a series of commuter conversations during which the trio planned their legislative strategy. At first Little was skeptical about working with a Republican member of the House, but the other two quickly persuaded him to give Jeffords a chance. As Jeffords's aide, Gray became the congressional staff leader on the issue and the point man for the new legislation.[5] Another link in the network was added when Neil Sampson, a troubleshooter for Norman Berg in the Soil Conservation Service with experience on the Seminar on Prime Lands, met Little at an Environmental Protection Agency (EPA) meeting on agricultural land protection called by Tom Mierswa. After the meeting Sampson agreed to help the group in working out a legislative strategy. Sampson had considerable flexibility in his job and not only represented a link to the bureaucracy but also had access to the unpublished *Potential Cropland Study* data and so provided the informal group with a more factual base for their concerns.[6]

The group began to discuss legislative possibilities at a number of informal meetings in late 1976 and 1977. An important early strategic decision was whether or not to include farmland protection in the general farm bill of 1977 or to "send it off on its own." The group decided to propose separate legislation as a way to "attract debate," to give the bill an "educational purpose." This purpose, the group reasoned, was more important than a quick and quiet legislative success. Early ideas centered on the creation of an Agricultural Land Resources Review Commission, a congressionally mandated commission "charged with studying and reporting to the Congress on the current status and trends affecting the agricultural land resources of the nation, along with recommendations for appropriate federal action." As originally conceived, the purpose of the commission would be to publicize the problem, to remedy the dearth of adequate data on trends affecting the supply of agricultural land, and to support a selected number of state and local farmland protection programs in order to "evaluate the cost and effectiveness of various approaches."[7]

This last purpose of the commission was crucial if the commission was to become a real policy laboratory, as these farmland preservationists hoped. They wanted to do more than research a problem; they wanted to assist local governments in experimenting with possible solutions. Also important, and ultimately more successful, was the idea that the commission would serve as a vehicle to bring greater public and policy attention to the problem. The ideas discussed in these early meetings between Fletcher, Little, Gray, and Sampson became the basis of the farmland protection bill soon to be introduced in Congress.

With the idea for a bill already in hand, the group moved to build legislative momentum with a CRS-sponsored Workshop on Agricultural Land, held on 8 February 1977 in the Library of Congress. Between thirty-five and fifty congressional staffers and two congressmen, Jeffords and George Brown of California, met to hear about the problem and to discuss possible solutions. Little presented the participants with a stark picture of the "cropland squeeze," his term for the intersecting trends of high rates of cropland loss and the increased demand for farmland to meet greater production demands. The loss of cropland to urban development, Little warned,

> comes at a time when exportable crop surpluses are increasingly needed to offset trade imbalances stemming from ballooning import costs for petroleum, and for humanitarian reasons in a starving world. Even as these needs have become more urgent in recent years, overall yields per acre seem to have stopped increasing, and may even be trending downward—for the first time in twenty years. Uncertain weather patterns, competition for water, air pollution, increasing costs and scarcities for fertilizers, fuels and other supplies, environmental constraints on farming practice—all these have their toll. What is becoming clear is that if high levels of productivity are needed, and if yields are not increasing, then it becomes important to look at the acres themselves. And the look SCS has taken suggests that at a time when it is more critical than ever before, the United States could actually be running out of its cropland reserves.[8]

Neil Sampson followed this alarming analysis with his report on the unpublished *Potential Cropland Study* data. He noted that three million acres of rural land, including one million acres of cropland, were being lost to urban and other uses each year. He concluded that the

situation was not a crisis but that "we have an ethical and moral responsibility" to "prevent the needless waste of prime farmland."[9] Robert Coughlin, brought in from the Regional Science Research Institute
in Philadelphia, summarized his research on the effectiveness of various state and local attempts to preserve farmland. Coughlin reported
that not only were most programs ineffective but that experience had
not yet shown what combinations of controls and incentives might
work.[10] By implication, then, federal legislation was needed to spur
states and localities to search for new and more effective policy solutions. By all accounts, the workshop was highly successful in ad-
vancing the issue beyond the small network of associates who planned
the event. The workshop presented the most concise and sobering
analysis of the situation possible at the time. In addition to educating
thirty-five to fifty congressional staffers, the workshop established Jeffords as the leader of farmland preservation in Congress.

In some ways Jeffords was not the person one would have predicted
for the part. Elected to Congress in 1974, he was still a new and relatively unknown Republican, not a likely person to lead a crusade.
Yet he had a record as an environmentalist: in 1973, as Vermont's
attorney general, he had helped to draft a statewide land planning
program. Jeffords was attuned to the problems of controlling development in a small state with a limited supply of farmland and was
especially concerned about the spillover from the rapid development
of Vermont recreational areas in the late 1960s and early 1970s.[11] In
addition to championing farmland legislation, Jeffords became an ar-
dent defender of price supports for dairy farmers and in time developed a reputation as a maverick Republican who was not afraid to
pursue liberal policies.

If Jeffords was ready for legislation, it was because his administrative assistant, Robert Gray, had pushed the issue before him. Gray
was a planner from upstate New York who had seen an interstate
highway and the subsequent construction around it take the best
farmland in the area. This experience left Gray determined to do
something to prevent the unnecessary conversion of cropland to urban-
oriented uses.[12] His opportunity came as legislation surfaced after the
CRS workshop. With Jeffords as an enthusiastic sponsor, Gray as the
key congressional staffer, and a growing number of people on Capitol
Hill becoming aware of the problem, a farmland protection bill was
ready for launching into the House machinery.

On 7 March 1977, Representative Jeffords introduced the first of seven nearly identical bills in the House of Representatives. Because of his strong personal backing, this bill—the National Agricultural Land Policy Act—came to be known as the "Jeffords bill." It emerged directly from the January discussions of the Little-Fletcher-Gray-Sampson network, which produced the ideas for the bill. One weekend Little typed the first draft over, then the group revised the bill before it was sent on through Gray to Jeffords and then to the floor of the House. The bill was based on three main ideas, two from the farmland network's January discussions of an Agricultural Land Review Commission and the third borrowed from the earlier policies of USDA. Title I declared "that it is the policy of the federal government . . . to use all practical methods to retain, protect, and improve agricultural land."[13] This title would assert that retaining farmland was a goal of federal policy and require all federal agency policy to be consistent with this goal. In effect, it would do for the entire federal government what Butz's policy memorandum had suggested for the Department of Agriculture. It was designed to address the perception that the federal government, with its subsidies for development, was a major cause of farmland loss. It did not intervene in the marketplace, but it restricted federal subsidies in the marketplace. This consistency title required that the federal government clean up its own house, that it alter what it was already doing to influence the market.

The other two central ideas of the Jeffords bill, embodied in Titles II and III, were an outgrowth of the ideas generated in the January discussions of the farmland network. Title II established the Agricultural Land Review Commission, while Title III authorized demonstration projects as part of the laboratory for "demonstrating and testing methods of reducing the amount of land which is annually being converted from agricultural to nonagricultural uses." Funding was set at $15 million for the commission and $50 million for financial support to the demonstration projects. Jeffords referred to Title III as the "guts of the bill" because he considered it essential to begin assisting local governments with the expensive task of protecting farmland. He was not interested in simply creating a commission to study the problem but wanted also to put federal funds behind the search for effective policy solutions. The purchase of development rights seemed to be the only politically acceptable yet effective solution, but this approach proved to be prohibitively expensive for most localities. Federal funding would be much more important than a federal consistency policy or a study commission in terms of providing farmland protection with the boost it needed.[14] Title III ran afoul of the stiffest criticism because it raised the specter of more federal intervention in private land use decisions. Opponents of the Jeffords bill feared that this title would mean federal funds, then federal guidelines, and finally federal control of local and state land use plans.

The bill anticipated this fear with a precise statement that it was not a federal land use bill and did not authorize the federal government to regulate private property. This disclaimer stated simply: "This act does not authorize the federal government to regulate the use of private land or to deprive owners of land of their rights to property or income from the sale of property and does not diminish in any way the rights and responsibilities of the states and political subdivisions of the states." This statement was a tacit admission that federal farmland protection legislation was running uphill against two related traditions in American political culture—opposition to public regulation of private property and the fear of centralized authority. This section of the bill was made necessary by the legislative climate following the failed federal land use bill. These were years of reaction against anything that smacked of federal land use controls, even if the approach was different than that of the earlier bill. The federal land use planning legislation came out of an era when effective environmental management invariably meant more federal control. By 1977 state and local initiatives had made this assumption no longer necessarily true; on many environmental issues, including farmland protection, some states and localities were now ahead of the federal government.[15] Moreover, farmland protection was tied to a different department than earlier federal land use bills had been. Together these changes suggested that federal legislation on farmland protection would inevitably be more decentralized than before, in line with the organization of USDA and the dictates of a mixed farmer and environmentalist constituency. Yet, as Neil Sampson remembers, the "land use bugaboo" stayed with the Jeffords bill so that "basically what emerged was that you can't say land and wise use and conservation and federal government in the same piece of legislation."[16] The antistatism and localism of the political culture resisted even a mild challenge.

If the Jeffords bill had a legislative analogue, it was the 1972 Coastal Zone Management Act, not the attempts at federal land use planning. This act arose out of a public and scientific concern for the ecological uniqueness of the nation's estuaries and seashores. The coastal act became law during the height of environmental activity in Congress and at a time when comprehensive federal land use planning also seemed certain. It provided the states with federal funds for planning in coastal areas and included a section that required the siting of large-scale federal projects to be consistent with state plans. Titles I and III of the Jeffords bill were essentially patterned after this law, although the comparison was never made explicit. The real difference was that the coastal act, even though it was sometimes co-opted by development interests, was still significantly stronger than the Jeffords bill. Of course environmentalists could not expect as tough a bill in the more conservative climate of 1977 as had passed five years earlier, but there were some who worried that the Jeffords legislation was too weak, that it appeared to address a problem without really doing so.[17] While the Jeffords bill would have provided an opportunity for states and localities to protect agricultural land, it certainly would not have forced either local governments or private landowners to keep their lands in farming. In comparison with the Coastal Zone Management Act, farmland protection offered only limited federal assistance in protecting a unique piece of the American landscape.

While the Jeffords bill was making its debut, farmland protection advocates advanced their cause in another piece of legislation—the Surface Mining Control and Reclamation Act of 1977. Environmentalists saw strip mining as a threat to the agricultural potential of alluvial valleys in the West, while surface mining in the Midwest placed coal extraction in direct conflict with corn production. Machines such as Central Ohio Coal Company's "Big Muskie" removed 220 cubic yards of soil in one shovelful and allowed prime farmland to be destroyed with alarming speed. Concern was strongest in Illinois, a state where 12 million acres of prime farmland lay right on top of strippable coal reserves. In February 1977 two studies, one funded by the Department of Health, Education, and Welfare and the other by a public interest group called the Environmental Policy Center, concluded that prime agricultural lands could not be reclaimed to their original production value after being mined. This conclusion, combined with pressure from farmers and farm organizations upset over the loss of their land and livelihood, led some to suggest a moratorium on strip mining of prime farmland. According to a zoning administrator from Peoria, Illinois, "Reclamation of prime agricultural lands is very questionable at best. It is in the nation's best interests . . . that all highly productive farmland be declared unsuitable for strip mining."[18] Another local official warned that strip mining would prove "fatal" to the "agricultural heartland" and urged federal action because local zoning, in his experience, was not able to stop the stripping of farmland.[19] A spokesman for the National Farmers' Union supported the moratorium concept: "Any land not fully restorable to its original agricultural use should be banned to stripping. All land already subjected to strip mining must be restored to its original use."[20] Democratic representative John Seiberling of Ohio hinted at a larger problem than simply the loss of valuable farmland: "Everyone is concerned about the energy crisis and if we keep on destroying our agricultural lands years from now we will have a food crisis that will make the energy crisis seem tame. We seem to rush from crisis to crisis because no one does any long-range planning."[21] Congressman Morris Udall echoed the theme that "choice farmland" was "being chewed up for highways and shopping centers and strip mining," and noted with some bitterness that the "one bill that offered hope for preserving agricultural land" was the failed national land use planning bill that he had earlier sponsored.[22]

This support enabled farmland preservationists to get a part of what they wanted in the final legislation. The new law required coal companies to revegetate and to reclaim lands to their approximate original contours but still allowed surface mining on steep slopes, alluvial valleys, and prime farmlands. An amendment by Senator Charles Percy of Illinois mandated the restoration of prime farmlands—a compromise between no protection and a complete moratorium on mining prime farmlands.[23] This limited recognition of the need for agricultural land preservation came in part through the work of the emerging core of farmland preservationists. Neil Sampson worked on an Interagency Task Force that forged the compromise on restoring farmlands;[24] the recent USDA definition of prime farmland became a part of the new law; and the *Potential Cropland Study* was essential ammunition for the Percy amendment. Thus, the passage of the first federal strip mining control bill reflected the emerging importance of agricultural land preservation and represented a victory of sorts for environmentalists. Critics noted, however, that the new federal bill was in some ways weaker than existing state laws and still sacrificed the permanent productive capacity of prime land to the "one-time harvest" of coal, leaving farmland to depend on the unproven hope of soil restoration.[25]

Meanwhile, the Jeffords bill began its slow march through Congress. On 26 May, Senator Dick Clark of Iowa introduced a Senate version of the same bill. A logical sponsor for the bill, Clark was from a farm state with strong urbanization pressures. This combination had led to an innovative farmland protection program in Iowa's Black Hawk County that had caught national attention. The Senate version authorized only half of the funding that the House version did, and Senator Clark also felt obliged to deal with the legacy of the national land use planning debate. On the floor of the Senate he argued that "the federal government is the single largest contributor to the needless waste of prime agricultural lands." This legislation, he emphasized, did not put the federal government "in the business of planning land use on the private farmlands of the nation" but merely forced the federal government to "exercise full responsibility for the land use impacts of its own policies and actions." If he truly believed, as he claimed, that "we are almost certainly facing a squeeze in productive capability only a few years from now," this was indeed a cautious remedy.[26] Emphasis on the notion that federal projects and activities were the chief villain—more a reasonable assumption than a proven fact—served to distance a federal farmland protection policy from a federal land use policy. Clearly this antistatist emphasis was required if farmland protection was to have a chance in either body of Congress.

The first critical moment for the Jeffords bill came on 15 and 16 June 1977, when hearings on the bill were held before the House Subcommittee on Family Farms, Rural Development, and Special Studies. During these two days positions were staked and arguments made that set the tone for the next three years of legislative discussion on the issue. The hearings were carefully planned by Jeffords and his aide, Bob Gray, with the help of Jim Swiderski of the committee staff. Interest in the legislation was so great that there was time for only half of the local groups and special interests who wanted to testify to do so. State and local environmental groups generally supported the legislation, and the farm lobbies split on the issue, while the new Democratic head of the Department of Agriculture, Bob Bergland, sent the committee mixed signals. Except for some minor shuffling, the positions settled on during these two days remained much the same for four years.

Advocates for farmland protection presented the case for the Jeffords bill in strong terms. On the one hand, they emphasized the severity of the coming cropland crisis, while on the other they insisted that this was a moderate bill and not the beginning of a federal land use policy. To do the former, Jeffords and some witnesses compared the farmland situation to the most visible resource problem of the 1970s—the energy crisis. Whereas gas lines made energy problems painfully obvious to Washington policymakers, the loss of agricultural land was not immediately felt on Capitol Hill. The case for a local interest in farmland protection was apparent to those who lived in areas with heavy losses of farmland, of course, but the case for a national interest in it rested to a large degree on what became almost a numbers game—the data generated by USDA. Jeffords accepted the *Potential Cropland Study*'s figure that two million acres were lost to urbanization, doubled that to include land lost to "buckshot urbanization," added another million acres of land the *Potential Cropland Study* calculated as lost to water development projects, and painted this numerical picture:

> Recent Soil Conservation Service research shows that some five million acres of rural land are being converted to urban uses, are isolated by development, or are inundated by new water development projects every year. A third of these acres lost every year are valuable cropland, which must be replaced from a cropland reserve that is smaller than anyone suspected—a third of the 1967 estimates. In fact 80 percent of usable cropland in the United States—400 million acres—is already in cultivation. As for the reserves, the high-quality land amounts to only 24 million acres—an amount that, at current rates of conversion, isolation, and inundation could be depleted in as little as fourteen years.[27]

Thus the case for farmland protection became tied to a specific set of numbers. These numbers became the focus of intense debate between advocates and opponents of farmland protection and in some instances obscured the real controversy. What was really a struggle between competing philosophies, between a conservation mentality and a production mentality, between ecology and economics, between the SCS and the ERS, too often became a dispute over the validity of a set of statistics. Jeffords's testimony also included talk of "the moral imperatives" to "protect and conserve what is acknowledged as the greatest body of prime agricultural land on the face of the earth," but this ethical argument received less attention than the statistical one. Jeffords was compelled to rely on dire statistics and the energy crisis comparison because that was the only way in which Congress could be budged. In the spirit that nothing should be fixed until it is broken,

Jeffords had to first prove that the market for allocating the use of prime farmland was broken. Thus Jeffords consistently claimed that the loss of farmland was the nation's next energy crisis in the making, that it was "one of the most compelling resource conservation issues in the postwar era." In 1980 Jeffords asked, "Do we need an urgent crisis to form responsible public policy that would balance the need for agricultural land with economic growth? . . . Few of us want national land use planning. Yet, if we continue to wait, as we did with energy, a massive federal response is inevitable."[28] The claim that the farmland crisis was the next energy crisis never persuaded many who were not already believers, though, and Jeffords and his friends were left with data on land loss substituting for a crisis.

After Jeffords had painted this grave picture, the second half of his selling job seemed almost out of place. Having described a resource issue of major proportions, Jeffords then had to defend his bill as a "modest" approach, as a solution barely adequate to the nature of the problem. As Jeffords assured the hearing, his bill was not "any kind of land use bill dressed up in overalls." In private some of the bill's supporters feared that the legislation might be too weak, that it appeared to address an issue without really doing so.[29] The reason for an almost embarrassingly small response to such a severe problem was the need, as the bill's sponsors saw it, to dissociate the Jeffords bill from the Jackson land use initiative. As Iowa's Republican congressman Charles Grassley made clear, the bill was acceptable to him only if it was entirely noncoercive—that is, only if it gave something to farmers without taking anything away.[30] He and others would (and did) oppose anything tainted with the stain of federal land use controls.

This issue provided the context for the most dramatic event of the two-day hearings. In a well-meaning but near-disastrous testimony, the speaker for the Sierra Club, Wilma Frey, gave the Jeffords bill the kiss of death: "Since Congress and the administration are not moving on a comprehensive land use bill, it is imperative that the crucial issue of farmland preservation be handled separately. . . . Since agriculture has deep roots in America, with many people feeling an affinity for farmland, it may be that developing a program for protection of farmland could be a tool for paving the way for acceptance of more comprehensive land use legislation."[31] Whatever truth there was in this view, Frey's testimony proved to be a serious tactical error. Neil Sampson, who was present at the time, later recalled, "You could have thrown a box car full of ice cubes in the House Agriculture Committee room and not caused the same chilling effect."[32] This testimony confirmed the suspicions of those who feared that federal land use was sneaking in the back door, that the land use planners, having failed with a general approach, were proceeding with a piecemeal approach. This ill-advised testimony became standard reference for the opposition for the next four years and proved more damaging than any that the opposition could possibly have given.

There were some groups, including some farm groups, who needed no help in finding reasons to oppose the bill. To the fringe farm groups of the libertarian right, the legislation was a dangerous extension of federal control and, as the National Livestock Feeders Association warned, "could easily become the springboard for land use regulation and control by the federal government."[33] The National Cattlemen's Association opposed the bill out of a reflexive opposition to anything supported by environmentalists. More worrisome to supporters of the bill was the position of the American Farm Bureau Federation, the nation's largest farm organization and a traditional Republican ally. While giving lip service to farmland preservation, the Farm Bureau argued that this should be addressed and, in fact, was being addressed adequately at the local level. A federal role, the bureau reasoned, "inevitably carries with it federal rules, regulations, and eventually, federal control." With logic that challenged the conservationists' notion of prime farmland and neatly summarized the antistatist view, one Farm Bureau lobbyist asserted, "There's nothing magic about any one patch of ground. Farmers resent the threat that bureaucrats will steal their future by regulation."[34] Getting Farm Bureau support was an important goal for farmland preservation advocates, who wanted to show the support of a unanimous farm lobby. The Jeffords bill received the support of other farm groups, including the National Farmers Union, the Grange, and many state Departments of Agriculture, but the inability to command the support of a unified farm constituency continued to hurt the chances for a bill that was meant, among other things, to help farmers.

The conservation movement was similarly split in its reaction to the Jeffords bill. Soil conservationists and planners naturally rallied to the cause, but the more traditional resource economists remained cool to the notion of a federal policy dealing with private lands. The Soil Conservation Society of America sponsored a conference on land use in March 1977 that floated many land use ideas and was sympathetic to a federal role in preserving agricultural lands. The list of cosponsors—those groups who shared an institutional interest in the issue—included the National Association of Conservation Districts, the National Association of Departments of Agriculture, the Urban Land Institute, the American Institute of Planners, the American Society of Planning Officials, and the Council of State Planning Agencies.[35] Planners were not always convinced of the threat to the nation's food supply but often had more immediate reasons for supporting farmland protection, such as maintaining rural economies, producing food locally, preserving open space for aesthetic reasons, reducing the energy costs of sprawl, protecting groundwater, and providing "green lung" air filters adjacent to polluted cities.[36] The soil conservationists' view complemented this picture, as evidenced in Neil Sampson's argument: "We know, therefore, that a disproportionate share of America's prime farmland lies within areas of urban pressure; is served by the most intensive network of transportation, energy, and communications systems; and has soil qualities that minimize development costs. This combination of factors serves as convincing proof that without some sort of public intervention normal market forces will continue to remove prime farmland—often irreversibly—from the nation's agricultural base."[37] Farmland preservation directly challenged the notion that the market was the best place to decide land use questions, as Sampson recognized: "There are, after all, higher values than money and better measures of good and evil than costs and profits. But to find such measures, we must look to ethical, not economic values."[38]

Market interference was precisely the matter about which some resource economists took issue. Often located in the Department of Agriculture's ERS, the land grant universities, or traditional conservation organizations such as Resources for the Future, these economists, who had been reared in decades of surplus, questioned the idea that farmland could become scarce and remained suspicious of farmland preservationist concerns. Marion Clawson, senior economist at RFF, suggested that the new emphasis on food supplies was a facade used by preservationists to mobilize political support for open space preservation. "To many who know and love good land," Clawson wrote, "there is something close to sinful about any action which takes highly productive soils out of farming. Those who hold this view typically reject economic tests as a measure of land use."[39] Don Paarlberg, former adviser to Secretary of Agriculture Earl Butz, attacked the "scarcity syndrome" and argued that, in a strictly economic analysis, "the loss of agricultural land is reduced from a national issue, involving the nation's food supply, to a series of local issues involving the differing interests of farm and city people."[40] Other economists held that farmland preservation was an attempt, misguided at best and deliberately distorted at worst, to gather political support for otherwise unattainable open space goals.[41] Tinkering with the land market was not justified, one economist argued, because the "economic costs and benefits" and the "philosophical rationale for removal of the market from land use decisions" had not been considered. The free land market would provide more than enough land to meet future food demands, and the Jeffords bill was "the wrong thing at the wrong time and for the wrong reasons."[42] Yet economists were not monolithic in their position. Ideological arguments combined with disciplinary disagreements to produce mixed professional advice.

The Carter administration was also less than unanimous in its support of farmland legislation in 1977. Carter himself was sympathetic to environmental ideas but never gave strong leadership to this federal initiative. Secretary of Agriculture Bob Bergland's primary interests lay elsewhere, but he nevertheless supported the notion that agricultural lands should be conserved. A familiar line in Bergland's speeches dramatized the issue: "In my lifetime, we've paved over the equivalent of all the cropland in Ohio. And before the century is out, if we keep on at the same rate, we'll pave over the equivalent of all the cropland in Indiana. This can't go on."[43] Bergland created an atmosphere in USDA that permitted others to pursue the issue, but at several key points he did not pursue the issue as hard as supporters had hoped. Jeffords believed that Bergland provided "pretty good support" for the legislation, yet Bergland was inclined to see a minimal role for the federal government, limited primarily to restricting government subsidies for development, as Title I of the Jeffords bill mandated. Bergland considered farmland protection an "important commitment" of USDA but also held that the "proper federal role" was "research, education, data collection, and federal assistance."[44] Next in line was M. Rupert Cutler, assistant secretary for research, conservation, and education, who was in a position to shape departmental policy. Cutler's commitment to environmental ideas was firm, and he played a key role in trying to make USDA more ecologically sensitive on such diverse issues as the protection of wilderness and regulation of pesticide spraying in national forests, SCS stream channelization, and erosion control, as well as farmland protection. Cutler did not shrink from the essential ideological point: "The day was, not too long ago, when the word 'planning' was a scareword, a term so controversial that it was used only behind closed doors, never in 'polite society.' Today, land use planning, for example, is an accepted concept, an essential element of a national program of conservation and development of our national resources and protection of our environment."[45] Perhaps in 1977, when he gave this speech, Cutler did not perceive all of the obstacles to making planning a reality; in the end he was not able to convince even his own administration to support the Jeffords bill.

Cutler's testimony was easily the most important given during the June hearings for the Jeffords bill, and the Carter/Bergland administration's position raised questions as to who would determine administration policy. Cutler agreed with the concerns of the bill and placed "the future of the nation's prime farmlands at the top of the priority list." Yet after a lengthy description of the problem, he concluded that the demonstration projects called for in the bill were too expensive and that the commission would be an unnecessary proliferation of bureaucracy. If this testimony was cryptic, it was because Cutler personally and the administration generally were sympathetic with the aims of the bill but unexpectedly were forced by the Office of Management and Budget (OMB) to oppose the bill. Under questioning this situation became obvious: Cutler repeatedly expressed support for the goals of farmland preservation but, because of the Carter administration's hopes for a balanced budget, had to hold back from fully endorsing the bill. OMB also objected to the creation of another commission and suggested that the necessary information could be gathered within the existing departments and without adding to the bureaucracy. This conflict began two years of discussion about whether, as Jeffords asked, "one department studying this problem, matched against all the other departments who are trying to maintain their own programs, would be successful."[46] Jeffords preferred an independent commission with a congressional mandate and an authority not tied to one department. The Carter administration remained at odds with itself, sympathetic to the need for agricultural land protection yet wary of increased funding and an independent commission. This ambivalent support was a major cause for the ultimate failure of the Jeffords legislation.

The funding issue proved to be the least resolvable of the two conflicts. The OMB remained firm in its opposition to any spending initiatives, especially at a time when the president was committed to curbing the growing federal deficit and when the 1977 omnibus farm bill was already overrun by $1 billion. As one congressman pointed out, $50 million for resource conservation was a pittance compared to the billions spent to increase production, but this logic held no sway with the OMB. William Haffert, still anxious for federal funds to help protect New Jersey farmland, suggested including the Jeffords bill in the general farm bill, with the funds for farmland preservation coming from a one- or two-cent reduction in commodity price supports. Neil Sampson discussed this idea with Peter Sorensen, Cutler's assistant, and USDA considered the proposal carefully. Ultimately, however, the OMB and the Carter White House could not agree with the idea.[47] Including farmland protection in the general farm bill was a tactic that achieved a partial success in 1981, without funds and after the bill's political education purpose had been fulfilled. But in the Ninety-fifth Congress, this tactic failed because advocates of the bill were more anxious to raise popular support for the idea than to quietly secure federal funds and because the OMB dominated the Carter administration's thinking on resource protection.

There was considerably more compromise shown on the creation of a commission, primarily because Secretary Bergland and the Agriculture Department genuinely liked the idea. Bergland personally supported the idea that federal projects should not contribute to farmland loss and was determined that the department take a positive response on the issue.[48] He floated the idea of a "Blue-ribbon Commission" that would serve for a shorter time and have a different focus than the commission envisioned in the Jeffords bill. Bergland's Blue-ribbon Commission was intended to be "a sounding board for the secretary on a broad range of land and water issues" but not to deal with the specific issue of agricultural land in as much detail as the congressional commission specified.[49] The original department plan was to have this commission regardless of the requirements of the Jeffords bill, but during late 1977 and early 1978 this idea got sidetracked in a tangle of legislative wrangling. Despite the overlap in function, the two ideas were sufficiently different to be treated separately, as Secretary Bergland recognized.[50] Nevertheless, because of the department's urge to respond favorably on the issue, Cutler's staff drafted their own bill, which was more modest in funding, left out the demonstration projects, replaced Jeffords's Agricultural Land Review Commission with Bergland's Blue-ribbon Commission, and satisfied no one.[51] The substitute bill never got very far as legislation but was a signal that the department was searching for a constructive response.

At issue was not only the focus of the commission but the independence of its research and policy recommendations. The Jeffords bill called for a commission outside of the normal bureaucracy, a commission that would allow a more comprehensive and more critical review of existing policies. USDA was anxious to maintain its role as the lead agency concerning agricultural lands and at first wanted to keep the commission largely in house. By early 1978 this view began to change as the department felt more of "the public and political pressures growing in this country" and recognized that an independent review would have more credibility in "calling national attention to the situation."[52] Later the department would take an important initiative by creating the National Agricultural Lands Study (NALS), which showed both independence and expertise. This later action came with no help from the OMB, which remained steadfastly opposed to the creation of a commission because it believed, based strictly on an economic perspective, that the loss of agricultural land was not a problem. With administration politics thus deadlocked between a willing USDA and an intractable OMB, it was up to Congress to move ahead without a clear signal from the executive branch.

On 21 February and again on 2 March 1978, the House Subcommittee on Family Farms, Rural Development, and Special Studies met to discuss and act on the Jeffords bill. Chairman Richard Nolan was unsuccessful in getting a meeting with or a clear policy statement from Secretary Bergland and decided to push on without USDA support.[53] The subcommittee approved the bill by a nine-to-four vote (split along party lines) and sent it on to the full Agriculture Committee. On 18 May, 7 June, and 12 July this committee discussed, amended, and voted on the Jeffords bill. The most controversial part of the bill, the demonstration project program, was deleted on a close vote after the committee heard Bergland's view that "it would be premature to expend federal funds in establishing, carrying out, or testing pilot projects" before the commission had reported on the severity of the problem.[54] The bill's supporters, confident that the commission would find the problem a serious one, argued that the demonstration projects were part of the research needed to find solutions to the problem. They cited evidence that existing state and local programs were not effective and maintained that the nation needed a sort of policy laboratory to test which kinds of land use policies might be effective at a local level.[55] The opponents, less sure that a problem existed, responded that spending federal funds on solutions prejudged the commission's research on the nature of the problem. While Jeffords must have been disappointed to see what he called the "guts of the bill" deleted, the scaled-down bill at least should have had a better chance of passing. It was now without its most costly provision and the one that raised the most fears of federal land use control. Even so, the Jeffords bill barely squeaked out of committee, on a close vote of 22–19. The opposition echoed the words of the Sierra Club testimony that "developing a program for protection of farmland could be a tool paving the way for acceptance of more comprehensive land use legislation."[56] Whereas Jeffords, backed by a network of committed farmland preservationists, was ready to commit federal funds to a federal policy to find land use solutions, other representatives were still carefully measuring the problem. For Jeffords and his backers, the commission was a way to bring attention to what they already knew. For others, the commission was to be an investigation of whether or not the loss of agricultural land merited serious federal concern.

At the same time as farmland protection legislation was crawling through the House Committee on Agriculture, similar legislation was faring even worse in the Senate. The Senate version of the bill had no supporter as active as Jeffords and no staff as interested as Gray or Swiderski. Repeating its ambivalence about the House version, the Department of Agriculture could not agree to support the bill. Neil Sampson, who tried to forge ways for the agencies in USDA to reach consensus on the bill, finally was forced to concede: "I don't think the department can fight its way through to a position on this bill. It just seems to have tied everybody in knots."[57] With these obstacles, and with no one to fight through or around them, the Senate bill did not even make it out of committee.

In 1978 farmland protection found a strong supporter in the Senate in the person of Senator Magnuson of Washington. On 16 March, Magnuson introduced his version of the Jeffords bill in the Senate and made clear his urban orientation on the issue. He emphasized that the "loss of agricultural land has been especially severe near our urban areas" and pointed to the "economic and aesthetic asset" of "preserving a green belt of farm lands around our urban areas" for a "fresh supply of agricultural products" and for the "expanses of open, unfettered land" that would enhance "the natural beauty and quality of life for everyone." Magnuson's support for the bill was influenced by the experience of the farmland preservation program in King County, in his own state. This local PDR program had met with some success but, as Magnuson noted, was "discovering that the preservation of agricultural lands is very expensive."[58] Magnuson's emphasis was not so much on national productive capability as on local and regional reasons for preserving farmland. He was looking for a way to get federal dollars to support the preservation program in his home state. This sort of pork-barrel politics ("bringing the bacon home") added support to the idea of farmland protection[59] but did little to move the bill through the Senate.

While the legislation to protect agricultural land languished in the Ninety-fifth Congress, the Department of Agriculture, under the leadership of Bob Bergland, tried a different tactic. Bergland's interest in protecting agricultural land led him to consider drafting a stronger position than the one adopted by Secretary Butz in 1976. In fact, the 1976 policy was enforced so little that the Bergland officials did not even know it existed.[60] Norman Berg and the Land Use Committee were anxious to strengthen the department's commitment to farmland preservation. At Bergland's direction, they drafted a stronger statement, which was then modified ("watered down," according to Rupert Cutler) after a series of meetings with local and state officials. Released on 30 October 1978, the revised Secretary's Memorandum required "that USDA agencies adjust their technical and financial programs to minimize the adverse effects of their actions on important agricultural lands." The memorandum, out of political necessity, stated that it did not imply any federal land use powers or interfere with the rights of private property, yet it did pledge the department's efforts "philosophically and substantially on this important issue."[61] In effect, this policy was the same as the Title I consistency clause of the Jeffords bill, except that it applied only to one department. Whether because of timidity or astute political calculations of what was possible, Bergland did not push the protection of agricultural land beyond his department. Yet if the federal government was going to stop assisting in the loss of farmland, if it was going to clean up its own house, then at least Bergland could move toward that end in the one department where he clearly had jurisdiction. At the end of 1978, this was more than Congress had been able to do.

The Demise of the Jeffords Bill

There was reason to believe that farmland protection legislation might be more successful in the Ninety-sixth Congress than it had been in the Ninety-fifth. Although it could hardly qualify as a mass movement, the cause of preserving agricultural land did seem to be generating some momentum. The *Des Moines Register* ran a week-long front-page series titled "Vanishing Acres" that gave full sway to the preservationists' cause. Referring to the *Potential Cropland Study,* the newspaper reported that "USDA's computers . . . show that five million acres of land—including one million acres of prime crop land—are being lost to urbanization and other uses each year" and suggested that a food "disaster" might be in store by the end of the century. Cutler labeled the land destruction "unassailable and brutal," Little warned that "each new subdivision, highway, dam, factory, power plant or shopping center threatens permanently to reduce the productive capacity of American agriculture," and an Iowa farmer admonished, "We dare not kidnap the earth from our children."[62] George McGovern, South Dakota's senator, enlisted in the cause and warned that erosion and the loss of farmland taken together would create "a crisis . . . so profound and so less easy to remedy than our energy problems that soil conservation and cropland conversion deserve to be the environmental 'glamour issues' of this decade."[63] The Conservation Foundation wondered aloud if "America's mighty agricultural machine will break down" and listed the loss of prime farmland as one of several serious threats.[64] The editors of *Harper's* doubted that "urban sprawl is choking America's food-producing capability" but concluded, "In the end, the future of the land appears neither as bleak nor as bright as it does uncertain."[65] This theme of uncertainty led some to argue for farmland protection in order to ensure an adequate agricultural base even if it were not needed. Sterling Brubaker, a senior economist at RFF, wrote, "I am not convinced that agricultural land requirements and demographic trends are on an early collision course, but it still seems wise to give more attention to land-sparing urban forms." Others called for farmland protection to provide a margin of food safety based on a "contingency reservoir of protected cropland."[66]

Other measures of support trickled in from around the countryside. A trucking strike and a snowstorm in 1978 dramatized New England's food vulnerability (90 percent of its food was imported) and sparked purchase of farmland development rights in Massachusetts, Connecticut, and New Hampshire. A Louis Harris opinion poll found that 53 percent of the public regarded the loss of farmland to be "very serious," while a GAO survey revealed that officials in twenty-five states considered the loss of farmland to be a serious problem in their state.[67] In states such as Illinois and New York, even the Farm Bureau supported state programs to preserve agricultural land. Yet as the number and variety of state programs grew, many problems remained. A truly effective state or local program was still elusive. Agricultural districts, the best of the voluntary programs, had yet to prove that they could do more than provide benefits to farmers who were distant from cities and not likely to sell their land in any case. The purchase of development rights, while undeniably effective, was prohibitively expensive in most areas, and both New Jersey and Long Island's Suffolk County were forced to curtail significantly their original ambitions. Suffolk County's experience also demonstrated that a PDR program could artificially inflate land values and provide a guaranteed market for land speculators—hardly the intended results. If farmland protection was to succeed, either farmers were going to have to accept more compulsion or states and localities were going to have to pay more money.[68]

This background of state and local experimentation added to the optimism of those who believed the Ninety-sixth Congress might bring the federal assistance that was crucial to effective farmland protection. Jeffords, backed by the enthusiastic staff work of Bob Gray, was again the leader of the cause in the House, while Senator Magnuson had joined in as the sponsor of the Senate version of the legislation. With two years of experience, supporters of the bill were now better prepared and knew the lay of the congressional landscape. The issue also had greater visibility because of the public discussion of the Jeffords bill in the Ninety-fifth Congress. But despite all of these reasons to hope for success, farmland protection advocates were again disappointed. Although it was in some ways simply a repeat of the arguments and positions taken before, the legislation put forth in 1979 did bring some new elements into the ongoing policy discussion.

The legislation did not get off to as smooth a start as its sponsors had hoped, and the delay came from an unexpected source—farmers. Advocates of the new Jeffords bill had been careful to get the proposed legislation high on the agenda of the Agriculture Committee, but in the early months of 1979 the federal government was preoccupied with farmers who brought their protests to Washington. Their tractors blocked traffic, and they filled the committee rooms lobbying for congressional help to meet their crisis. Five years of all-out production under favorable price conditions had finally produced a surplus of agricultural commodities on the market, and farmers' incomes had taken a dive. The uncontrolled boom of the 1972–75 years was heading into bust for farmers who expected permanent high prices. So Washington dropped its usual business and listened to farmers for three months. When the confusion cleared and the farmers left to plant their spring crops, the House and Senate Agriculture Committees began their normal agenda three or more months late and with a sense that a food shortage was not as imminent as it had seemed only several years before.[69]

When Jeffords introduced his legislation in March 1979, he addressed this changing agricultural context. While he acknowledged the problem of "agricultural glut," he argued that "the real problem comes later," that temporary surpluses did not change the general conditions of the "post-surplus era." Because of the continuing world food shortage, Jeffords reasoned, "agriculture and the land base that supports it is our most durable source of strength and world leadership." In Jeffords's view, as agricultural exports played an ever more dominant role in reducing the nation's trade deficits, the conservation of farmland became the basis for diplomatic strength. Moreover, local reasons for protecting farmland were growing more powerful—so much so that Jeffords reported, "There has been a good deal of pressure brought to bear on the Congress and the Carter administration to take more dramatic steps than my proposal currently envisions."[70] Temporary surpluses aside, the overall conditions for farmland protection were stronger in 1979, both locally and globally, than they had been in 1977, Jeffords insisted, and this bill was a "cautious" approach to a growing problem. The continued importance of agricultural exports gave substance to this view: by 1980 nearly one-third of all crops were harvested for export. Agricultural exports totaled nearly $40 billion and were crucial in offsetting a $90-billion petroleum deficit. Farmland protection, some analysts argued, was therefore a national and international concern that could not wait for state and local governments. With food aid becoming an essential part of foreign policy, federal action was justified.[71]

Jeffords and others made much the same argument in committee hearings, but a few new wrinkles kept these sessions from being a simple repeat of the 1977 hearings. In 1979 the SCS's National Resources Inventory (NRI) provided new and more authoritative data on the loss of cropland. The Rural Development Act of 1972 had authorized the SCS to collect this data, but funding had been delayed for several years. The new study was more comprehensive than the Conservation Needs Inventory because it not only examined erosion problems but looked at other land and water problems, including the conversion of agricultural land to other uses. The NRI supplied plenty to worry about: it reported a worsening erosion problem and a loss of agricultural land at essentially the same rate as the *Potential Cropland Study* had revealed. The NRI's finding of an annual loss of 2.8 million acres of agricultural land, one-third of it prime farmland, confirmed the previous data and strengthened the case for farmland protection. The NRI also provided a link between erosion and land use because, as was suggested in the Senate hearings, soil erosion worsened as prime farmland was converted to other uses and marginal farmland was brought into production.[72]

Another new wrinkle in the debate was the focus of the Ninety-sixth Congress on the Jeffords bill's Title I, the federal consistency title. The accepted wisdom of the Ninety-fifth Congress was that actions of the federal government in the form of highway construction, sewer development, or Farmers Home Administration rural development loans were a chief contributor to the loss of farmland, and this situation was certainly one of Jeffords's personal concerns.[73] That the federal government needed to make its own actions consistent with the goal of farmland retention went unchallenged. What had seemed the only secure part of the bill in the Ninety-fifth Congress met stiff criticism in the Ninety-sixth Congress, however, and survived the committee process only in much-diluted form. The problem with Title I, as expressed by the Farm Bureau, was that it might "allow obstructionists to preclude activities of the federal government . . . just for the sake of precluding activities."[74] In the House Committee on Agriculture markup session in November 1979, committee chairman Thomas Foley substituted a new Title I that replaced the requirements of the Jeffords approach with softer recommendations. Instead of being required to have their programs comply with the goal of farmland protection, the amended bill encouraged cooperation between federal, state, and local governments in this regard and recommended that "to the fullest extent possible," federal agencies should inform state and local governments of plans that involved converting agricultural land to other uses. The rationale for this emasculated version was that the original was so broad that it might have unintended results, just as the Environmental Policy Act and the Endangered Species Act, according to opponents of environmental protection, "were being construed by the courts to have results often at variance with the intent of many of their original supporters."[75] This argument prevailed in committee, and when the bill went to the floor of the House it was without federal consistency requirements. As Representative Charles Grassley commented on the floor of the House, the bill "evolved from one that had a very strong provision for protection of agricultural land . . . into a bill that is a toothless tiger."[76]

This was not the last word on Title I, however, and the proponents of tough federal consistency standards prepared for the coming floor debate. While the backers of the Foley amendment appealed to the conservatives' fears of the unforeseen results of public policy and the power-aggrandizing tendency of the judiciary, proponents of stricter consistency regulations also built their case on a conservative instinct—the need to limit federal power in relation to state and local control. Representative Leon Panetta of California raised the fear that the federal government would "ride roughshod" over land use protection policies of state and local governments.[77] On an issue such as farmland preservation, on which some states and localities were ahead of the federal government in protecting the environment, liberals could join with conservatives in championing the rights of states and localities against the federal government. Environmental legislation had come a long way from a decade before, when environmental protection necessarily meant federal control.

For the first time, Congress saw more than impressionistic evidence that federal actions really were a major cause of the loss of farmland. One of the consistently mentioned deficiencies of data concerning agricultural land was the lack of a precise measure of how much land was lost due to federal actions and what specific agencies or programs were guilty. Neil Sampson, who had recently been made the executive vice president for the National Association of Conservation Districts, helped the NACD to gather survey evidence on both of these points just in time for the Senate hearing in July. The survey indicated that, in those districts that considered the loss of prime farmland to be a problem, "over half (54 percent) of these districts call federal actions either a significant or a major cause of the farmland conversion." Heading the list of guilty agencies were the Farmers Home Administration (loans for rural development) and the EPA (construction of sewage waste treatment plants). The survey concluded that "the USDA [consistency] policy is on the right course" and that "reducing the impact of federal actions on farmland conversion will have some beneficial effect, even if it will not address the problems identified in all conservation districts."[78] This support for the consistency requirement provided a factual basis for the dissent from the Foley substitute for Title I.

The Ninety-sixth Congress also had reason to take a new look at Title II, which created the Agricultural Land Review Commission. After the failure of the Jeffords bill in the Ninety-sixth Congress, some farmland protection advocates began to explore what could be accomplished within the executive branch. Some advocates felt ambivalent about working with the executive branch; they rightly feared that it might undercut support for the Jeffords bill. Nevertheless, the idea of creating a presidential commission went forward with the support of Malcolm Baldwin at the Council on Environmental Quality, Secretary Bergland of USDA, and some USDA staff members. Protection advocates in the department, such as Neil Sampson, favored the idea of a commission because they were confident that the commission would support their position. Others wanted to preempt the bill in Congress, establish executive control of the issue, and avoid a congressionally mandated commission. Opponents of farmland protection used the existence of an executive branch study as an argument against the Jeffords bill.[79] The Department of Agriculture and the CEQ cosponsored the National Agricultural Lands Study, and ten other federal departments or agencies participated, so all were assured that the study would not be too closely tied to the Department of Agriculture. Thus it met some but not all of the specifications of the Jeffords bill. Those who feared a bureaucratic whitewash of the issue insisted that NALS was too limited in its eighteen-month time period and its relatively small staff and budget. They added that it was charged only with reviewing existing efforts to protect agricultural land and would not generate the innovative protection methods that they believed were needed. They argued successfully during committee markup sessions that Title II was needed to expand the time, budget, and staff of the study and thereby allow a more comprehensive analysis and the generation of new and innovative techniques.[80] In short, for those who did not completely trust the secretary of agriculture or the bureaucracy, Title II was a means of insisting on a more thorough and creative study.

Whatever Bergland's intentions, the immediate effect of the creation of NALS was to hurt the chances of the Jeffords bill. Despite the arguments of its defenders, Title II now duplicated, at least in part, a study already underway. NALS also provided an excuse for critics of the Jeffords bill to delay the entire bill. They argued that any legislative response to the problem (if indeed it was a problem) should wait until after January 1981, when NALS was scheduled to issue its final report. Neil Sampson and others testified against this view at the Senate Committee on Agriculture hearings, arguing that the dimensions of the problem were already fully documented and that NALS could contribute most by adding ideas about solutions, not by restating the problem.[81] Despite these arguments for the necessity of immediate congressional action, opponents of the legislation continued to argue that Congress should wait until the results of the new study were in. NALS was thus turned into an inadvertent excuse for delaying action.

Title III, establishing the demonstration projects, was again the focus of the attack by those who saw in the bill the beginnings of federal land use planning. Representative Charles Grassley, the bill's most careful and active opponent, argued in the House Agriculture Committee hearings that the funding for demonstration programs would inevitably bring federal restrictions along with federal funding and eventually would mean that local and state land use controls would be superseded by federal dictates. In the Senate the bill, especially Title III, was described as a backdoor approach to federal land use planning, or sometimes as a "camel's nose under the tent," meaning that it was the start of something that would inevitably grow larger and more odious.[82] Jeffords and others countered this argument by claiming that if state and local action were encouraged now, federal action would be unnecessary later. If the problem could be effectively managed at the state and local levels, supporters reasoned, the federal government, in its "customary role as crisis manager," would not be necessary.[83] This argument was good enough in committee to defeat Grassley's amendment to delete the demonstration projects, but the "camel's nose" theory followed the bill onto the floor of the House.

In other ways, support and opposition to the bill were much the same as in the Ninety-fifth Congress. Rupert Cutler again gave USDA's schizophrenic opinion: he agreed that the loss of farmland was serious, but at the direction of OMB, he again withheld support for the bill. As Senator Leahy of Vermont summarized USDA's position during the hearings, "The department was for it and OMB was against it."[84] Support from farm organizations was ambivalent. The American

Farm Bureau Federation moved from a tentative opposition to a hesitant favorable position, only to back away from the bill at the last minute. The Farm Bureau approved the bill but suggested enough amendments to leave the bill's body looking like a skeleton.[85] Strong support continued from an array of other farm groups, including the conservative National Grange, the liberal National Farmers' Union, the NACD, the National Association of Counties, various state departments of agriculture, and numerous state and local farmland preservation groups. In the Senate the bill received an extra dose of publicity when Senator Gaylord Nelson convened his Select Committee on Small Business to consider the preservation of agricultural land as it related to the preservation of the family farm.[86] Nevertheless, farmland protection never became as popular or as salient at the federal level as it was in many states and localities.

The debate on the floor of the House of Representatives on 6 and 7 February 1980 marked the climax of over three years of legislative activity. The debate offered little that was new in terms of substance but rather was a telling sign of the strength of the antistatism embedded in the nation's political culture. The most frequent charge was that the bill was "a dangerous first step towards national land use planning," a charge backed by the three-year-old ill-advised Sierra Club testimony that the bill "might be a tool paving the way for more comprehensive land use legislation." The fear of centralized regulations moved opponents to charge that the bill meant "nothing less than the long hand of Washington, D.C., hovering over every acre of land within a three-thousand-mile radius," that it was a "social engineer planning scheme," or that it was "the father of [federal] land use planning." Supporters of the bill reiterated their position that this was a "sensible, rational approach" to the problem and was "cooperative" rather than "coercive." One thing on which there was agreement was that the federal government was the "most flagrant abuser of agricultural land" and, as such, the most in need of regulation. In this context, an amendment by Leon Panetta of California to restore a strong federal policy in Title I easily passed with support from conservatives who later opposed the bill for its other aspects. Having agreed that the federal government was "one of the primary villains involved in eating up agricultural land in the country," the House could not agree that this was even a serious problem. Opponents argued that the study commission was "unnecessary, duplicative, and unwarranted" in light of the ongoing NALS research, that the Title II demonstration projects were "premature" pending the results of NALS, and that the whole bill was too costly. Supporters of the bill repeated their position that farmland loss was "the most serious resource problem facing the country" and that the Jeffords bill was a "moderate" effort—one supporter even called it a "faint-hearted" step—to address the problem. This reasoning failed to persuade, and the House first voted to delete the Title III demonstration grants by a vote of 227–163 and then rejected the remainder of the Farmland Protection Act by a vote of 210–177.[87]

The *Washington Post* reported the next day that "an innocuous-looking bill" was "treated brutally and finally killed." According to the *Post,* "the main trouble was that it sounded to many members like a first step toward national land use planning which they fear would lead ultimately to a situation where government tells every landowner what he or she may do with property."[88] Some representatives simply wanted to put off legislation until the results of NALS were in. One observer claimed that the chief reason for the bill's failure was that most members of the House were still not familiar with the bill and voted "no" simply to protect themselves in an election year.[89] Jeffords believed that the bill fell victim to the last-minute opposition from the Farm Bureau and to the lingering perception that it was part of an effort to implement federal land use planning.[90] The vote showed both party and regional patterns along generally predictable lines. Republicans overwhelmingly opposed the bill (28 for, 115 against), while Democrats displayed a weak preference for the act (150 for, 98 against). This was hardly a party vote (House Speaker Thomas P. "Tip" O'Neill voted "no"), and the more meaningful division came along regional lines. New England and the Pacific coast states voted nearly two to one in favor of the bill (94 to 53), and the Great Lakes states gave the measure a strong majority (23 to 10). Majorities in all other regions opposed the legislation, with southern and western states voting three to one against (24 to 74) and the midwestern Corn Belt voting "no" in nearly the same proportion as New England voted "yes" (23 to 45). Thus the Jeffords bill found the most support from the most urbanized regions of the country, regions that had already lost the most farmland. Political support responded to, but did not anticipate, the loss of farmland.[91]

Meanwhile, the Senate version of the bill, introduced by Senator Magnuson, remained stalled in a Senate subcommittee chaired by Senator Roger Jepsen of Iowa, who feared that the bill would be the first step in the creation of a federal "land czar." He promised that if anyone "showed up on my land to tell me what I could do with it, I'd meet him with a double-barreled shotgun."[92] This did not mean that four years of legislative activity and hours of dedicated work by a handful of farmland preservationists had come to nothing. The Jeffords bill had, as its sponsors intended, served as a vehicle for increasing public and policymaker awareness of the issue and in creating a political context that encouraged a bolder reaction from the Department of Agriculture. The broad support for the consistency clause of Title I showed the way for successful legislation in the next Congress. The bill also helped to forge some new political alliances between environmentalists and farmers at both the local and national levels, alliances that were not as productive as they might have been in exploring areas of mutual interest. For all of this, however, the Jeffords bill failed to do what it needed to do—that is, it failed to convince Congress that a genuine "crisis" existed. Nevertheless, as one supporter wrote to Jeffords, the discussion may have "raised the level of consciousness of many" and brought more attention to the National Agricultural Lands Study, which would perhaps provide "the clincher for another try."[93] With farmland protection stalled in Congress, attention turned to NALS as the next best hope for preserving agricultural land.

5

The

National

Agricultural

Lands

Study

Bids for Support in the Carter Years

On 16 January 1981, four days before Ronald Reagan became president, the National Agricultural Lands Study released its final report. The report was both a warning and a call to action. It warned that U.S. agriculture was losing farmland to nonagricultural uses at a rate that jeopardized future food production, and it called for federal initiatives to help state and local governments enact land use measures to prevent the continued loss of agricultural land. The study was sponsored by the Council on Environmental Quality and the Department of Agriculture, but it was more a reflection of fundamental changes in U.S. agriculture than of the leadership of the executive branch. The NALS was the finale for farmland protection in the 1970s, and the political context of its release guaranteed that it would have no encore.

Even before Reagan's election foreshadowed the certain death of an active federal farmland protection policy, the Carter administration was not eager to enter into the politics of farmland preservation. Rather, the issue percolated up from the middle layers of the bureaucracy and from Congress, where the determined minority of farmland pressurizations was beginning to have some success in convincing others that demographic and agricultural transformations were making agricultural land suddenly more vulnerable. Carter's secretary of agriculture, Bob Bergland, had a reforming impulse and gave some support—certainly more than his predecessor, Earl Butz, had—to conservation initiatives. Yet Bergland's primary interests were with the economic and social structures of agriculture, not with land use. Leadership on land use issues in the department came from the departmental Land Use Committee created by Norman Berg and others during the Butz administration. During Bergland's term this committee was chaired by Assistant Secretary for Conservation, Research, and Education M. Rupert Cutler, whom one insider called one of "only two officials in the Carter administration who seem at all interested in the politics of private lands."[1] The Land Use Committee's first effort was the 30 October 1978 memorandum on agricultural land use (discussed in chapter 4), whose object had been to force all department agencies, such as the Farmers Home Administration and the Agricultural Stabilization and Conservation Service, to make their lending and spending activities consistent with the goal of preserving farmland. Yet when agency pressures weakened the wording, Secretary Bergland, who had been in Congress in 1974 when conservative reaction rallied to defeat the federal land use planning bill, hesitated to push hard on the politically risky issue of land use. The result was that the policy had proven extremely limited in several ways. As an intradepartmental statement, it lacked the binding power to force its own agencies to comply and could too easily be brushed aside as a "wise use policy" with no teeth.[2] As a statement to other departments, it lacked the authority to intervene in their affairs. It became, as one critic noted, a "do good, avoid evil" statement with enforcement that was "spotty at best."[3] The acknowledged ineffectiveness of so mild a policy left some members of the Land Use Committee dissatisfied and looking for ways to move the administration to a more activist stand.

The Land Use Committee also felt pressure from the ongoing inter-agency dispute within USDA over the issue of agricultural lands. The controversy unleashed by the 1977 publication of the *Potential Cropland Study* still pitted the Soil Conservation Service against the Economic Research Service, the conservationists against the economists. In part this was another turf struggle within the byzantine corridors of the department, but it was also a contest of competing disciplinary perspectives on resource questions. On the basis of data distilled from the Census of Agriculture, the ERS argued that the *Potential Cropland Study*'s finding of three million acres of agricultural land lost each year was too high. The economists held that the real rate of conversion of agricultural land was much lower, probably less than one million acres per year. Thomas Frey, chief geographer for the ERS, believed that the *Potential Cropland Study* used "deficient" data and presented a "faulty interpretation" of land use changes.[4] The Land Use Committee thought an external study might at least resolve some of the internal "confusion" so that a common understanding of the dimensions of the problem might emerge.[5] If the experts could agree, then that professional consensus might give the department a less clouded authority on land use questions.

Even as these internal reasons for a study were building, the Agriculture Department began to feel the external pressure applied by the Jeffords bill. Secretary Bergland wanted to avoid the congressionally mandated commission called for in Title II and preferred an in-house study, one that could be controlled by the executive branch. Protection advocates, increasingly frustrated with the reluctance of Congress to consider the Jeffords bill, were happy to achieve by executive decree what appeared to be increasingly difficult to accomplish legislatively.[6] In 1978 these pressures gelled into specific suggestions for what was to become the National Agricultural Lands Study. In August of that year, representatives of the National Association of Counties met with Secretary Bergland to propose the formation of a "National Study Commission on Agricultural Land Retention." Bergland had seen his earlier efforts to establish a Blue-ribbon Commission on a wide range of conservation and agricultural issues squelched by the Office of Management and Budget, but he now endorsed this more specific proposal. Bergland sent the idea to Rupert Cutler with a note: "I like this idea and would like to explore it with the department's Land Use Committee."[7] The committee welcomed the idea and pushed eagerly ahead.

The CEQ joined the momentum for a commission in October 1978 by agreeing to be a cosponsor. The council had shown a strong interest in land use issues and in 1976 had issued a memorandum directing all federal agencies to include the loss of cropland in their environmental impact statements. The memorandum had more symbolic effects than actual results, and the CEQ was anxious to find a more effective policy. When council chairman Charles Warren received the Land Use Committee's proposal for a commission, he responded that the idea "could provide significant opportunity for the administration to address a difficult but critical issue" and announced that "the council would be pleased" to cosponsor the commission.[8] The cooperation of the CEQ meant that the funding burden on the Department of Agriculture would be reduced and that the study would have more credibility than if it were simply a departmental product.

In early 1979 the Land Use Committee, backed now by Secretary Bergland and CEQ chairman Warren, proposed to the White House some ideas for administrative initiative on the protection of agricultural lands. Within the White House Lynn Daft, Carter's adviser on agriculture, made contacts with the network of farmland advocates in Congress and pushed the idea with Stuart Eizenstat, one of Carter's domestic affairs advisers.[9] The memorandum sent by Bergland and Warren to Eizenstat and to Jack Watson, another of President Carter's domestic policy advisers, emphasized that past "policy statements have had no discernible effect" on the problem and further warned that "if the administration does not take more visible steps to address the problem, then Congress may shortly do so." The message to the White House suggested two actions. First, the memorandum urged that the president "direct agencies explicitly" to consider the loss of farmland in their environmental impact statements. In effect, this move would have given presidential authority to the ineffective and limited policies of USDA and the CEQ. Second, the memorandum proposed the creation of a Presidential Commission on the Retention of Agricultural Lands; three implementation options were listed in order of preference and effectiveness. The preferred choice was to act by executive order "because it would provide the strongest authority and endorsement." The second option was to send a presidential memorandum to agency heads, while the third and weakest option was to set up an interagency agreement, which, the memorandum accurately predicted, "would produce less definitive results."[10]

The Carter administration responded sympathetically but stopped short of full support. Cutler suggested that the president might mention the new study on agricultural lands preservation in his 1979 Environmental Message,[11] and this theme fit neatly into Carter's environmental rhetoric:

> America's land and natural resources have nourished our civilization. Because our natural heritage was so abundant, we sometimes take these natural resources for granted. We can no longer do so. Our land and natural resources do have limits, and our demands upon them are growing at increasing rates. . . . A second critical issue for American farmers and consumers [erosion was the first] is the availability of agricultural lands—particularly prime farmlands—and their conversion to other uses. . . . [The] administration and Congress will work together to develop and implement appropriate actions.[12]

As a question of resource scarcity, farmland preservation had a certain resonance in the Carter vocabulary, and a few staffers in the Carter White House even saw some political benefit in the issue. Following Daft's lead, Eizenstat and Watson recommended that the president support the idea of a commission: "Agricultural land is viewed as an important issue within the farm community, particularly in certain parts of the Northeast and Midwest. It is the sort of non-price issue we should be stressing over the next year or so, given the increasing difficulty we will encounter in realizing further increases in farm prices and farm incomes. We think there is an opportunity for considerable political payoff for such a commission, if it is well done." But Carter's staffers also warned that the commission should not be weighted too much toward planning and conservation, that it should avoid "preservation for preservation's sake" but should take a production-oriented perspective in considering the "use and conservation" of farmland.[13] In terms of funding, the idea of creating a commission to study private land use ran afoul of the more conservative side of the Carter administration. The result turned out to be far less than the rhetoric had promised or the Land Use Committee had requested. The White House, following the guidance of the OMB, dropped altogether the idea of issuing a presidential order to force federal agencies to consider the loss of farmlands and accepted the commission only in its weakest form. Skeptical of the severity of the problem, the OMB convinced the White House that the study should not carry presidential authority. Not only was the president removed from the commission, but the idea of a commission itself was altered to become a less prestigious study group. The original proposal envisioned a commission of department heads, legislators, and representatives of local governments and conservation organizations. This commission would direct the study project and presumably give weight to the study results. But NALS, as it evolved, came to consist of only a study, without the authority of a commission, and was thus hampered from the start in fulfilling its promise as a vehicle for publicizing the need for farmland protection.

Once the administration had granted approval for an interagency study, Bergland and Warren proceeded with the one important decision that remained—selecting a director for the study. An original list of twenty was quickly pared to four and then to two, Robert Gray and Michael Brewer. The choice was not so much between qualifications as between perspectives. Gray was a planner by training and an activist by instinct; he had helped to draft the Jeffords bill and was clearly an advocate of farmland preservation. Brewer was an economist who was less inclined toward public policy solutions and tended rather to emphasize the virtues of market mechanisms. Both sides recognized that the choice of a director was more than a choice of personnel, for it would determine the tone and direction of the study. A compromise of sorts emerged: Gray was appointed Executive Director and Brewer Research Director. But what seemed at the time like a way to bring the two sides together only heightened the disagreement and the bitterness between the two men and the two perspectives.

Bergland and Warren launched NALS on 14 June 1979 with a plan of study, $2.2 million, eighteen months, and a staff of twenty to cover a broad research agenda. The plan of study charged the staff with determining the extent and causes of the loss of agricultural land, inventorying current state and local efforts to save farmland, and recommending any necessary and appropriate federal actions. The study agenda was broad enough that different meanings were attached to the same words. Conservationists wanted the study not only to explore the nature and extent of the problem but, even more, to carefully research and creatively generate possible policy solutions. Economists wanted the study to determine whether a problem indeed existed and only then to consider policy remedies.[14] The differences between the two camps soon split the staff into two groups, Brewer's people and

Gray's people. The split moved from differences in ideas to personal acrimony and ego confrontations that in turn impeded progress and clouded the outcome of the study.

The differences in expectations, styles, and approaches became more apparent as the study progressed. Brewer perceived the study as a disinterested analysis and hoped to find in Gray a "scholarly colleague." He later complained of being "under pressure to conduct research that I did not feel was appropriate."[15] Political differences became personal as some environmentalists came to see Brewer as an "impediment" to the study and even worried that he "developed a paranoia."[16] Farmland advocates held that NALS was not "established for the purpose of delaying action," that it should be "a much more visible type of study."[17] For his part, Gray maintained that NALS "was not a pure research kind of study." Rather, it combined the goals of research, policy proposals, and public education.[18] To those accustomed to quiet research, this mixture seemed like an illegitimate combination. Bergland gave some legitimacy to the activists' interpretation when he suggested that NALS conduct a series of regional meetings to discuss concerns about agricultural land away from a Washington perspective. In the White House there was even some discussion of President Carter attending one of these meetings in order to be "associated with the issue and with this particular enquiry." Carter's advisers were "very favorably impressed with [NALS's] high caliber of staff" and saw the publicity as a benefit: "Politically, we are getting the mileage we need out of the USDA/CEQ study."[19] Nevertheless, these meetings attracted criticism from some staffers who saw them as a means of establishing political support for government intervention before the problem was thoroughly studied. Similarly, a NALS public relations pamphlet titled *Where Have All the Farmlands Gone?* seemed to some to be more concerned with shocking statistics than with scientific inquiry. Worst of all, its critics believed, the pamphlet prejudged the conclusion of a scientific study whose research was not yet complete. Shirley Foster Fields, the energetic publicity director for NALS and author of the pamphlet, considered it her job to bring the study out into the open, to give it the benefit of public scrutiny rather than let it remain a matter for government experts only. Thus the pamphlet reported, "Every day in the United States, four square miles of our nation's prime farmlands are shifted to uses other than agriculture. The thief is urban sprawl." It also advanced a prediction that revealed the need for publicity: "Ten years from now, Americans could be as concerned over the loss of the nation's prime and important farmlands as they are today over shortages of oil and gasoline." This often-repeated (and not entirely accurate) comparison with the highly visible energy crisis showed again that if the conservationists were to succeed, they needed to generate some sense of a "crisis" before the political system would respond. But to those who expected dispassionate policy analysis, the language of "the war between the bulldozer and the plow" presupposed the results of the study.[20]

The NALS Final Report

Despite this internal dissension, NALS released its final report in January 1981, on budget and on time. The language reflected somewhat of a compromise between the two groups, although Gray held the upper hand. Charles Benbrook, a staff member on loan from the CEQ, drafted most of the initial version of the final report, and Gray made sure that this draft was sufficiently alarmist so that some sense of urgency would be left in the report after "Brewer's people" called for revisions. The staff went through seven drafts before they could all sign off on one version, which everyone did, even those who later criticized the report.[21] The principal problem for NALS—what Gray later called the "most difficult problem I faced with this study"—was to resolve the numbers dispute between the SCS and the ERS. NALS accomplished this task only by "getting down below the guys with egos to the numbers crunchers."[22] In some long sessions with the computer printouts of the conflicting numbers, staff from both groups went through the contradictory databases and established some legitimacy for the statistical measures of the problem that appear in the final report.

More than most policy issues, the debate on agricultural land hinged on numbers. Based largely on SCS surveys, NALS concluded that cities and suburbs were moving onto rural lands at a rate that caused a loss of nearly three million acres of agricultural land per year. Nearly one-third of this loss, or one million acres, came directly from cropland. The three-million-acre figure, based on the 1977 *Potential Cropland Study* and the NRI, became the most-quoted and most-criticized part of the NALS report. Farmland protection advocates, including Gray, sometimes used the figure carelessly, not distinguishing between losses of agricultural land—defined by NALS as a broad category including range, forest, and pasture as well as cropland (totaling 1,361 million acres)—and the much smaller losses of cropland only (totaling 540 million acres). Economists preferred to emphasize the one-million-acre (actually 875,000-acre) annual loss of cropland from a base of 540 million acres. Both figures, if used properly, represented the best data then available.

NALS contributed to the policy discussion in perhaps a more important way by giving substance to the concept of farmland as a limited resource. Integrating as well as possible the conflicting data sources available to them, NALS researchers concluded that the nation's "cropland base"—that is, the amount of good-quality land either currently used or with the physical and economic potential to be used for growing crops—stood at about 540 million acres. The data showed that 413 million acres were then in use, while another 127 million acres had the potential to be used if needed. This concept of a cropland base rested on the SCS land capability classification system (see chapter 2) and implicitly accepted the conservationists' perspective, which stressed the importance of physical characteristics in determining good farmland. The economists, in contrast, usually began discussions of the supply of agricultural land by mentioning the 1.5 billion acres of private rural land in America, thus emphasizing the abundance of land.[23] In identifying a cropland base NALS gave some precision to the notion that good-quality farmland was not a boundless resource.

Using this fixed figure of 540 million acres of potential cropland, NALS showed how agriculture was expanding into this cropland base even as demographic shifts were reducing it. With exports rising and productivity (yield per acre) stationary or growing slowly, NALS predicted that most of the potential cropland would be in use by the end of the century, when farmers would have cultivated between 77 million and 113 million additional acres. The principal cause for this cropland expansion, NALS explained, was the U.S. plunge into the world food market: "Exports are expected to dominate the growth in overall agricultural demand. The volume of U.S. agricultural exports increased an average of 10 percent annually during the 1970s. The harvest from one in three acres is now exported. In 1979, the market value of U.S. agricultural exports reached a record $40.5 billion. Agricultural exports now account for almost one-fifth of the nation's total exports and play a key role in the U.S. balance of payments."[24] NALS thus accepted and even applauded continued high export levels and maximum-production agriculture in the nation, because this clearly made the case for agricultural land protection stronger. Although NALS recognized that this maximum-production effort had some negative environmental consequences—soil erosion, in particular—NALS never challenged the wisdom of continuing such a substantial level of exports and never addressed whether the balance-of-payments benefit, the trade of "soil for oil," was worth the cost. In this sense, NALS was a land protection document that, unlike the best of the conservation thinking of the 1930s, never challenged the dominant production mentality.

NALS also made some less-controversial contributions to the policy discussion. The study compiled a handbook with a sampling of the hundreds of various state and local programs to preserve farmland.[25] Designed to help state and local officials, the handbook was the most comprehensive collection of farmland protection programs available. It took a more optimistic tone about the effectiveness of these programs than most other recent research and, in particular, brought attention to agricultural zoning as a surprisingly common approach. The lack of federal coordination was clearly demonstrated by another NALS research project, which explored the impact of federal actions on local land use patterns. This study identified thirty-seven federal agencies with over ninety programs that contributed to the loss of agricultural land. Only two of these—the EPA and USDA—even considered the effects of their projects on agricultural land. The federal government, NALS showed, already intervened in local land use by subsidizing highways, waste disposal plants, and housing developments that often blindly contributed to the loss of farmland.

To address the limitations of state and local land use activities and to remedy the existing federal contribution to the loss of farmland, NALS recommended a series of policy initiatives. The proposed initiatives included the articulation of a policy requiring all federal agencies to consider farmland in their actions; federal spending incentives to encourage development away from good agricultural land; technical and financial assistance to state and local governments; and provision for more consistent and reliable data collection. These were fairly modest ideas that emphasized "putting the federal house in order," as most analysts called it, and did not envision a heavy federal involvement in local land use matters. In contrast to the situation earlier in the decade, when federal leadership implied federal involvement (at least with funding and general guidelines), in 1981 federal leadership on land use seemed confined to providing information when it was requested and staying out of harm's way. In this sense NALS represented a retreat from earlier, more activist versions of farmland preservation, which called for increased public regulation of the private land market, with federal leadership made more visible through federal funds and technical assistance to states and localities. NALS emphasized instead the idea of inducing the federal government not to do harm, of restricting federal subsidies for projects built on prime farmland—that is, of compelling the federal government to better coordinate its planning efforts. This shift moved the argument from a debate about private property rights to a discussion of the wisdom of various public subsidies. NALS thus inadvertently contributed to the sense, which grew strong in the late 1970s and 1980s, of an incoherent government, at odds with itself and incapable of effective intervention without unintended consequences. With ninety federal programs contributing to the loss of farmland, one possible interpretation of NALS was that the federal government needed to do less, not more.

The reception given to the final report showed that instead of settling the controversy over the dimensions of the problem, NALS simply raised the emotional pitch of the debate. With a clear target at which to aim, the economist critics quickly began criticizing the data from NALS. Brewer, in order to "clear the decks with my scholarly colleagues," rushed into print with his view of the alleged problem. He first collected twelve of the seventeen research reports done by the staff and arranged their publication as a sort of minority report through the Senate Agriculture Committee, chaired by Senator Jesse Helms.[26] These papers contained much of the same data as the NALS report but phrased the problem in more cautious terms. Instead of mentioning the three million acres of agricultural land lost annually, Brewer stated that the less than one million acres of cropland lost each year from the cropland base of 540 million acres was so "modest" a trend that public intervention was hardly justified. Elsewhere, Brewer suggested that the three-million-acre figure for the loss of agricultural land was exaggerated because NALS defined agricultural land to include almost all undeveloped rural land, even hillsides, deserts, and other lands with no practical potential for crop production. The effect of this "expansive" definition of agricultural land, Brewer alleged, was that NALS did not really measure urban encroachment onto farmland, as it claimed. Rather, according to Brewer, the study measured urban encroachment onto nearly all rural lands, whether farmland or not.

Brewer further charged that NALS deliberately confused the important distinction between agricultural land and cropland in order to attract attention to the higher figure. Brewer maintained that NALS used its statistics "incautiously" and that a proper reading of the numbers "need not conjure up images of houses gobbling up children's cropland."[27]

Other critics and even some conservationists blamed NALS for abusing the statistics on the loss of farmland to urban uses in order to create a false impression of the magnitude of the problem. Gray sometimes juxtaposed the 3 million acres being lost each year from agricultural land with the 540-million-acre cropland base, thereby creating the erroneous impression that 3 of 540 million acres, rather than 3 of 1,361 million acres, were lost to farming each year.[28] Pierre Crosson, a senior fellow at RFF, explained why even some conservationists were uneasy with the report: "The NALS Final Report distinguishes between the conversion of cropland and potential cropland—the real issue—and conversion of all agricultural land. But somehow in press reports about the study the distinction was lost, and the three-million-acre figure is firmly embedded in the popular literature as the key measure of the conversion problem. Those responsible for NALS perhaps were not as careful as they might have been in assuring accurate reporting on this issue."[29] Privately, mainstream conservationists and agricultural economists were not so charitable and charged NALS with deliberately obscuring the research results in order to magnify the problem. As one Washington insider noted, "The report doesn't cry wolf, but Bob Gray has gone all around the country crying wolf."[30]

Not surprisingly, most economists in the USDA came out against NALS. The SCS stood as the department's lone bastion of support for agricultural land preservation. Most other agencies, such as the Farmers Home Administration and the Agricultural Stabilization and Conservation Service, simply proceeded with business as usual in the absence of broader support for NALS concepts. Similarly, the ERS, originally a supporter for the idea of a study, became disenchanted with the NALS data. Partly because of their different disciplinary perspective and partly because of their ongoing interagency rivalry, the ERS held to its lower rates of urban expansion.[31] Brewer collaborated on a number of articles in professional journals with other USDA researchers, notably David L. Brown, Robert F. Boxley, and Calvin L. Beale, which together characterized NALS as a "morass of inconsistent and conflicting numbers that left issues more confused than previously."[32] In an interesting indictment, they concluded: "The farmland issue has become highly politicized in recent years. It is a proxy for numerous agricultural concerns (especially the preservation of small farms) and has been lumped with environmental issues such as soil erosion and wildlife preservation. . . . Yet the scientific basis for this political movement is questionable. Alteration of property rights and other land preservation remedies appear extreme when compared to available evidence."[33] For these researchers, expert opinion did not justify the popular conclusion. Their concern was that exaggerated figures and the symbolism involved in farmland preservation would allow popular support to run ahead of the social scientists' knowledge. Thus, these researchers lumped farmland preservation together with other environmental causes, while some of NALS critics from the left made the opposite charge that the farmland preservation movement had not made the necessary linkages with kindred causes.[34]

The three-million-acre figure became a litmus test of support or opposition to farmland preservation and received attention far out of proportion to its significance. Philip Raup, an agricultural economist at the University of Minnesota, attributed this phenomenon to "the demand for shocking statistics," which led to "a serious misuse of NALS data, a misuse that has been fostered by the confusing way in which the data have been presented."[35] The most vigorous attack on NALS came from William Fischel, a Dartmouth economist, who went beyond the criticisms of Brewer and others that NALS abused its data to challenge the accuracy of the data itself. In a wide-ranging attack on NALS, the SCS, and conservationists in general, Fischel argued that the conservation surveys on which NALS relied were substantially flawed. He maintained that these surveys drastically overestimated the growth of urban land because they counted some forty-acre plots with scattered developments as land lost to agriculture and because they defined urban land more inclusively than had earlier inventories to which the most recent data was compared. If inventories in 1957 and 1967 tended to exclude from the urban category some land that had been partially developed, while the 1975 and 1977 surveys erred toward the inclusion of similar land, the effect would be to vastly overstate the incremental growth of cities and suburbs. He also noted that the data NALS used was inconsistent with the Census of Agriculture and with some spot-check aerial photographs from the U.S. Geological Survey. For instance, NALS estimates on total urban area were higher than the Geological Survey data by 29 percent in Pennsylvania, 41 percent in West Virginia, and 74 percent in Florida. From this information Fischel concluded that NALS overestimated urban growth by two or three times the actual rate.[36] Julian Simon, the Illinois economist who built a career on the premise that scarcity in economic terms is impossible, joined the criticism of NALS by describing the whole event as the conspiratorial work of some malicious and misguided "Washington politicos" bent on destroying the private property rights of local developers. A self-proclaimed "cornucopian," Simon labeled NALS the product of "eco-freaks" and an "obvious scientific fraud" suffering from "glaring internal inconsistencies."[37]

Behind the difference over the numbers lay more basic differences in ideology and in beliefs about the role of social science expertise. Some critics of NALS seemed at least as concerned that their scientific authority might be questioned as they were that the public might get a false notion of the severity of farmland loss. Brewer objected to "the press and the pamphleteers" who used NALS to support the exaggerated notion that "the country is running out of farmland." The local problems of land use and growth management, Brewer maintained, "do not add up to a national crisis with a bumper sticker campaign to 'save our farmlands.'"[38] Brewer wrote that the crusading style of NALS "furnished graphic examples of difficulties researchers can encounter in exploring subjects that many perceive as articles of faith, and that are suffused with vested interests and foregone conclusions." NALS's approach "robbed science of its authority," Brewer claimed, and left the country "without an accurate compass" to guide it on the issue. Brewer and Boxley criticized NALS for "conflicts in scientific faiths" and held that their own views rested on "the rigorous scientific analysis which is the dominant methodological approach of contemporary agricultural economics." Brewer framed the issue in terms of "whether the future consequences of current trends in land use warrant policy intervention in the processes that now allocate the resource."[39] Government policy was an "intervention" in the otherwise natural, even scientific, working of the free market.[40] Also implicit in these criticisms was a view of science as a politically neutral fund of information to guide public policy, with social scientists in the elevated role of experts. NALS was thus a double threat for some social scientists who were critical of the study. Ideologically, it lacked sufficient respect for private land markets and raised the prospect of a liberal, interventionist government. Professionally, some feared that the mix of science and conviction in the farmland preservation cause might work to devalue the role of professional expertise.

Conservative critics of NALS also shared in the rising antistatism of the late 1970s and 1980s. Responding to the claim that farmland loss was analogous to energy consumption in the 1950s, Fischel responded, "Well, there is a crisis in the making, but it is a crisis in the control of private property, not a crisis in food and fiber production."[41] He also helped to explain why NALS drew such a furious response by noting that the NALS "recommendations should not be taken lightly; they have far more power to restrict all forms of development than any previous grant of entitlements to anti-development interests (e.g., environmental impact statements and coastal zoning requirements)."[42] Fischel voiced his distaste for land use controls in general, not simply for federal involvement in land use. His sentiment revealed a strong bias toward development interests and against the entire concept of a public interest in the use of private property. These ideological themes—the sanctity of private property, the value of the free market, and the state as clumsy and coercive—were part of the larger shift in national values that culminated in Reagan's election in 1980. What Reagan insider David Stockman wrote of Carter's energy and resource policies might just as well have been written about agricultural land: "The 'moral equivalent of war' was really a front for the state control of resources and the economy. It was a neo-Malthusian ideology that held that we were running out of everything."[43]

As the rhetoric began to subside it became apparent that NALS estimates of farmland loss were indeed too high. Evidence from the 1982 NRI and from census surveys confirmed the charge that the three-million-acre figure was too high, as many agricultural economists had insisted. The 1982 inventory differed in several significant ways from the previous surveys, so that they were not strictly comparable. Some errors apparently came from different data-collecting procedures followed by the field personnel; some workers included land that was zoned or idled for development, but that was not yet built on, as "urban." There was no convincing evidence that this practice involved deliberate falsification of data, but it did mean that NALS had significantly overestimated the loss of agricultural land. Even so, the 1982 NRI did not include rural land lost to water storage, land parceled in expectation of urban development, or rural houses constructed on less than ten acres. This left some uncertainty as to a precise measurement of the loss of agricultural land, and estimates in the early 1980s ranged from 1.2 million to 2.1 million acres lost annually.[44] Taken together, the evidence suggested that the pace of agricultural land loss had quickened during the 1970s, but not as rapidly as NALS had reported. This was confirmed by USDA's 1987 resource inventory, which reported that the conversion of farmland went from one million acres annually during the 1960s to about two million acres annually during the decade from 1967 to 1977. Then, at the end of the 1970s, the farmland conversion rate dropped back to the traditional one million acres per year.[45]

Coming during both the conservative ascendancy of the early 1980s and the return of farm surpluses, this downward revision of farmland loss rates helped to close the lid on the coffin of agricultural land use planning. But the fixation on an aggregate national statistic concealed many aspects of the problem and inevitably understated the qualitative dimensions of the loss of agricultural land. The "impermanence syndrome" that accompanied the revival of population growth into the countryside meant that development would affect more acres, perhaps twice as many, as were actually counted as "developed" in a survey. The rate of farmland loss was measured by the increase in the land counted as urban and suburban. Measuring the expansion of cities and suburbs into the countryside assumed that conventional patterns of growth still operated; however, the demographic transition of the 1970s suggested that growth no longer occurred as a spreading, or even a sprawling, from a central point. The trend toward "buckshot urbanization" meant that farmland loss could not be measured simply by counting the increase in urban land and that existing data was altogether inadequate for measuring the impact of population settlement patterns on the productivity of agriculture. One study, for instance, found that six counties lost land to agriculture at the rate predicted by NALS even though the area experienced very slow population growth. Rising affluence led to more decentralized living patterns, so that suburban acreage grew by 45 percent from 1964 to 1975, while population grew only by 5 percent.[46]

Moreover, measurements of national net changes in land use missed entirely the substitution of quantity for quality and the regional variations in type of land lost to agriculture. An increase of 160 acres of hilly, highly erodible land with thin topsoil could not compensate for the loss of 160 acres of flat, fertile land, just as a gain of 500 acres of Kansas prairie could not offset the urbanization of 500 acres of California citrus groves or Massachusetts cranberry bogs. The nature of the land resource dictated that aggregate statistics of any sort could be only a partial measure of the problem. If the conservationists were guilty of dogmatically holding to the three-million-acre figure even in the face of contrary evidence, the economists were likewise guilty of being reluctant to admit that any quantitative evidence from surveys might understate the true dimensions of the problem.

The great data debate also displayed very little sensitivity to changes over time. Farmland conservationists became set on establishing a fixed annual rate of farmland loss, the three-million-acre figure, and projected this past rate into the future, often without attention to the historical period from which the data came. Opponents faulted them on this point by noting that the data came from a decade of dam building and interstate highway construction (1967–1977).[47] Yet this viewpoint too ignored the changing pattern of development (and the changing pattern of household formation, which would influence the rate of new construction) and looked for a constant rate of farmland loss. Often obscured was the fact that both conflicting sets of data agreed on an increase in the rate of farmland loss in the seventies over previous years. This agreement should have suggested that the seventies marked a period with different patterns of rural land use and discouraged the ahistorical projection of past rates into the future.

The NALS debate also reflected a shortsighted mentality and, in particular, missed the potential impact of long-term population growth. Most NALS projections ran twenty years ahead, or until the end of the century.[48] The background papers generally looked ahead fifty years, to a date probably within the lifetimes of some participants. This short time frame left out any truly intergenerational questions of resource use. NALS considered the availability of land for our children, but any serious analysis of the supply of land for our grandchildren's children was missing, especially considering the probable impact of population growth. NALS projected a domestic population level of 253 million by 2000, with the annual growth rate slowing to 0.6 percent. Global population, NALS projected, would reach 6.35 billion by 2000.[49] The continued growth of population beyond this time was not considered; neither were the possibilities of increased domestic fertility rates or continued immigration.[50] One has only to remember that the demographic projections of the 1930s called for a stable U.S. population by 1980 to realize that this sort of forecasting is inevitably inaccurate; nevertheless, it is historically shortsighted to assume that problems exist within the time frame of only one or two generations.

World population growth directly influenced NALS's thinking on exports, but more important was the mushrooming of agricultural exports during the 1970s. Farm exports amounted to nearly $40 billion annually by decade's end and compensated for 62 percent of the nation's expenditures on imported oil.[51] The consensus during the 1970s was that exports were crucial to the nation's balance of payments and were a tremendous boon to farm incomes. NALS joined this consensus and uncritically projected that farm exports would nearly triple during the next two decades and would therefore require at least another 75 million acres,[52] which would obviously make the case for farmland protection stronger. Most economists expected a slower growth in exports, as noted by Pierre Crosson of RFF: "This difference in growth of export demand is the main reason for the difference between the NALS conclusion that the adequacy of agricultural land is now a crucial national concern and my own—which is that it is not. If I believed that exports were likely to grow as fast as projected by NALS, I would share their view that the country faces a serious shortage of agricultural land."[53] Crosson calculated that exports would demand another 62 million acres by the year 2005, less than the NALS predictions but still a significant number. In addition, the view that exports were entirely benign began to break down in the early 1980s as it came under attack from a variety of sources. Reagan's farm policy of increased reliance on markets required higher exports to maintain farm incomes, but this policy put farmers on a "price roller-coaster" that critics began to question.[54] Conservationists began to realize that "surplus madness" led to soil degradation and that U.S. farmers were misled in what they viewed as their mandate to feed the world.[55]

The push for all-out production during the 1970s carried with it the cost of higher than acceptable rates of erosion—that is, more than five tons per acre, according to the SCS standard for most soils—on nearly one-quarter of the nation's cropland. Higher exports, as agricultural journalist and author Lauren Soth noted in *Foreign Affairs,* threatened "the nation's agricultural resources. . . . Limits to growth are anathema to Americans. . . . But the oil is clearly running out, and so is the most precious of our resources—topsoil."[56] Thus the consensus for exports to grow as fast as NALS projected had crumbled by the early 1980s, but U.S. cropland steadily became more of a global resource. The "gradual but steady disappearance" of agricultural productivity could undermine some foreign policy objectives, which pointed to the importance of "land use ethics on a global scale."[57]

The key variable in predicting future demand for cropland was technology. NALS emphasized the leveling off of current yields, the decline of irrigation, and limits imposed by rising energy and fertilizer prices. The rest of the century, NALS guessed, would see annual growth in yields between .75 percent and 1.5 percent. This estimate was in line with the 1.1 percent accepted by other economists in USDA, although some held out hope for a major technological breakthrough that would dramatically raise this level.[58] At the extreme, such breakthroughs as crop hybrids, genetic engineering, or artificial stimulation of photosynthesis claimed the "promise of virtually limitless horizons in food production" that would greatly reduce the amount of land needed for agriculture.[59] Most estimates did not count on such breakthroughs and were correspondingly much lower. Pierre Crosson wrote that increased petrochemical costs and expansion onto poorer-quality land would most likely lead to a continuation of the slower pace of productivity growth that had marked the 1970s. Earl Heady, a respected agricultural economist from Iowa State University, noted that yields had increased at 3.8 percent from 1939 to 1965 but only at 1.8 percent from 1965 to 1979. He predicted that this leveling-off trend would continue so that annual productivity increases by the end of the century would average only 1.0 to 1.3 percent. Only a major breakthrough in technology would change this trend, and as both Heady and Crosson realized, such a sudden technological advance would require increased funding for agricultural research, and it would likely take at least a generation for the productivity gains to be felt.[60] Vernon Ruttan of the University of Minnesota responded that "the sources of future productivity growth are unclear" and argued that the nation was entering a period similar to the first three decades of the century, when there was virtually no increase in yields.[61] Thus NALS and its critics largely agreed that technology would provide a smaller part of the answer than it had in the past.

Despite the ongoing academic controversy, NALS received a modest welcome from a variety of sources. The *Washington Post,* the *New York Times,* and the *Christian Science Monitor* all gave NALS publicity, and the *Post* editorialized, "For once an impending problem has been identified before it reaches crisis proportions. It remains to be seen whether the will to do something about it can be summoned while the solutions are still relatively painless. The government needs to get its own house in order by formally recognizing the national interest in preserving farmland and redirecting programs that do the opposite."[62] Most farm groups also supported the NALS findings, although to different degrees and for different reasons. The president of the National Farmers' Union spoke in favor of NALS at the group's annual convention: "That's three million acres that are gone [annually], and it represents a loss of opportunity for hundreds of young people who would like to farm that land. Family farms are being threatened by unplanned developments that consume some of the best farmland."[63] In a similar vein, the *Progressive Farmer* announced that "farm folks are upset about cities spreading over prime farmland."[64] The *Farm Bureau News* reported that the NALS findings were flawed because environmentalists dominated the final report, yet still encouraged states to proceed cautiously with programs to protect agricultural land.[65] The Farm Bureau's official statement on land use planning declared, "We are opposed to the continued encroachment of federal and state agencies and local governments on prime agricultural and forest lands."[66] Casting the issue this way—with the government as the intruder—was a limited view of the problem, yet this version of the story accurately foreshadowed the shape of federal policy.

A Cold New Era for Land Use Reform

In 1981 farmland preservation appeared to have a most unlikely hero in President Reagan's newly appointed secretary of agriculture, John Block. This was both because Block proved to be somewhat of an anomaly in the new conservative administration and because farmland preservation found a conservative face that lingered into the 1980s. An astute political maneuverer, Bob Gray built a bipartisan base of support for farmland protection and separated the study from the Carter-Bergland administration. As a former aide to a Republican congressman, Gray cultivated a base of congressional support in both parties. Gray also deliberately did not include in the NALS report the customary "Note to the President" or "Message from the Secretary," so that the report would have greater credence in the new administration. All of this made it easier for the new secretary of agriculture, John Block, to support farmland preservation. Block had favored farmland preservation as state secretary of agriculture in his own state, Illinois, and on coming to Washington he framed the issue in these terms: "All the statistics, legislation and studies mean nothing without a basic understanding that in the next twenty years we cannot meet a 60 to 85 percent increase in demand for U.S. agricultural products while urbanizing three million acres of productive land each year and maintaining current low productivity rates."[67] Farmland preservation flowed logically from Block's commitment to exports, but how forcefully Block would act and how much support he could command for a novel land use policy in the conservative Reagan administration was open to question. Still, Block announced in February 1981, "The NALS has built a strong case for establishing a national policy for protecting good agricultural land. I support such a policy. I support wrapping up the studies now and taking action."[68] Later, Block specified the federal role as "calling attention to the problem on a national scale" but specifically rejected "a more positive federal initiative."[69]

Encouraged by this initial endorsement, farmland advocates introduced the Farmland Protection Policy Act into the Ninety-seventh Congress. James Jeffords collaborated with Ed Jones to introduce the House version, while Patrick Leahy of Vermont and Roger Jepsen of Iowa cosponsored the Senate version. Supporters had learned from their legislative defeat of the previous year, and this year's bill faced little of the difficulty encountered by the Jeffords bill. Still, the bill proceeded without executive support, as the Reagan administration had arrived at a position on the issue that was directly opposed to Block's views. Early in 1981 Block proposed an executive order establishing a federal farmland protection policy, but at a cabinet council meeting on 10 September 1981, Block came under intense criticism, especially from officials at Housing and Urban Development and from Martin Anderson, Reagan's domestic policy adviser. Representatives from other agencies argued for trying to weaken the congressional legislation, and there was some sentiment for "doing nothing until Congress forces the administration to act and then to do only the minimum to comply with the law."[70] Despite these mixed signals from the administration, lawmakers worked their way toward a compromise solution. The final version was signed into law on 22 December 1981 as a subtitle in the 1981 Agriculture and Food Act. Including the bill in the general farm bill essentially reversed the decision on legislative strategy that advocates had made in 1977, and this certainly contributed to the bill's easy passage. More important to securing passage than the sponsors' legislative skill, however, was the fact the new bill did far less than the original Jeffords bill, so much so that Little accurately called it "a pale shadow of what we started with."[71] The act called for USDA to designate one or more farmland information centers and to develop a farmland educational program for widespread distribution through the extension service. The legislation also encouraged USDA to provide technical assistance to state and local farmland protection programs. The crucial part of the act was a mild version of the consistency title—the only one of Jeffords's original ideas to survive (unless one counts NALS as an ongoing study commission), since the federal financial support for local and state initiatives clearly was politically unacceptable. Yet, as Jeffords recognized, "even that got watered down fairly badly."[72] The law directed USDA to "develop criteria for identifying the effects" of federal programs on agricultural land loss, and federal agencies were to "take into account" the possible loss of farmland and "consider alternative actions, as appropriate."[73] Enforcement was left to existing agencies following existing procedures; there was no requirement for agencies to document their compliance, and there was no provision for agency oversight. Section 1548 even prohibited the law from becoming the basis of any lawsuits against an agency to compel enforcement, thus stripping local governments or conservation groups of their main avenue of legal redress. In short, the bill was a good faith measure that relied on the voluntary compliance of federal agencies who had already proven that they had no interest in preserving farmland. Nominally the bill was aimed at the ninety federal programs identified by NALS as contributing to the loss of agricultural land, but there was nothing in the bill to force federal agencies to change their farmland-consuming ways. Gray testified for the bill in Congress that "people at the local level are looking to the federal government for some leadership."[74] Instead, the bill offered an antifederal approach to policy and left leadership on the issue with the state and local governments.

It is conceivable that a vigorous administration might have given some life to such an anemic piece of legislation, but the reverse happened in the early Reagan-Block administration. Rules for implementing the Farmland Protection Policy Act remained bottled up in USDA for eighteen months before being released. Bob Gray charged that the department "dragged its feet" in complying with the act, and California representative George Brown complained, "It is becoming increasingly clear that this administration opposes a meaningful federal role in agricultural land protection efforts. . . . I fear that Congress can expect little in the way of concrete results in implementing the

Farmland Protection Policy Act."[75] In a progress report as mandated by law, Secretary Block designated the National Agricultural Library as the principal farmland information center, but no educational program was developed. USDA identified thirteen agencies whose programs contributed to the loss of farmland, but only one of those, the Tennessee Valley Authority, had requested help in reviewing its programs.[76] The proposed rule for implementation, released in July 1983, was a narrow reading of the act and consisted primarily of sixteen criteria that used the SCS's newly developed Land Evaluation and Site Assessment (LESA) system for determining whether a proposed action would affect valuable farmland.[77] Public comment was generally favorable, and some groups argued for a more stringent interpretation of the law. But John Crowell, assistant secretary for natural resources and environment, moved in the other direction. He dismantled the Land Use Division of the SCS, which had been USDA's center for land use ideas since 1977 and was responsible for implementing the act, and issued the final rules only under congressional pressure. In a speech before the National Cattlemen's Association, Crowell called the Farmland Protection Policy Act "unwanted" and essentially agreed with the western timber and cattle groups, public utilities, and conservative legal groups who opposed the law. Supporters accused Crowell of consulting with the Pacific Legal Foundation before publishing the rules, and Bob Gray charged that "James Watt is alive and well and living in USDA right now."[78] The final rules confirmed this view by further narrowing the scope of the law in three major ways. First, the rules prohibited federal agencies from using this law to refuse assistance to a private landowner in a project that might cause the loss of farmland. Second, the changed rules restricted the law's application to any land zoned commercial, industrial, or residential, even though much of the nation's best farmland was zoned rural residential. And finally, the rules clarified that federal permitting or licensing activities were not federal "programs" as defined by the law. As the rules candidly admitted, the act did not "mandate" any change, it only required agencies to consider alternatives. Nothing would prevent those agencies from proceeding normally after the farmland impact assessment had been completed. A former land use planner for the SCS rated the chances for the law to have any effect as "virtually nil."[79] Privately Gray informed Jeffords that the rule "basically 'guts' the law and at best pays only lip service to the original intent of Congress. . . . My own assessment of the final rule is that it will at most create more paperwork, while having no positive results" in actually restricting government subsidies for development on farmland.[80]

Clearly, NALS suffered from being released into the hands of the most conservative administration in fifty years. Had Bergland remained in office for another term, he would have pursued his plans for a major overhaul of farm policies, "including new directions in controlling soil erosion [and] soil loss, and including redefining the federal role and authority in the matter of trying to protect prime farming land from urban encroachment."[81] Instead, Reagan's emphasis on decentralized government and budget reductions made the chances for a federal spending or leadership initiative in a novel policy area nearly impossible. More important, agricultural surpluses returned and dampened any "crisis" thinking. Just as the idea of farmland protection emerged in the early 1970s in response to food scarcities, so the movement faded in the early 1980s under mounting farm surpluses. Failure at the national level left the movement without a focus, but state and local protection programs continued to sprout at a rate which suggested that local interest in farmland protection remained strong. Private institutions filled part of the leadership gap; the American Farmland Trust, headed by Douglas Wheeler and with Bob Gray and Norm Berg occupying important roles, provided limited technical and financial assistance to local conservation efforts. The failure of federal leadership meant that land use reform returned to the local arena and began to transform itself in new and interesting ways.

Conclusion

A historical assessment of the farmland preservation movement suggests three conclusions. On a political level, the movement for agricultural land preservation in the 1970s proved to be, for environmentalists, an important inroad into agricultural policymaking; and political coalitions begun in the 1970s produced legislative results in the 1980s. From the perspective of environmental history, the focus on preserving agricultural land was part of a renewed focus on the ecological restraints on agriculture, a partial recognition that agriculture was moving from an era of abundance into an era of uncertainty about land, water, and energy resources. Finally, farmland preservation represented an important example of the use of social science in policymaking and in particular showed that social science ways of thinking, though used by liberals in support of change, could have conservative results. Thus farmland preservation was an example of many social and environmental issues that rely on uncertain knowledge, the advice of experts, and the data provided by social science.

New Alliances for Farmland Preservation

Political changes resulting from the farmland preservation movement were immediately obvious, although the long-term significance of these changes was open to question. How important these changes might prove to be is part of an ongoing story with no settled conclusion in sight. Some observers consider the dominant trend in agricultural policymaking in this century to be the disintegration of the power of traditional farm groups as they have been joined by competing alliances of consumers, conservationists, even food stamp recipients, all vying to shape farm and food policy.[1] For veteran agricultural economist Don Paarlberg, this meant that agriculture was "being deprived of its preferred position, including its special claim on natural resources. . . . The conclusion is inescapable: farm organizations, the agricultural committees of Congress, the U.S. Department of Agriculture, and the land grant colleges have lost control of the farm policy agenda."[2]

Other observers saw the same trend in more favorable terms, as an opening up of the farm policy process to accommodate "an emerging alliance between progressive farm and environmental groups."[3] From this perspective the most important outcome of the farmland preservation movement was in the way this issue prepared the way for more significant conservation success in the 1985 farm bill. The farmland preservation movement served as a first attempt at an environmental focus on agriculture and provided experience, ideas, institutions, and leadership for the fledgling alliance between traditional agricultural conservationists and environmentalists who had only recently interested themselves in agriculture. When NALS folded up shop in 1981, some of the staff, including Bob Gray, moved to the American Farmland Trust (AFT), which formed in NALS's wake as a private farmland protection advocacy group. Norman Berg left the Soil Conservation Service and joined AFT, and together Berg and Gray began putting together a "conservation coalition" in anticipation of the 1985 farm bill. Working through AFT, the two men scheduled and chaired meetings, set agendas, invited participants, and provided background information. They included not only agricultural conservation groups such as the National Association of Conservation Districts or the Soil Conservation Society of America, which had supported farmland preservation, but also mainstream environmental groups such as the Sierra Club, the Natural Resources Defense Council, and the National Wildlife Federation, as well as government officials from Congress and USDA. By 1984 this coalition consisted of over twenty different interest groups who met regularly to discuss legislative ideas and strategy. The personal connections made during the farmland preservation movement of the late 1970s thus formed the core leadership for this new issue network in the 1980s.[4] The ideas that drew the group together came from the emerging "environmental critique of modern agriculture," which had become, one participant wrote, "more authoritative, more compelling, and much more widely accepted within the agricultural community."[5]

While the farmland preservation movement provided vital organizational leadership for the conservation components of the 1985 farm bill, political and environmental circumstances dictated that erosion rather than farmland preservation—what Berg called the other side of the same coin—would be the crucial motivating issue for the new law. Renewed concern about erosion combined with a budget-conscious political mood to force a rethinking of federal soil conservation efforts. Since the 1940s most policymakers had generally accepted soil conservation payments to farmers as consistent with farm income support, and these payments usually had unquestioning congressional backing. Budget-minded critics in the executive branch sometimes complained that conservation payments, particularly those of the Agricultural Conservation Program, were congressional pork-barrel projects, but when President Nixon refused to spend ACP funds in 1972, Congress rallied and passed a new law requiring that these funds be spent. This congressional support weakened as the production boom of the early 1970s put production enhancement in conflict with conservation goals. As new lands were plowed and conservation measures forgotten, it became increasingly difficult to justify conservation payments that apparently had more to do with enhancing farmers' incomes and production levels than with reducing erosion.

In 1976 Congress asked the Department of Agriculture for evidence of the effectiveness of these conservation expenditures, and the department discovered that it could provide no such evidence. The result was the Soil and Water Resources Conservation Act of 1977, a congressional mandate for the department to review soil conservation programs and suggest changes.[6] By the early 1980s the data showed an annual soil erosion rate of three billion tons, with about 40 percent of all cropland eroding at a rate greater than the tolerance level (T-value) established by the SCS. The rate of erosion was continuing, perhaps even worsening, in spite of fifty years's worth of federal conservation policy, which cost more than $1 billion annually in the early 1980s. Further, the surveys showed that although the national average for erosion on all cultivated cropland was 4.8 tons per acre annually (slightly under the SCS T-value for most soils), the most severe erosion was concentrated on a relatively small amount of land: about 12 percent of all land was eroding at four times the SCS tolerance level. To calculate it differently, 70 percent of all "excess" eroded sediment came from only 9 percent of all cropland. One estimate held that 85 percent of all wind erosion came from only 1 percent of cropland— land that the SCS judged not to be "treatable."[7] These sorts of numbers led to the idea that soil conservation initiatives should be targeted to these especially erosive lands, and one obvious suggestion was to remove these lands from production.

In addition, there was mounting evidence that not only was erosion a productivity issue but that it caused considerable environmental and economic damage as well. The traditional soil conservation argument rested on the concept of intergenerational equity and called for conservation measures as a way to protect soil fertility for future generations. This land productivity rationale, because it did not yield neatly to economic analysis, did not always convince those who argued that the costs of erosion control were greater than the marginal long-term social benefits. New evidence in the early 1980s on soil erosion's damage to water quality provided a more persuasive rationale. One respected analysis put the damage from soil runoff into streams and reservoirs at between $3 and $13 billion annually, with $6 billion a likely midrange figure. Researchers estimated that soil erosion was the major polluter for 64 percent of the nation's lakes and 57 percent of the nation's rivers. Soil runoff from agricultural land silted reservoirs, clogged hydroelectric facilities, damaged water quality, caused algal blooms, decreased oxygen supplies, and contributed to nitrogen, phosphorus, and bacteria pollution. Navigation, recreation, water supplies, and freshwater fisheries all suffered directly from soil erosion.[8] Agriculture was demonstrably a source of serious environmental degradation, and these costs of sedimentation from farmland provided environmentalists with a persuasive argument that water quality goals required more effective soil conservation policies.[9]

The conceptually innovative move conservatives made in the 1985 farm bill, based on this environmental critique, was to link commodity policies with conservation policy—that is, to integrate resource conservation into larger agricultural goals. This shift was facilitated by widespread disenchantment with the high cost and the marginal effectiveness of USDA subsidy programs. The export explosion of 1972–81 had seen exports grow by an annual average of 9.4 percent, and farm commodity exports reached a value of $43.8 billion in 1981. This strong export demand meant relatively high crop prices and therefore comparatively small federal price support payments to farmers. This situation changed in the 1980s, as the 1980 grain embargo of the Soviet Union, the high value of the dollar, high feed grain prices, and shrinking foreign markets all drastically slowed the growth in the volume of U.S. commodity exports; the dollar value of exports actually declined 40 percent from 1981 to 1986. As a result, commodity prices, farm income, and the value of farm assets—especially agricultural land—were all down significantly in the early 1980s. As market prices for crops fell, federal price supports for agricultural commodities grew. Federal subsidy payments totaled $27.7 billion over the four-year period from 1977 to 1981 but skyrocketed to $63.3 billion from 1981 to 1985. From 1984 to 1987 these payments averaged nearly $23 billion annually—nearly four times the cost from the late 1970s. Senator Roger Jepsen of Iowa introduced a series of hearings directed toward a "new generation" of farm policies by denouncing existing farm programs as "costly" and "ineffective"; Secretary of Agriculture John Block proposed phasing down federal subsidies and moving toward a market-oriented policy; and some farm organizations favored mandatory production controls. The solutions were different, but all parties agreed that current farm programs were fundamentally flawed.[10] In these circumstances, environmentalists saw an opportunity to blend conservation goals with the more general aims of crop supply management and budgetary restraint. Especially troubling to environmentalists (and anyone concerned with rational policymaking) was the conflict between federal price supports, which encouraged the cultivation of marginal lands, and federal conservation policies, which tried to limit the soil damage inherent in cultivating these same lands.[11] Ralph Grossi, president of the AFT, put the dilemma this way: "During the decade of the 1980s these [price support] payments averaged more than $40 million a day for the entire ten years. . . . One has to wonder whether we have really accomplished any lasting public objectives with that money."[12] The

Department of Agriculture's receptiveness to conservation ideas was made clear in a remark Assistant Secretary of Agriculture John Crowell made to a group of conservationists in 1983: "The need as we see it is to downsize the U.S. agricultural production machine. If you conservationists can help us do it in such a way that we reduce agricultural subsidies and also benefit the environment, we have an opportunity to cooperate."[13]

The conservation title of the 1985 Food Security Act was thus designed to address the simultaneous failure of both commodity and soil conservation policy. Widely touted among agricultural conservationists as a move that ushered in a new environmental era for agricultural policy, even as a "radical departure" from past legislation,[14] this conservation title contained "sodbuster" and "swampbuster" provisions, a Conservation Reserve Program (CRP), and the promise of "conservation compliance," a provision that would require farmers to implement an SCS-approved soil conservation plan as a requisite for receiving federal subsidies. The sodbuster and swampbuster provisions were a specialized form of conservation compliance, designed to discourage the plowing of wetlands or highly erodible lands by refusing USDA benefit payments of any kind to farmers who cultivated these lands without an approved conservation plan. Farmers were given five years to design a conservation plan and ten years to implement it. The most visible part of the plan was the CRP, under which USDA would contract with farmers to remove highly erodible lands from cultivation for ten to fifteen years. This program was a tacit admission that the agricultural expansion of the 1970s had been a disaster for soil conservation; it was also an attempt (similar to the Soil Bank of the 1950s and 1960s and the land acquisition program of the New Deal) to secure federal protection for the most vulnerable rural lands. These ideas had been circulating among conservationists for several years, especially in reaction to the renewal of concern about soil erosion in the late 1970s, but they were adopted in 1985 with a speed and a lack of political opposition that surprised everyone.[15] Part of the reason for this success was that the farmland preservation movement had initiated an issue network that had matured into an identifiable "conservation coalition" and was poised to take advantage of the opportunities presented in the 1985 farm bill. What appeared to be the sudden success of a new group was actually, for some farmland protection advocates, a second chance.

Considered by some conservationists "the most significant soil conservation legislation since the 1930s," the conservation title of the 1985 Food Security Act initially met with considerable success. After some confusion over exactly what farmlands would be eligible for the CRP, enrollment in the conservation reserve proceeded smoothly. By 1990 the Department of Agriculture had contracted for over 34 million acres in the CRP, short of the goal of 45 million but still a larger total reserve than the Soil Bank or any previous crop reserve program had established. By some measures the CRP could claim some success in meeting its multiple objectives of supply management, erosion reduction, and water quality improvement. The annual reduction in soil erosion amounted to 650 million tons, or a 20 percent reduction in the nation's total. One estimate of natural resource benefits arising from CRP came to $10 billion and included a reduction of the erosion damages to water supplies, enhancement of air quality in areas of wind erosion, and an improvement in wildlife habitats. Economists calculated the net social benefits, after the cost of federal rental payments, at between $3.4 and $11 billion.[16] The conservation coalition that had supported the legislation, including the NACD, the AFT, the National Wildlife Federation, and the Sierra Club, applauded these successes. Ralph Grossi, president of the AFT, claimed "a taste of success" in the 1980s that had eluded conservationists in the 1970s; Ken Cook, an influential analyst on agricultural and conservation issues, argued that in terms of reducing soil erosion the 1985 law might bring "more progress in the next four or five years than in the previous fifty."[17]

Despite this enthusiasm, the first half decade's experience with implementing the new legislation revealed some significant problems in transforming law into practice. This was not simply a matter of finding the most efficacious way of carrying out what Congress had willed but to a large extent involved recognizing the wide range of discretionary power that administrators possessed. As historian Samuel Hays has argued, regulatory administration has become a major arena for the continuing political process of give and take, not simply a policy neutral way of executing congressional mandates. The "conservation coalition," farm organizations, and commodity interests all monitored the implementation phase of the law carefully, in effect verifying Hays's observation that when a law is passed the political struggle simply moves to the bureaucracy.[18] The CRP, generally accepted as the centerpiece of the conservation title of the 1985 Food Security Act, was the focus of most debate. Some found fault with the multiple objectives of the CRP and noted that some of these objectives could be in conflict. The implementation of CRP emphasized erosion control for the sake of maintaining productivity, and this standard left out some erosive lands where water quality and wildlife habitat were potential benefits.

In particular, CRP enrolled large areas in the Great Plains in order to reduce wind erosion, but the program did not work as well as conservationists had hoped in the Corn Belt or in the Chesapeake Bay regions, where CRP had little apparent effect on eroded sediment in water supplies.[19] CRP rental payments were highest in wheat-producing areas, sometimes as much as two to five times the market rental rate for the same land, but relatively lower in corn-producing areas. This meant that comparatively little farmland from the Corn Belt was enrolled in the CRP, while in some Great Plains areas these high rates attracted land speculators who found that the rental payments over ten years could actually cover the costs of buying the land.[20] This encouraged land speculators from outside the region to become absentee plains landowners and allowed many plains farmers, especially those near retirement age, to simply put their land into the CRP, sell their equipment, and retire from the farm with CRP payments as retirement income. Despite the law's provision that no more than one-quarter of the land in any given county should be enrolled in the CRP, over 80 percent of all CRP land came from only 18 percent of the nation's counties. This local concentration left some rural residents, especially in the Great Plains, worried that the program would contribute to regional depopulation. One study found that the CRP and cross-compliance combined would result in a 37 percent decline in the agricultural economy of the Southern Plains. Other economists estimated that the CRP would lead to a 21 percent decline in both economic activity and employment in eastern Montana.[21] Thus, by enticing farmers to leave marginal farmland, the new program had the unintended result of carrying on the work of the New Deal land acquisition and farm rehabilitation program.

The most significant problem of all was that the program did not provide for what should happen to retired lands once the contract period was over and thus left farmers with uncertain future incomes and the land with only temporary protection. This was analogous to California's Williamson Act and other agricultural districting programs that provided benefits to farmers in exchange for contracts not to develop farmland (see chapter 3) but that proved ineffective in slowing the loss of farmland once the contract period ran out. Unlike the New Deal's land acquisition program, the CRP rented the land for ten years only, and some conservationists feared that the land could be plowed again as soon as the rental contract expired. The 1990 farm bill moved in the direction of long-term conservation by specifying that CRP lands would be subject to conservation compliance at the end of the contract period and by authorizing USDA to purchase long-term voluntary easements on retired lands, although funding for this project was uncertain. Surveys from the Northern Plains region revealed that nearly half of all farmers planned to return their CRP land to normal cropping after the ten-year contract period was over.[22] The memory of the Soil Bank, which saw nearly 30 million acres diverted from production during the 1950s and 1960s only to be put to the plow again in the 1970s, suggested that without some follow-up the CRP could become a very expensive subsidy without lasting conservation benefits.[23]

Other provisions of the farm bill's conservation title met with similar problems in implementation. Conservation compliance had the potential to affect more land than any other provision. The USDA identified between 140 and 160 million acres of highly erodible cropland that would be subject to conservation compliance. To implement conservation compliance on this large amount of land would require the completion of over one million conservation plans—a staggering amount in relation to the number of existing SCS field personnel—and raised the possibility that conservation compliance implementation would be slowed and other conservation programs sidetracked by this tremendous workload.[24] A more important issue than the speed with which conservation compliance could be implemented was the prospect that it might be implemented with such flexibility as to become virtually meaningless. Wilson Scaling, Reagan's choice for chief of the SCS, argued that private landowners "have the right to manage their land in the way they know best" and certainly did not want conservation "crammed down their throat." Lenient federal standards, Scaling reasoned, were necessary because "centralized authority does not work" and "common sense" would lead farmers voluntarily to reduce erosion. Following these principles, the SCS announced in 1987 that the agency would use flexible standards that would allow a great deal of local discretion by SCS field personnel and move SCS from a regulatory toward an advisory role. Specifically, the SCS rules implementing the law abandoned the service's established T-value for measuring excess erosion and allowed field personnel to make exceptions in cases where reducing erosion to T-value was "not economically or technically feasible," a judgment to be made by local SCS agents.

This decision for lenient enforcement rested in part on the fact that the scientific basis for T-values had come under increasing attack from some specialists who charged that the standard was arbitrary and lacking in rigorous scientific backing. This absence of a scientific consensus thus became part of the conservative argument against vigorous enforcement of conservation compliance. While some conservationists charged that this move was "taking the teeth out" of conservation compliance and left a system that was "substandard to the professional conservationist," the Farm Bureau argued for a lenient implementation or, failing that, legislative repeal.[25] Similarly, some conservationists charged that USDA enforcement of the sodbuster and swampbuster provisions was so lenient as to have little effect on actual farming practices. Because there were so few swampbuster violations reported, one soil conservationist concluded, "The Reagan administration simply ignored the swampbuster provisions."[26]

In 1990 the conservation title of the Food Security Act was reauthorized with only minor changes. The conservation coalition that had been so surprisingly successful and unified in 1985 had begun to show some division between the more traditional agricultural conservationists, especially the NACD, and the newer environmental groups. The commodity groups, which had virtually ignored the conservation title in 1985, played a significant role in 1990 and were especially irked by the swampbuster provisions. With the quiet support of the Farm Bureau, these groups succeeded in amending the 1990 law to define wetlands more restrictively, so as to include less land, and to reduce the penalties for wetland offenders. Even so, most conservationists were happy with the ongoing program, which, by being reauthorized basically intact, began to take shape as a more permanent part of federal agricultural policy.[27]

Still, it remained to be seen whether this new program could become a fixture of agricultural policy. Marty Strange, director of the

Center for Rural Affairs in Nebraska, questioned whether the new agricultural conservation was a matter of federal principle or budgetary expedience: "When production is surplus and prices low, conservation is convenient; when export sales are brisk and prices robust, the commitment to conservation withers. Nothing in the current set of policies suggests anything substantially different."[28] Despite some conservationists' talk of a "revolution" in agricultural conservation, questions remained about how much had been accomplished and whether these accomplishments could survive the next export boom. The farmland preservation movement initiated a policy dialogue in the 1970s between environmentalists and agriculturalists, and this conversation became a farm conservation alliance that yielded innovative legislation in the 1980s. The claim that these new players in the agricultural policymaking arena represented a revolution in agricultural policymaking that was similar to the changes of the 1930s reflected more the hazards of participant assessment than a realistic historical judgment. It was too early to tell whether this conservation coalition could transform success in Congress into fundamental conservation improvements in the rural countryside.

The New Sense of Environmental Limits

A second conclusion to draw from this study is that the farmland preservation movement was part of an emerging awareness of the resource scarcity and ecological instability of modern agriculture. The middle decades of the twentieth century represented a remarkably productive era for both U.S. and world agriculture. This productivity came from two sources—technology-induced gains in yield per acre and increases in acreage under cultivation. By the end of the 1970s most of the obvious gains from these sources had been reaped. Also, while the total farmland acreage in the United States remained relatively unchanged in the twentieth century, the world's cultivated acreage grew rapidly during the same period. According to one estimate, more than 470 million hectares (1,161 million acres) worldwide were converted into cropland between 1920 and 1978.[29] Future increases of this magnitude would prove impossible, and even more modest increases would entail high environmental costs, as in the conversion of tropical rain forests into farmlands. Moreover, aggregate gains in cropland often concealed the decline in land quality that came with erosion, deforestation, salination, and desertification.[30] The other major source of agricultural growth was higher yield per acre through intensive farming methods; the green revolution increased global grain production 260 percent from 1950 to 1980. Between 1950 and 1984 the world's fertilizer use increased by nine times, the irrigated acreage across the globe tripled, and higher-yielding crop hybrids were adopted in many countries. Yet by the 1980s fertilizer use had stabilized, irrigated acreage per capita was declining, and some nations saw their agricultural base jeopardized. China, for instance, had less cropland than the United States for its 1.1 billion people (240 million acres); each year it was losing 2 million acres to nonfarm uses and 1.16 billion tons of topsoil to the Yellow River alone. Grain production in China grew steadily in the 1960s and 1970s but peaked in 1984 and leveled off for the rest of the decade. India tripled its wheat harvest from 1965 to 1983, but here too production hit a plateau, while erosion continued at a rate of six billion tons annually. Overall, as much as one-third of the Third World's cropland suffered from serious soil erosion, while growth in global food production in the 1980s had slowed to less than 1 percent annually, compared with a growth in demand of 1–2 percent in industrialized countries and 3–5 percent in Third World nations.[31]

The middle decades of the twentieth century also benefited from a generally favorably climate, with warm temperatures and only moderate variations. The return of greater annual fluctuations in weather (the nineteenth-century pattern) or human-induced climactic change resulting from such factors as ozone depletion, increased carbon monoxide, particulate air pollution, and acid precipitation could all introduce stresses into the agricultural ecosystem.[32] The specter of global warming due to the greenhouse effect had particularly troublesome implications for agriculture. Scientists predicted that increased carbon dioxide in the atmosphere would cause a global temperature rise of between three and nine degrees Fahrenheit. Whether this change would occur suddenly or gradually and how well technology could adapt to the changes was difficult to predict. Global warming in the 1980s was thus a topic for intense scientific debate but little political action.

Yet if the dimensions or the speed of climate changes were uncertain, there was no doubt that global warming would introduce new stresses into agricultural systems. A temperature rise of three to nine degrees Fahrenheit would likely melt polar ice caps and raise sea level by 0.5 to 3.5 meters. Even a one-meter rise in sea level could, unless checked by dikes and seawalls, inundate 3 percent of the world's land area, including dense coastal cities that together contained over one billion people. One study projected that global cereal production would decrease by 1 to 7 percent by 2060, with a corresponding 150 percent price increase. Tropical countries, already poorer and with stressed agricultural systems, were expected to suffer most of the damage. In the United States, climate models suggested that the midwestern farm belt might shift north and that the Southern Plains would be especially subject to desertification. Of the two remedies suggested most frequently, new drought-resistant crop varieties and increased irrigation, one depended on scientific breakthroughs, and the other would likely be limited by energy and water shortages— especially in the Southern Plains, where irrigation water came from the Ogallala aquifer, a supply already being rapidly depleted.[33]

While any modeling of the specific future effects of global warming on agriculture remained clouded, two troubling generalizations about global warming came clear. One was that the lag time between carbon dioxide buildup (on a hundred-year rise with no end in sight) and temperature increases (which would come years or decades later) virtually guaranteed that global warming would be essentially irreversible. A second was that even if long-term averages proved susceptible to accurate modeling techniques, climate change would likely be highly unpredictable in the short term. Temperatures oscillating widely around a slowly rising average could send farmers into bankruptcy, grain markets into chaos, and world food supplies into jeopardy.[34] Compared with such a scenario, the twentieth-century pattern of relatively small annual fluctuations in weather patterns might appear to be a beneficial anomaly. The possibility of great uncertainty in future weather patterns thus highlighted the way in which relatively stable weather combined with favorable technology and land availability to make the 1930s through the 1970s look like a remarkable era of exceptional agricultural growth rather than the historical norm.

By the 1970s this growth curve of the middle decades of the century was beginning to level off as the sources of that growth reached their limits. One limit to further agricultural growth was the ongoing degradation of soil and water supplies. Erosion, desertification, and the salination and waterlogging of irrigated lands contributed to the global loss of an estimated 15 million acres of cropland, an amount equivalent to more than half of the annual acreage of newly cleared forests. The worldwide erosion of cropland meant thinner soils, more water runoff, less nutrient and organic matter available for crops and, ultimately, an agriculture that was less productive. One estimate was that at erosion rates current in the 1980s, the worldwide loss of productivity between 1975 and 2000 would fall between 15 and 30 percent. Nationally, estimates of erosion's negative effect on soil fertility ranged from 2 percent over thirty years to 10 percent over a century. Damage estimates of erosion's onsite costs in lost fertility and increased demands for fertilizer and labor ranged from $1 to $18 billion per year.[35]

Water supplies were a related limit to the potential growth of agricultural production. Around the world, irrigated acreage tripled between 1950 and 1980, but by 1980 21 percent of the world's irrigation water came from groundwater overdrafts, and 26 percent of the world's irrigated cropland suffered from either waterlogging or salinity problems.[36] In the United States, irrigated acreage doubled from 25 million acres in 1950 to 50 million in 1978, then declined to 45 million acres by 1983. Irrigated lands accounted for 13 percent of all cropland yet contributed nearly one-third of the value of all crops, because yields per acre were significantly higher—in some cases twice as high—on irrigated than on nonirrigated lands. Much of this irrigation expansion came on the Great Plains, where center-pivot irrigation systems made possible the watering of large areas of corn, cotton, sorghum, and wheat from underground water supplies. Groundwater overdraft became a serious problem in some places, especially in the Texas and Oklahoma panhandle region overlying the Ogallala aquifer, and the decline of the water table in these areas accounted for the decline in irrigated acreage after 1978. In parts of California irrigation was lowering the water table at the rate of 1.5 acre-feet per year, and the depleted aquifers caused land subsidence of up to ten feet in some places. The surface water available for irrigation was likewise declining. A large portion of the Colorado River's water—85 percent—went to agriculture, but the river was coming under increasing demands for urban uses. In the 1980s Arizona and Colorado were among the states that were pressuring agriculture to reduce its consumption of the Colorado River's waters.[37] Scarcely a trickle reached the river's end in Mexico as it was, and this increased competition for the waters of the Colorado could only mean that there would be less water for irrigation in the West.

Not only was agriculture's exploitation of abundant soil and water beginning to play out by the end of the 1970s; its use of fossil fuel was also beginning to pay declining dividends. During American agriculture's growth surge from the 1930s through the 1970s, overall yield per acre more than doubled; the labor requirement per acre declined by 75 percent; and cheap fossil fuel for tractors, machinery, and petroleum-based fertilizers and pesticides replaced labor as the most expensive ingredient in agricultural production. From 1945 to 1985 the energy input into agriculture quadrupled. The use of nitrogen fertilizer alone increased by twenty times and by 1985 equaled the total fuel input of 1945. As U.S. farming increased its productivity, it decreased its energy efficiency, so that to produce one calorie of food energy required three calories of fossil fuel energy, while another six or seven calories were spent in food processing, distribution, and preparation. This sum represented more than ten times the energy consumption of farms in developing nations, and one estimate suggested that if other nations followed the energy-intensive pattern of the United States, the world's petroleum supplies would be exhausted in one decade.[38] This energy-intensive system proved economical for farmers so long as energy prices were low, but fuel prices rose during the 1970s at the same time that many farmers began to realize the productivity plateau inherent in this technology (see chapter 2). Fertilizer prices (sensitive to petroleum prices) rose sporadically, and fertilizer use peaked in the late 1970s, then declined during the 1980s. What for four decades had been a source of growth in the agricultural system had become a source of potential disruption.[39]

Intertwined with energy use was American agriculture's persistent trend toward monoculture and an increasingly narrow genetic base. Much of the productivity of the middle decades of the century came from the spread of hybrid seed varieties that responded well to synthetic fertilizers and made possible the continuous planting of major cash crops such as corn or wheat. These monocultures in turn required the increased use of pesticides and herbicides in order to control the greater concentrations of unwanted insects and weeds that accompanied the loss of crop diversity. This system had obvious advantages in productivity, in the efficient use of specialized machinery, and in marketing, but by the 1970s the weaknesses of this system were becoming apparent. Critics noted that monoculture increased erosion and was less productive in some fields than multiple cropping or intercropping.[40] Selectively bred monocultures also dramatically reduced genetic diversity and thus raised the prospect that genetically uniform crops might be particularly susceptible to disease or insect epidemic. This hazard was illustrated in 1970 when a mutant fungus leaf blight ruined about 10 percent of the nation's corn crop. Insects and diseases coevolved with pesticides to develop immunities, and by the 1980s more than four hundred insect species had developed immunities to insecticides. Both the amount and the toxicity of pesticide use increased tenfold between 1945 and 1985, but the damage to crops from insects nearly doubled—from 7 to 13 percent—during the same years.[41] The National Academy of Sciences concluded in 1972 that American agriculture was "impressively uniform genetically and impressively vulnerable," and two respected agricultural analysts in 1980 reasoned, "The stability that comes from ecological diversity has been reduced, perhaps significantly."[42]

Perhaps the most visible vulnerability in the ecology of this agricultural system was the environmental and public health damage done away from the farm. The erosion of sediment and the leaching of farm chemicals into streams and rivers increased turbidity, caused algal blooms, poisoned aquatic ecosystems, and diminished water's recreational opportunities. Agriculture contributed over half of all surface-water pollution, causing the siltation of 1.5 million acre-feet of reservoir capacity each year, damaging 30 percent of the nation's inland fish populations, and making municipal water treatment more expensive. Estimates of the annual off-farm damage to surface waters ranged from the Conservation Foundation's $3 to $13 billion to USDA's $2 to $8 billion.[43] Agriculture's damage to groundwater was harder to detect but potentially more threatening. Between one-third and one-half of all counties and at least 50 million people, mostly rural, were susceptible to groundwater contamination from agricultural sources. Studies of groundwater contamination were just beginning in the 1980s, and complete knowledge of the situation was impossible, yet preliminary tests suggested an enormous problem. California reported twenty-two different pesticides in its groundwater, and altogether, thirty-eight states found seventy-four different agricultural chemicals in groundwater drinking supplies. In one study 20 percent of all wells showed elevated levels of nitrates. It was no wonder that the 1980s saw increased calls for pesticide controls, even from some farm groups.[44] Agriculture's damage to the environment also included the annual loss of more than 400,000 acres of wetlands from the 1950s through the 1970s and grazing damage from western beef cattle to riparian zones and trout habitats.[45]

Given this range of environmental problems associated with modern agriculture, many critics began to search for alternative agricultural systems that would be more organic, sustainable, or regenerative. Defenders of the conventional system pointed to its productivity and held onto the possibility of breakthroughs in biotechnology that could reduce the ill effects of chemical agriculture and perhaps even unleash

a new round of yield increases in both animal and plant production. What the two sides shared was a sense that the engines of agricultural growth that had propelled the productivity surge from the 1940s through the 1970s were beginning to lose power—not that the system was necessarily near collapse but that growth was slowing and problems were growing. Even mainstream resource economists began to recognize, as Resources for the Future reported in 1986, that "modern agriculture" was more ecologically "disruptive" than traditional agriculture because of energy, fertilizer, and pesticide dependence, which were essentially "subsidies from other ecosystems" and created a "legitimate concern about the long-term sustainability of modern agriculture."[46]

A Broader View of Policy and History

Farmland protection also provided an intriguing example of the uses of social science research in making policy decisions. Since the beginning of the century, the promise of the policy sciences has been their supposed potential to discover universal truths of human behavior that would allow impartial policy analysts to replace the complexity and selfishness of partisan political disputes with objective solutions based on the disinterested search for scientific knowledge. The most important statement of these ideas was Robert Lynd's *Knowledge for What?,* published in 1939. Lynd believed that modern society had developed large and complicated economic and political structures that individuals were unable to understand and powerless to change. Traditional forms of individualist democracy had created a "dangerously undemocratic vacuum" between private citizens and powerful political and corporate elites. This breach could be filled, Lynd thought, by public-minded policy scientists who could understand the complexity and overcome the partisanship of the present situation. He counted on applied social scientists to reform the political and economic structure in the direction of democracy and rationality.[47] Lynd's ideas both shaped and were shaped by the Progressive and New Deal experiences with social scientists in government. World War II and the Cold War enhanced and legitimated the role of social science research, and the Great Society spawned a legion of policy analysts in the federal government. Federal funding for domestic social science research went from $73 million in 1960 to $380 million in 1967 and, according to one estimate, reached $1.8 billion by the late 1970s.[48] The usual perception has been that this social science, dominated by leftist academics, has exercised a liberal influence on policymaking. This perception stems partly from the conservative opposition encountered by key individuals or organizations, such as the New Deal's Rexford Tugwell or the Bureau of Agricultural Economics,[49] and partly from the fact that social science researchers are more liberal than both the public as a whole and their academic colleagues in other fields.[50]

The opposite perception—that social science research exerts a conservative influence on policymaking—is best stated in Henry Aaron's underappreciated 1978 classic, *Politics and the Professors: The Great Society in Perspective*. Aaron, an economist at the Brookings Institution, argued that "research reflects prevailing political moods at least as much as it influences them" and ultimately that "research . . . tends to be profoundly conservative in its impact."[51] The main contribution of social science research was not in specific findings, he argued, but in providing a perspective for evaluating programs in terms of demonstrable effects.[52] This way of thinking about problems, Aaron wrote, would be an intellectually conservative force for a variety of reasons. The continual battle of competing theories, the academic awards for anomalous findings, and changing political climates guaranteed that research would nearly always yield conflicting results and thus that knowledge would be incomplete. The nature of research would also tend to narrow the focus of study away from unresolvable questions of political values toward technical problems capable of solution. This would mean that public opinion was valued less than expert knowledge. Social science research, Aaron concluded, "corrodes the kind of simple faiths on which political movements are built." In such a context, decision makers simply sifted through the available research to find results that confirmed predetermined positions. Conflicting research, then, reinforced the "instinct to delay," while what passed as "scholarly impartiality" was in reality an assortment of fundamental political positions "clad in the jargon of academic debate."[53]

Aaron provided important examples of this thesis in the fields of poverty and education research. The War on Poverty initiated a host of new programs and came along at a time when cost-benefit analysis and program evaluation, borrowed from Robert McNamara's Defense Department, carried great prestige. Consequently, the legislation establishing these new programs generally included a mandate for evaluation. Aaron found, however, that these program evaluations were not decisive in determining the ongoing political success or failure of programs. Rather, "evaluation was a political instrument to be trotted out" when it supported existing political positions for or against these programs. Moreover, it tended to focus attention toward technical problems and away from more fundamental political problems, and insofar as results were never conclusive, it reinforced the tendency to delay action.[54] President Nixon in particular used program evaluations very skillfully to rationalize decisions for cutbacks in antipoverty programs. More recently, the decline of poverty research under President Reagan confirms the notion that researchers have reacted to political trends, not led them.[55]

Aaron found a similar phenomenon at work in federal education policy, where researchers tried unsuccessfully to unsort the tangled matrix of poverty, racial discrimination, and educational performance. The result of decades of research on this relationship between race, poverty, and education has been increased knowledge, more sophisticated analysis, and a greater store of empirical evidence. Instead of clarifying this relationship, however, the research has rendered it more complex. The result of this growing complexity has been that social science has no clear advice for governmental action, and indeed, the perspective of social science research has made any action seem premature and any political advice shaky. Thus the major contribution of social science research in this field has been, again, to delay action.[56]

The case of farmland protection may be seen as another example of how the influence of social science research has reinforced the policy status quo. This was not simply because the agricultural research establishment tended to be conservative, as some researchers have accurately pointed out.[57] Much of the research for farmland protection came from the environmental perspective, from advocates of policy reform. These reformers based their case on the national dimensions of farmland loss, that is, on the results of social science survey data. Framing the issue primarily in social science terms required a statistical certainty that was difficult to obtain and virtually invited technical disagreement. This dispute over the exact dimensions of farmland loss provided a perfect delaying argument for those who wanted absolute certainty before justifying an intervention in the status quo. The effect of the great data debate was to narrow the focus of debate from what was really struggle over competing ideologies into a technical dispute over whose numbers were more accurate. This move, of course, implied that only the experts had a valid contribution to make, so arguments based on "bumper sticker campaigns"[58] or "emotional appeals"[59] could easily be rejected. In a reversal of the usual criticism of planners as elitists, this issue saw the antiplanners in the role of technocrats giving supposedly impartial advice from the pedestal of science.

Not only was the game of social science essentially a conservative one, albeit with many liberal players, but the social science research on farmland issues published in the 1980s confirmed Aaron's contention that social science is essentially reactive. The decade saw growth in the number of state and local farmland protection programs, some encouraging evidence of the partial success of some of these programs (notably Oregon's statewide mix of incentives and controls), and surprisingly strong public sentiment in favor of farmland protection, even if that meant higher taxes.[60] Yet the federal government was absent from this discussion, and the problem of farmland loss was generally phrased not as a national issue but as a state and local concern.

Recent research has tended to scale back the definition of the issue, to see it as primarily one of maintaining agriculture near cities—that is, as a series of local concerns rather than a national problem. Because the discourse of social science research invites contradictions, this recent research has also turned on its head the notion that urban sprawl hurts agriculture. While the 1970s produced literature on the "impermanence syndrome," the 1980s have challenged this concept with the idea that specialized agriculture might benefit from encroaching cities. Researchers have enumerated some of the "mutual benefits" that farm and city have to offer each other and have elaborated on the "positive adaptation" of some farmers to nearby cities. The old language was of the city as a predator preying on the defenseless rural countryside; the newer biological metaphor is that of symbiosis, and of course each interpretive metaphor can find empirical support.[61] Other research has suggested that public policies to reduce urban sprawl might have unintended and even contradictory effects.[62] This emphasis on the accidental and unknown effects of public policy have reinforced the tendency to require absolute certainty before acting. The scaled-down definition of the problem and the emphasis on the negative outcomes of policy show that the questions social science researchers were asking in the 1980s reflected the more conservative mood of the decade. Social science research did not guide policy but instead reacted to it.

Farmland loss is thus an example of a widespread and particularly difficult environmental problem. The issues are complex, and experts tend to dismiss public perceptions as simplistic and overdrawn. The damage is slow but irreversible, the problems are not easily recognized, and the statistical measurements of the problem are the subject of great debate. Whether it involves global warming, acid rain, groundwater contamination, or the paving of farmland, the call for science to provide more data can delay and even deny effective policymaking. Because the problem is dynamic, it may be different before it is fully described. Different theoretical perspectives will produce different data, so scientific disputes may go on for years, or even decades, before any consensus emerges. To wait for more research may mean that the problem is not understood until the damage is done. As James Sundquist recognized in 1970, "The country cannot afford to wait until all of the analyses have been completed and all the facts are in. Action must precede research. . . . In driving to the Pacific, one need not have a road map of the entire route to know that he begins by heading westward."[63]

Although history is unlikely to provide that road map, a history of the farmland preservation debate might offer some points of orientation. One might expect that historical case studies would reinforce the conservative tendency of social science research because they almost inevitably match a fallen reality against a platonic ideal. Thus the past would become a burden, an archive of failure, or, as Friedrich Nietzsche wrote in the nineteenth century, a "great and continually increasing weight" that paralyzed action and inhibited thought. The sense of human frailty that history often provides could lead to hopelessness and disillusionment over the prospects for human progress. But there is another possibility, which Nietzsche described as "the strength to break up the past, and apply it too, in order to live." Historians "must bring the past to the bar of judgment, interrogate it remorselessly, and finally condemn it." There was, Nietzsche believed, a "right time to forget and a right time to remember."[64] Historian Otis Graham offers some suggestions as to how historians can help policymakers discern what to forget and what to remember, how to escape the burdens of the past and sense the life-giving applications. Graham suggests that we should not look for "lessons" from the past by way of simple analogies, but rather that history should provide a "special sensitivity to two dimensions of human life—the dimension of time and of context, . . . the diachronic and the synchronic . . . , or sequence and setting."[65] Policy history ought not to aim for the predictive power of policy sciences but instead should find its role in a narrative sensibility that traces the stages of policy development without being misled into thinking that the passage of a law represents the final act of the drama. The historical narrative should pay special attention to what happens after a law is passed and should see the intricacies of implementation and the unanticipated turns of program administration as a vital part of the story of the modern administrative state. Similarly, policy history is well situated to understand the rich context of policymaking—that is, to bring insight to the institutions, the political culture, and the full range of economic, social, and environmental variables that shape the policy process.[66]

With this awareness of sequence and setting, a policy history of farmland preservation ought to suggest that agricultural land protection should be viewed in the scope of a larger range of federal and state policies. Export policy, agricultural research, federal grants for highways or sewage plants, tax policies on home ownership, federal interest rates, and even birth control policies all stand as components of a de facto federal rural land use policy. This eye for context ought to be paired with a sense of timing that sees not only continuity but also discontinuity, that separates the unique from the general. Thus we should beware of extrapolating past trends into the future and should be especially sensitive to the unusual features of the agricultural era that began in the 1930s and continued through the 1970s. This period appears as an anomalous era of spectacular growth in comparison with the last several centuries of agricultural history, and a policy informed by history should view this growth as a novelty, not the norm. In this way history might be transformed from Nietzsche's unbearable burden into a contribution toward a vision of a better future.

Notes

Introduction

1. Quoted in Schlesinger, *Robert Kennedy,* 226.
2. The second version comes from an interview with Watt in *Public Opinion,* "Conservatives at Court," 12; Fletcher, in an interview with the author (2 December 1982) reported the uncensored version.
3. U.S. Department of Agriculture, *Will There Be Enough Food?*; Ebeling, *Fruited Plain.*
4. See, for example, Hightower, *Hard Tomatoes, Hard Times*; Hightower, *Eat Your Heart Out*; Commoner, *Poverty of Power,* especially pp. 155–75; Schumacher, *Small Is Beautiful,* 14; Lappe and Collins, *Food First*; Berry, *Unsettling of America*; Youngberg, "Alternative Agriculture Movement," 227–46.
5. Examples of this approach include Robbins, *Our Landed Heritage,* and, more recently, Wyant, *Westward in Eden.*
6. Gates, "Overview of American Land Policy," 227–28.
7. Hawley, "Social Policy and the Liberal State in Twentieth-Century America," 117–39; Leuchtenburg, "Pertinence of Political History," 585–600; Karl, *Uneasy State*; Balogh, "Reorganizing the Organizational Synthesis"; Galambos, *New American State*; Evans, Rueschemeyer, and Skocpol, *Bringing the State Back In*; Skowenrek, *Building a New American State*; McCraw, *Regulation in Perspective.*

Chapter One

1. Lord, *Behold Our Land,* 304.
2. Conkin, *FDR and the Origins of the Welfare State,* 73.
3. Lord, *Behold Our Land,* 77; McDonald, *Early American Soil Conservationists*; Danhof, *Change in Agriculture,* 253–75; Rasmussen, "History of Soil Conservation," 3–18; Held and Clawson, *Soil Conservation in Perspective,* 29–40.
4. U.S. Department of Agriculture, Economic Research Service, *Farm Real Estate Historical Series Data,* 2. See also Saloutos, "Land Policy," 448. For a more favorable view of this period of settlement see Cochrane, *Development of American Agriculture,* 78–121.
5. Saloutos, "Land Policy," 445.
6. Powell, *Report on the Lands of the Arid Region of the United States,* 8. The best description of Powell's ideas and the obstacles they faced is Stegner's *Beyond the Hundredth Meridian,* 202–42.
7. Marsh, *Man and Nature,* 42, 233, 280, 259. See also Lowenthal, *George Perkins Marsh.*
8. Magee, "Overworked Soils," 327, 328; Strong, "Cotton Experiments in California," 333; Hoskins, "New England Agriculture," 700. On the timber famine fears see Pisani, "Forests and Conservation," 340–59.

9. Hays, *Conservation and the Gospel of Efficiency*, 66–73.

10. U.S. Congress, Senate, *Report of the National Conservation Commission*, 18, 79.

11. Martin, *James J. Hill*, 550; Hill, *Highways of Progress*, 16.

12. Wiley, "Conservation of the Fertility of the Soil," 274.

13. *Report of the Commission on Country Life*, 83; see also Danbom, *Resisted Revolution*, 36, and Ellsworth, "Theodore Roosevelt's Country Life Commission," 155–72, especially p. 166.

14. Gates, "Comments," 214.

15. Quotations are from, in order, Gray et al., "Utilization of Our Land," 415; Gray, "National Land Use Policies," 231. See also Kirkendall, "L. C. Gray," 206–7.

16. Ely, *Foundations of National Prosperity*, 10.

17. Ely, "National Policy for Land Utilization," 113, 116; "Report of Committee No. 10, National Land Policy," 179.

18. Other members were O. E. Baker, F. J. Marschner, and B. O. Weitz from the BAE and W. R. Chapline, Raphael Zon, and Ward Shepard from the Forest Service.

19. Taylor and Taylor, *Story of Agricultural Economics*, 863, 848–53.

20. Gray et al., "Utilization of Our Land," 415–18, 502–5.

21. Ibid., 442, 433.

22. Baker, "Changes in Production and Consumption," 97–146; Baker, "Outlook for Land Utilization," 220–21.

23. Gray, "Land-Utilization Problem, Intensified by Depression," 457–58.

24. Gray et al., "Utilization of Our Land," 503–4, 423.

25. Quotations are from, in order, ibid., 506, 504; see also Kirkendall, "L. C. Gray," 207.

26. Letter from L. C. Gray to Dr. A. F. Woods, 1929, Record Group 16 (hereafter cited as RG), National Archives (hereafter cited as NA).

27. Black, "Research in Agricultural Land Utilization," 7–9; Ely, *Report of the National Agricultural Conference*, 115; Gray, "National Land Use Policies," 235.

28. Kirkendall, *Social Scientists*, 15–20; Christgau, "Adjustment for Production in Agriculture," 1–8.

29. Lord, *Wallaces of Iowa*, 305.

30. Kirkendall, "L. C. Gray," 210–11.

31. Hyde, "Developing a National Policy of Land Utilization," 36.

32. Cooper, "Extent and Emergence Character of Problems of Submarginal Land," 52; Knight, "Soil Conservation as a Major Problem of Agricultural Readjustment," 154; "National Land-Utilization Program," 240–49; Ely, "Adjusting the Tax Burden," 126.

33. Gray, "Our Land Use Problem," 457, 461–62; Soule, "Planning for Agriculture," 204–6.

34. Bennett and Chapline, *Soil Erosion*, 2046, 2043.

35. Brink, *Big Hugh*, 15–22, 48–60; Swain, *Federal Conservation Policy*, 148–53; Bennett, *Soil Conservation*, 313.

36. Burner, *Herbert Hoover*, 236–44; Fausold, *Presidency of Herbert C. Hoover*, 106–12; Hamilton, *From New Day to New Deal*, 216–36.

37. Ladd, "New York's Land Utilization Program," 53–58.

38. Roosevelt, *Public Papers,* 699; see also Kirkendall, *Social Scientists,* 53–58.

39. R. G. Tugwell, "Farm Relief and Permanent Agriculture," 273–74; R. G. Tugwell, "Place of Government," 55.

40. Wilson, "Agricultural Conservation," 3; Rowley, *M. L. Wilson,* 151.

41. R. G. Tugwell, "Place of Government," 59; Kirkendall, "New Deal and Agriculture," 83–110.

42. Kirkendall, *Social Scientists,* 28.

43. National Resources Board, *Report,* 8, 15, 105.

44. Ibid., 105. On Wallace and hybrids see Wallace, "Challenge to Science," 47–52; Schapsmeier and Schapsmeier, *Henry A. Wallace,* 20–21, 27–28; Kirkendall, "Second Secretary Wallace," 199–206.

45. Wallace, "Soil and the General Welfare," 111–16.

46. National Resources Board, *Report,* 92–95, 114–34; Clawson, *New Deal Planning,* 108–11.

47. National Resources Board, *Soil Erosion,* 4; Schmude, *Development of Nationwide Resources Inventories,* 2–4.

48. National Resources Board, *Report,* 161.

49. Ibid., 175.

50. Ibid., 185, 187.

51. Wehrwein, "Discussion," 53, described the report as a "landmark"; Clawson, *New Deal Planning,* provides a more recent assessment. For Wilson's comments see Wilson, "Report on Land of the National Resources Board," 39–50. Kirkendall, *Social Scientists,* 85, reports Roosevelt's response. See also Warken, *History of the National Resources Planning Board.*

52. National Resources Planning Board, *Public Land Acquisition,* 17; Saloutos, *American Farmer,* 197–98.

53. Baldwin, *Poverty and Politics,* 92–107; Kirkendall, *Social Scientists,* 108–29; Saloutos, *American Farmer,* 150–63.

54. National Resources Planning Board, *Public Land Acquisition,* 16, 19; Saloutos, *American Farmer,* 159–61; Kirkendall, *Social Scientists,* 82.

55. Franklin Delano Roosevelt to the Secretary of Agriculture, 25 August 1934, RG 16, NA; "Memorandum for the Secretary of Agriculture," 25 August 1934, Office File 732, Roosevelt Library.

56. Quoted in Kirkendall, *Social Scientists,* 87.

57. Director, Bureau of the Budget, to the President, 3 April 1934, RG 16, NA; Memorandum for the President from Lewis W. Douglas, Director of the Bureau of the Budget, 3 April 1934, Office File 1017, Roosevelt Library.

58. Kirkendall, *Social Scientists,* 85–86.

59. Wooten, *Land Utilization Program,* 29–34, 37.

60. Wilson, "Foreword," *Land Utilization Program,* i.

61. Cole and Crowe, *Recent Trends in Rural Planning,* 123–41; Williams and Price, "Law of the Land," 32–33; Wehrwein, "Public Control of Land Use," 74–85; Albers, "Progress in County Zoning," 393–402.

62. E. H. Wiecking to George S. Wehrwein, 8 December 1937, RG 16, NA.

63. Elliot, "Discussion," 86; Wehrwein et al., "Remedies," 241–45.

64. Morgan, *Governing Soil Conservation*, 8; Sampson, *For the Love of Land*, 24–29.

65. Trimble, "Perspectives on the History of Soil Erosion Control," 162–80.

66. Sears, *Deserts on the March*, especially chaps. 10 through 13.

67. U.S. Congress, House, Subcommittee of the Committee on Public Lands, *Hearings*, 3, 17, 23–24; Glick, "Soil and the Law," 296–318.

68. Franklin Delano Roosevelt, Memorandum for the Secretary of Agriculture, Warm Springs, Ga., 17 March 1937, Office File 732, Roosevelt Library.

69. Wilson, "Agricultural Conservation," 9–10.

70. Paul H. Appleby to G. W. Pugsley, 1936, RG 16, NA.

71. U.S. Congress, House, Subcommittee of the Committee on Public Lands, *Hearings*, 81–82, 68.

72. Henry A. Wallace to T. O. Walton, President of Texas A & M, 8 March 1937, RG 16, NA.

73. J. D. LeCron, Assistant Secretary of Agriculture, to R. W. Brown, Missouri Farm Bureau, 23 April 1937, RG 16, NA; Claude R. Wickard, "Statement by the Secretary of Agriculture Concerning Departmental Cooperation with Soil Conservation Districts," 21 September 1940, RG 83, NA; Wallace to Roosevelt, 16 February 1937, RG 16, NA.

74. Franklin D. Roosevelt, Draft of Proposed Letter from the President to the Governors, 19 February 1937, Office File 732, Roosevelt Library.

75. M. L. Wilson to Charles W. Eliot II, 2 October 1935, RG 16, NA.

76. LeCron to Brown, 23 April 1937; Wallace to T. O. Dalton, 8 March 1937, RG 16, NA.

77. Morgan, *Governing Soil Conservation*, 45.

78. Karl, *Uneasy State*, especially chap. 8; Hawley, "New Deal State and the Anti-Bureaucratic Tradition," 83; see also Otis L. Graham, Jr., *Toward a Planned Society*, 35–44.

79. Morgan, *Governing Soil Conservation*, 45–46.

80. Wallace to Robert H. Wood, 25 January 1937, Office File 1, Roosevelt Library.

81. Wallace to H. H. Bennett, 10 December 1937, RG 16, NA.

82. Bennett, "Field Memorandum SCS #769," 25 March 1939, RG 114, NA.

83. Morgan, *Governing Soil Conservation*, 81–83.

84. M. L. Wilson, "New Department of Agriculture," 13 January 1939, RG 114, NA; Sampson, *For the Love of Land*, 30–32.

85. "Progress Report, Land Committee," 25 September 1940, p. 4, RG 187, NA; A. E. Jones, "Soil Conservation Districts," 21 July 1941, RG 83, NA; Sampson, *For the Love of Land*, 32–33.

86. Wallace to Honorable J. T. Manley, 12 May 1937, RG 16, NA; Hardin, *Politics of Agriculture*, 71.

87. Bennett to Wallace, 1 December 1938, RG 16, NA; Morgan, *Governing Soil Conservation*, 84–86; Sampson, *For the Love of Land*, 30.

88. Morgan, *Governing Soil Conservation*, 86–87; Hardin, *Politics of Agriculture*, 74–75; Sampson, *For the Love of Land*, 30–31.

89. Hardin, *Politics of Agriculture*, 74–75; Morgan, *Governing Soil Conservation*, 98.

90. Sampson, *For the Love of Land*, 31.

91. Bennett, "To All Ranking Field Officers," 29 April 1937, RG 16, NA.

92. Sims, *Soil Conservation Service,* 79.

93. Wallace to Bennett, 10 December 1937, RG 16, NA; Wallace to Walton, 8 March 1937, RG 16, NA.

94. Morgan, *Governing Soil Conservation,* 89–93.

95. Kirkendall, *Social Scientists,* 146.

96. Ibid., 166.

97. U.S. Department of Agriculture, Office of Information, "Source Material on Agriculture's Conservation Objectives," 1 November 1938, RG 83, NA.

98. National Resources Committee, *Progress Report—June 15, 1936,* 7.

99. National Resources Committee, *Progress Report—December 1938,* 27.

100. "Joint Statement by the Association of Land Grant Colleges and Universities and the United States Department of Agriculture on Building Agricultural Land Use Programs," 8 July 1938, RG 16, NA; Kirkendall, *Social Scientists,* 222.

101. National Resources Committee, *Progress Report 1939,* 9.

102. Wallace, "Memorandum for Chiefs of Bureaus and Offices," 6 October 1938, RG 16, NA; Wilson, "Facets of County Planning," 2.

103. Wiecking to S. H. Rutford, 27 February 1939, RG 83, NA.

104. U.S. Department of Agriculture, "Report on the Progress of Land-Use Planning during 1939," 30 January 1940; Land Committee, "Progress Report," 25 November 1940; "Cooperative Agricultural Planning," n.d., RG 187, NA; Kirkendall, *Social Scientists,* 179; Benedict, *Farm Policies of the United States,* 394–95; Barlowe, *Land Resource Economics,* 519.

105. Wallace, "Importance of Planning in the Development of the Department of Agriculture," 20 March 1939, RG 83, NA; Ensminger, "Community in County Planning," 47.

106. "Cooperative Agricultural Planning," n.d., RG 187, NA; Tolley, *Farmer Citizen at War,* chap. 5; Foster and Vogel, "Cooperative Land Use Planning," 1144–49.

107. Lewis and Lewis, "The Farmer Helps to Plan," 504–5.

108. Barlowe, *Land Resource Economics,* 519.

109. Kirkendall, *Social Scientists,* 182–84.

110. Ibid., 166–70.

111. Albertson, *Roosevelt's Farmer,* 231–52; Kirkendall, *Social Scientists,* 191–96.

112. Baldwin, *Poverty and Politics,* 240–41.

113. Hargreaves, "Land-Use Planning in Response to Drought," 574.

114. Hirst, "City Growing Pains in the Country," 20.

115. Minutes from Land Committee meetings, 3–4 November 1938, 20 January 1939, 27 October 1939, 22–23 March 1940, 5–6 February 1943, 25–26 June 1943, RG 187, NA; Alvin T. M. Lee, "Rural-Urban Fringe," 12 May 1941, RG 83, NA.

Chapter Two

1. The history of this transformation, especially of its ecological dimensions, has received insufficient scholarly attention. Useful perspectives are Cochrane, *Development of American Agriculture*; Fite, *American Farmers*; Shover, *First Ma-*

jority, *Last Minority*; U.S. Department of Agriculture, *Time to Choose*; and Vasey, *Ecological History of Agriculture*, especially chapter 10.

2. Schertz, *Another Revolution in U.S. Farming?*; Parker, "Agriculture," 373.

3. Cochrane, *Development of American Agriculture*, 126–28; U.S. Bureau of the Census, *Historical Statistics of the United States*, 469.

4. Cochrane, *Development of American Agriculture*, 130–36; see also Schertz, *Another Revolution in U.S. Farming?*, 13–20, 25–30; USDA, *Time to Choose*, 31–68; U.S. Bureau of the Census, *Historical Statistics*, 457; and USDA, *Agricultural Statistics, 1981*, 417.

5. See Ebeling, *Fruited Plain*; a strong dissent from a historian comes from Shover, *First Majority, Last Minority*.

6. Schultz, "Declining Importance of Agricultural Land," 725.

7. President's Materials Policy Commission, *Resources for Freedom*, 1, 5, 32–34.

8. U.S. Congress, Senate, Committee on Interior and Insular Affairs, *Stockpile and Accessibility of Strategic and Critical Materials*, 718; Report of the Mid-Century Conference on Resources for the Future, *Nation Looks at Its Resources*, 31, 60.

9. Nolan, "Inexhaustible Resource of Technology," 65–66.

10. Clawson, Held, and Stoddard, *Land for the Future*, 246. On the business influence on Resources for the Future see Fox, *John Muir and His Legacy*, 309–10.

11. Morgan, *Governing Soil Conservation*, 143–70. The quotation is from p. 155. See also Hardin, *Politics of Agriculture*, 102–3; Held and Clawson, *Soil Conservation in Perspective*, 69–75.

12. Worster, "Sense of Soil," 31.

13. Skocpol, "Bringing the State Back In," 3–37; Balogh, "Reorganizing the Organizational Synthesis," 119–72; Hays, "Politics of Environmental Administration," 21–53.

14. Morgan, *Governing Soil Conservation*, 132–33; Sampson, *For the Love of Land*, 49–63.

15. Helms, "Development of the Land Capability Classification," 60–73.

16. Schmude, *Development of Nationwide Resources Inventories*, 7. See also Held and Clawson, *Soil Conservation in Perspective*, 132–41; Kuhl, "1957 Conservation Needs Inventory," 84–88.

17. Held and Clawson, *Soil Conservation in Perspective*, 75–79; Morgan, *Governing Soil Conservation*, 179–89.

18. Held and Clawson, *Soil Conservation in Perspective*, 79–86; Helms, "Great Plains Conservation Program," 140–57.

19. See Bennett's classic *Soil Conservation* as well as Jacks and Whyte, *Vanishing Lands*; Shepard, *Food or Famine*; and Osborn, *Our Plundered Planet*.

20. Chase, "New Conquest," 27.

21. Lord, *Care of the Earth*, 19.

22. Lord, "Proceedings," 23.

23. DeVoto's monthly *Harper's* columns are compiled in DeVoto, *Easy Chair*; see especially 334. A concise description of DeVoto's conservation career is found

in Fox, *John Muir and His Legacy,* 223–29. For a thoroughly engaging full biography of DeVoto see Stegner, *Uneasy Chair,* especially pp. 298–322.

24. Eisenhower, "Earth and the Human Burden," 187, 185.

25. Osborn, *Our Plundered Planet,* 69, 61, 3.

26. Vogt, *Road to Survival,* 284. Vogt's impact is discussed in Fox, *John Muir and His Legacy,* 306–11.

27. In addition to the Resources for the Future reports already cited, see Dewhurst and Associates, *America's Needs and Resources.*

28. Ordway, *Resources and the American Dream,* especially 16–23. See also Ordway, Jr., "Are There No Limits?," 425–29.

29. National Resources Committee, *Problems of a Changing Population,* 6.

30. Commission on Population Growth, *Population and the American Future,* 16–21; U.S. Bureau of the Census, *Historical Statistics of the United States, Part 2,* 8. For a discussion on the causes of the baby boom see Easterlin, "American Baby Boom," 869–911; Sweezy, "Economic Explanation of Fertility Changes," 255–68; Bean, "Baby Boom," 353–65; Russell, *Baby Boom Generation,* chap. 1.

31. U.S. Bureau of the Census, *Historical Statistics of the United States, Part 2,* 639–40.

32. Jackson, *Crabgrass Frontier,* 231–45; see also Muller, *Contemporary Suburban America,* 51–60.

33. Whyte, *Last Landscape,* 15–21.

34. Quoted in Jackson, *Crabgrass Frontier,* 65, 79, 175.

35. Ibid., 249; see also Clawson, *Suburban Land Use Conversion,* 33–55.

36. Lord, *Care of the Earth,* 274, 275.

37. Gulick, "City's Challenge in Resource Use," 127.

38. D. A. Williams to State and Territorial Conservationists, "Fact Sheet; Conversion of Cultivable Land to Other Uses," 10 November 1955, Record Group 16 (hereafter cited as RG), National Archives (hereafter cited as NA); see also Lint, "Buildings or Farms?," 42–43.

39. Quoted in Sampson, *For the Love of Land,* 143.

40. Barlowe, "Our Future Needs for Nonfarm Lands," 478–79; Gaffney, "Urban Expansion," 511–12; Johnson, "Planning for the New Land Frontier," 569, 580–83.

41. For the 1958 inventory see U.S. Department of Agriculture, *Basic Statistics of the National Inventory of Soil and Water Conservation Needs,* and U.S. Department of Agriculture, *Soil and Water Conservation Needs,* 20–21, 74–75. For the 1967 inventory see U.S. Department of Agriculture, *Basic Statistics, 1967.*

42. Sampson, *For the Love of Land,* 145.

43. Miner, "Agricultural Land Retention," 1.

44. Coughlin, *Saving the Garden;* Fletcher and Little, *American Cropland Crisis,* 15–64.

45. A useful statistical summary is McEvedy and Jones, *Atlas of World Population History,* 342–51; for an ecological view see Ehrlich, Ehrlich, and Holdren, *Ecoscience,* 181–227. One provocative treatment of the causes of population growth is McKeown, *Modern Rise of Population.* On the persistence of the problem into the 1980s see McNamara, "Time Bomb or Myth," 1107–31, and Repetto, "Population, Resource Pressures, and Poverty," *Global Possible,* 131–69.

46. Bergstrom, *Hungry Planet,* xi, xiii.

47. Paddock and Paddock, *Famine 1975,* 9; Ehrlich, *Population Bomb.*

48. Ehrlich, *Population Bomb.*

49. Cochrane, *World Food Problem.*

50. Commission on Population Growth and the American Future, *Population and the American Future,* 47.

51. Paarlberg, in U.S. Congress, House, Committee on Agriculture, Subcommittee on Department Operations, *World Population and Food Supply and Demand Situation,* 16.

52. Lester Brown, *By Bread Alone,* 133–46; Humphrey and Buttel, *Environment, Energy and Society,* 210–12; Warnock, *Politics of Hunger,* 16; Dahlberg, *Beyond the Green Revolution,* especially chap. 3; Perkins, "Rockefeller Foundation," 6–18.

53. Quoted in U.S. Congress, House, Committee on Agriculture, Subcommittee on Department Operations, *World Population and Food Supply and Demand Situation,* 16. See also Cochrane, *Development of American Agriculture,* 151–53.

54. Lester Brown, *By Bread Alone,* 59–60.

55. Ibid., 3.

56. Cochrane and Ryan, *American Farm Policy,* 61, 66–67.

57. U.S. Department of Agriculture, *Statistical Abstracts 1985,* 390.

58. Sampson, *For the Love of Land,* 153.

59. Carter and Johnston, "Structure, Organization, and Control of American Agriculture," 745.

60. U.S. Bureau of the Census, *Statistical Abstract of the United States: 1986,* 657; for a discussion of how this "export explosion" turned into an "export bust" in the 1980s, see Galston, *Tough Row to Hoe,* 10–12.

61. Batie and Healy, "U.S. Agriculture as a Strategic Resource."

62. Bavel, "Soil and Oil," 3.

63. Crosson, "Demands for Food and Fiber," 54.

64. Heady, "Adequacy of Agricultural Land," 34–35.

65. U.S. Department of Agriculture, *Agricultural Statistics 1988,* 392.

66. Crosson, "Future Environmental and Economic Costs," 173; Heady, "Adequacy of Agricultural Land," 52–53.

67. U.S. Bureau of the Census, *Statistical Abstract of the United States: 1986,* 654.

68. Cochrane, *Development of American Agriculture,* 162.

69. Horsfall, "Fire Brigade Stops a Raging Epidemic," 105–15; see also Harlan, "Crop Monoculture," 225–50. Neither source shows much serious worry about increasing genetic vulnerability, and Horsfall sees the quick USDA response to the 1970 epidemic as a triumph of science. Such a sanguine view seems hard to maintain in light of his own mention of earlier, more devastating monoculture diseases, such as the Irish potato famine of the 1840s and the Bengal rice famine of 1943. Doyle, *Altered Harvest,* 30, reviews the same facts and concludes somewhat more pessimistically that the "trend toward centralization in food production—a trend which biotechnology is facilitating at a rapid rate—will mean greater vulnerability in the food system."

70. Lovins, Lovins, and Bender, "Energy and Agriculture," 73.

71. Statistics are from Durost and Black, *Changes in Farm Production and Efficiency,* 27, 31.

72. From Gever et al., *Beyond Oil,* 155, based on USDA statistics.

73. Lester Brown, *By Bread Alone,* 106–9.

74. Odum, *Environment, Power, and Society,* 116, 118.

75. Federal Energy Administration and U.S. Department of Agriculture, *Energy and U.S. Agriculture,* 1–2.

76. On the energy crisis see Franklin Tugwell, *Energy Crisis,* 97–101.

77. Pimental et al., "Food Production and the Energy Crisis," 446. See also Pimental and Pimental, *Food, Energy, and Society,* 68–70, 137–39. In this more recent estimate under the same scenario, the world's petroleum reserves would last only eleven years.

78. Steinhart and Steinhart, "Energy Use in the U.S. Food System," 307–15.

79. Doering, "Energy Dependence," 191–96; Lester Brown, *By Bread Alone,* 106–8; see also Lovins, Lovins, and Bender, "Energy and Agriculture," 68–86.

80. U.S. Bureau of Census, *1978 Census of Agriculture, Irrigation;* Frederick, "Irrigation," 117–23; according to Frederick (p. 129), farmers paid only 3.3 percent of the expenses of Bureau of Reclamation irrigation projects, 40 percent came from taxes and the remainder from the sale of electricity.

81. National Water Commission, *Water Policies for the Future,* provides an important criticism of cheap water policies in the past. On the use of the Ogallala aquifer in the High Plains of Texas see Green, *Land of the Underground Rain.*

82. Frederick, "Water and the West"; see also Frederick, *Cropland Crisis,* 129–49.

83. Held and Clawson, *Soil Conservation in Perspective,* 152, 232.

84. See, for example, Grant, "Land Use," 13–22.

85. Trimble, "Perspectives on the History of Soil Erosion Control," 162–80.

86. Carter, "Soil Erosion," 409–11; Pimental et al., "Land Degradation," 149–55; Brink, Dunsmore, and Hill, "Soil Deterioration," 625–30.

87. U.S. General Accounting Office, *To Protect Tomorrow's Food Supply,* 6, 10–17, 28–29.

88. U.S. Department of Agriculture, *Soil and Water Resources Conservation Act,* 3; U.S. Department of Agriculture, *National Program for Soil and Water Conservation,* 11; Batie, "Soil Conservation in the 1980s," 116–18; Cook, "RCA," 213–14; Cook, "Got Those GAO Blues Again," 346–50.

89. Meadows et al., *Limits to Growth,* 23; see also Warnock, *Politics of Hunger,* 32.

90. Meadows et al., *Limits to Growth,* 29.

91. Merrill, *Radical Agriculture,* xvii.

92. Bookchin, "Radical Agriculture," 8.

93. Berry, *Unsettling of America,* 33.

Chapter Three

1. Popper, *Politics of Land-Use Reform.*

2. Skocpol, "Bringing the State Back In," 4; Hays, "Political Choice," 124–54.

3. Balogh, "Reorganizing the Organizational Synthesis," 119–72; Balogh, *Chain Reaction.*

4. Leopold, *Sand County Almanac*; Carson, *Silent Spring*; for a lively introduction to the ideas of the movement's leaders see Fleming, "History of the New Conservation Movement," 7–91.

5. Hays, *Beauty, Health, and Permanence,* especially pp. 54–57.

6. Berg emphasized the continuity between earlier decades and the 1970s as well as the interconnectedness of land and water issues; Berg interview.

7. Quoted in Bosselman and Callies, *Quiet Revolution,* ii.

8. Graham, Jr., *Toward a Planned Society,* 159–66, 194–204; Rodwin and Susskind, "Land-Use Research Issues"; see also Graham, "National Growth Report," 68–76, and Graham, "White House Conference," 52–59.

9. Hawley, "Social Policy and the Liberal State," 125.

10. Barbara Ward, quoted in United States Department of Agriculture, *National Growth and Its Distribution,* 30.

11. Advisory Commission on Intergovernmental Relations, *Urban and Rural America,* 12–13, 59–60.

12. *Final Report, White House Conference on Balanced Growth and Economic Development,* 2:55.

13. On the weakness of the growth reports see U.S. Congress, House, Committee on Banking, Currency, and Housing, Subcommittee on Housing and Community Development, *National Growth and Development, Hearings.* Very useful on both the problems and prospects for national growth policy is a series of articles in Scott, Brower, and Miner, *Management and Control of Growth,* vol. 3.

14. Moynihan, "Toward a National Urban Policy," 3–20.

15. Carter, "Land Use Law," 691–97; Graham, *Toward a Planned Society,* 219–24; Noone, "Resources Report," 1192–1201; Popper, *Politics of Land-Use Reform,* 27–55.

16. "New American Land Rush," 83.

17. Plotkin, "Policy Fragmentation and Capitalist Reform," 409–45; for an expanded version of Plotkin's argument see Plotkin, *Keep Out,* 149–200.

18. Real Estate Research Corporation, *Costs of Sprawl,* 7.

19. Reilly, *Use of Land,* especially pp. 33–73, 145–75.

20. Presto, "Shrinking Farmlands."

21. *New York Times,* 26 June 1972, A24.

22. Council on Environmental Quality, *Environmental Quality, 1970,* xii, xiii; Council on Environmental Quality, *Environmental Quality, 1973,* vi.

23. Bosselman and Callies, *Quiet Revolution,* 1. The Council on Environmental Quality, which commissioned this document, intended it to stimulate support for an enlarged state role in the federal land use legislation.

24. Carter, "Land Use Law"; Lyday, *Law of the Land*; U.S. Congress, Senate, Committee on Interior and Insular Affairs, *Land Use Policy and Planning Assistance Act.*

25. U.S. Congress, Senate, Committee on Interior and Insular Affairs, *Land Resource Planning Assistance Act,* 2.

26. U.S. Congress, House, Morris Udall, 94th Congress, 1st sess., *Congressional Record,* 4 March 1975, E 862.

27. U.S. Congress, Senate, George Aiken, 93d Congress, 1st sess., *Congressional Record,* 19 June 1973, 20276–77.

28. Lyday, *Law of the Land,* 41–51; Plotkin, "Policy Fragmentation and Capitalist Reform," 435–40.

29. Plotkin, *Keep Out,* 199–200.

30. Hawley, "Social Policy and the Liberal State," identifies policy fragmentation and political localism as two of the key characteristics of the modern American state.

31. Plotkin, "Policy Fragmentation and Capitalist Reform," 433.

32. David Calfee, quoted in Lyday, *Law of the Land,* 43; see also U.S. Congress, Senate, Committee on Interior and Insular Affairs, *Land Use Policy and Planning Assistance Act, Report,* 47–49.

33. Downie, Jr., "Move to Save What Is Left," 649–52.

34. Berg interview.

35. David A. Witts, quoted in U.S. Congress, House, Committee on Interior and Insular Affairs, Subcommittee on the Environment, *Land Use Planning Act of 1974,* 207; Weldon Barton, National Farmers' Union, in U.S. Congress, Senate, Committee on Interior and Insular Affairs, *National Land Use Policy,* 375–77.

36. Office of the Secretary of Agriculture to Morris K. Udall, 24 April 1975, Record Group 16 (hereafter cited as RG), National Archives (hereafter cited as NA).

37. *Farm Bureau News* 52, 1 January 1973, 1; Clifford G. McIntire, American Farm Bureau Federation, in U.S. Congress, House, Committee on Interior and Insular Affairs, Subcommittee on the Environment, *National Land Use Planning, Hearings,* 293.

38. Lyday, *Law of the Land,* 46.

39. U.S. Congress, Senate, Committee on Interior and Insular Affairs, *Land Resource Planning Assistance Act,* 335; see also Sampson, *For the Love of Land,* 204–8.

40. Magida, "Environment Report," 367–69.

41. Demkovich, "Perils of Petaluma," 588–96; Supalla, "Land Use Planning," 895–901.

42. Quoted in Popper, *Politics of Land-Use Reform,* 61.

43. Little, "Toward a Land Resource Policy Agenda," 19.

44. Freeman, "Citizen's Stake in Soil and Water Management," 14.

45. Robert C. Wood, "Soil, Water and Suburbia," 6.

46. Quoted in Berg, "Programs to Help People Make Land Use Choices," 44–45.

47. Berg interview.

48. Don Paarlberg, in U.S. Congress, House, Committee on Interior and Insular Affairs, Subcommittee on the Environment, *National Land Use Planning,* 180–84.

49. Berg interview; Graham, *Toward a Planned Society,* 209–13; Arnold, *Making the Managerial Presidency,* 290–302.

50. Berg interview; Zitzmann interview; Corrigan, "Environment Report," 597–607.

51. Berg interview; Tankersly interview; Cotner interview.

52. U.S. Department of Agriculture, "Secretary's Memorandum 1897," 26 March 1973, in the files of Tankersly.

53. U.S. Department of Agriculture, "Secretary's Memorandum 1827," 26 October 1973, in the files of Tankersly.

54. Berg, "Evolution of a Land Use Policy in USDA," 154.

55. T. K. Cowden to Senator Thomas J. McIntyre, 14 February 1973, RG 16, NA.

56. Berg, "Evolution of a Land Use Policy in USDA," 157; M. Rupert Cutler, "USDA's Revised Land Use Policy," statement for the 30 June 1978 seminar on USDA's revised land use policy memorandum, in the files of Howard Tankersly.

57. Senator Carl T. Curtis to Quentin M. West, 28 April 1975, Earl Butz to Curtis, 12 June 1975, and Melvin Cotner to Don Paarlberg, 12 August 1974, RG 16, NA.

58. U.S. Department of Agriculture, Committee on Land Use, *Recommendations on Prime Lands,* 11.

59. Ibid., 12.

60. U.S. Department of Agriculture, *Perspectives on Prime Lands,* 3; Sampson interview.

61. U.S. Department of Agriculture, "Secretary's Memorandum 1827, Supplement No. 1," 21 June 1976.

62. Cotner interview; Sampson interview.

63. Council on Environmental Quality, "Memorandum for Heads of Agencies," 30 August 1976, in *Environmental Quality 1977,* 387–88.

64. This characterization is based on author's interviews with Cotner, Anderson, and Boxley of the Economic Research Service and with Berg and Zitzmann of the Soil Conservation Service.

65. Bowers, "Economic Research Service," 243.

66. Dideriksen and Sampson, "Important Farmlands," 195–97; Sampson, "Ethical Dimension of Farmland Protection," 13–28; Sampson interview; Gray interview.

67. Hart, "Urban Encroachments on Rural Areas," 15.

68. Otte, "Farming in the City's Shadow," 111.

69. Hadwiger, *Politics of Agricultural Research,* 32, 59–66. See also Busch and Lacy, *Science, Agriculture, and the Politics of Research,* 187–205.

70. Anderson, Gustafson, and Boxley, "Perspectives on Agricultural Land Policy," 36–43; Anderson, Boxley, and Cotner interviews.

71. For a vigorous, concise statement of this view see Raup, "What Is Prime Land," 180–81; see also William W. Wood, "Prime Lands," 909–13; Anderson and Boxley interviews.

72. Schiff, "Land and Food," 56.

73. Balogh, *Chain Reaction,* especially 302–26.

74. Bogue, *Metropolitan Growth,* 1–13; David L. Brown, "Agricultural Land Use," 83.

75. Otte, "Human Considerations in Land Use," 126.

76. Frey, *Major Uses of Land in the United States.*

77. Cotner to Paarlberg, 12 August 1974, RG 16, NA; Sampson interview.

78. Frey and Otte, *Cropland for Today and Tomorrow.*

79. Cotner, *Land Use Policy and Agriculture.*

80. Dideriksen, Hidlebaugh, and Schmude, *Potential Cropland Study.*

81. Butz to R. Long, 10 October 1974, RG 16, NA; Sampson interview.

82. Frey interview; Crosson interview; Schmude, *Development of Nationwide Resources Inventories in the United States,* 16–19.

83. Fletcher interview; Sampson interview.

84. Beale, *Revival of Population Growth in Non-Metropolitan America,* 3.

85. Beale, "Population Turnaround," 47–59.

86. Berry and Dahmann, *Population Redistribution,* 7–14; Morrison and Wheeler, "Rural Renaissance in America?," 1–26; Healy and Short, *Market for Rural Land,* 30–35.

87. Doherty, "Public and Private Issues," 51. Some recent evidence suggests that the population turnaround of the 1970s may have been fairly short-lived. See Brown and Zuiches, "Rural-Urban Population Redistribution," 1–18.

88. Hart, "Urban Encroachment on Rural Areas," 1–17.

89. Zeimetz et al., *Dynamics of Land Use in Fast-Growth Areas,* 13–15.

90. Coughlin, *Saving the Garden,* 48.

91. Ibid., 53.

92. John T. Buck, quoted in "Population Horror Stories." See also Fitchen, *Endangered Spaces, Enduring Places,* 100–107.

93. Little, *Land and Food.*

94. Paul Vander Myde to Steve Lundin, 13 May 1975, and Cowden to McIntyre, 14 February 1973, RG 16, NA. See also Cotner, *Land Use Policy and Agriculture.*

95. Council on Environmental Quality, *Untaxing Open Space,* 10–13.

96. Whyte, *Last Landscape,* chap. 6.

97. Hady, "Differential Assessment of Open Space and Farmland," 91.

98. Council on Environmental Quality, *Untaxing Open Space,* 77–79.

99. Reilly, *Use of Land,* 128–29.

100. Conard, "Conservation of Local Autonomy," 224–39; see also Fellmeth, *Politics of Land* (especially pp. 36–42), the report of Ralph Nader's study group on land use in California.

101. Gustafson and Wallace, "Differential Assessment as Land Use Policy," 379–89; see also Hansen and Schwartz, "Prime Land Conservation," 198–203.

102. Bryant and Conklin, "New Farmland Preservation Programs," 390–96; see also Sullivan, "Agricultural Districts," 122–30.

103. Healy and Rosenberg, *Land Use and the States,* 6.

104. Optimistic appraisals can be found in Clark, "Agricultural Zoning in Black Hawk County, Iowa," 149–54; see also Wall, "California's Agricultural Land Preservation Program."

105. For examples see Fellmeth, *Politics of Land,* 32–35, and Whyte, *Last Landscape,* 47–50.

106. For examples of this hopeful reading of constitutional law see Bosselman, Callies, and Banta, *Taking Issue,* and Reilly, *Use of Land,* 145–75.

107. Platt, "Loss of Farmland," 93–101.

108. Dunford, "Saving Farmland," 19–21.

109. See, for example, Toner, *Saving Farms and Farmlands;* Lapping, "Agri-

cultural Land Retention Strategies," 124–27; Little, "Farmland Conservancies," 204–11; and National Agricultural Lands Study, *Protection of Farmland*, the most complete survey to date.

110. Borrows and Yanggen, "Wisconsin Farmland Preservation Program," 209–12; Pease and Jackson, "Farmland Preservation in Oregon," 256–59; Schiff, "Saving Farmland," 204–7; "TDR: What's Happening Now," 10–14.

111. Raup, "Urban Threats to Rural Lands," 376.

Chapter Four

1. Esseks, "Politics of Farmland Preservation," 199–215.

2. Klein, "Preserving Farmland on Long Island," 11–13.

3. Lester Brown, "Vanishing Croplands," 6–14, 33–34; Lester Brown, *Twenty-Ninth Day,* 46–50; see also Eckholm, *Losing Ground,* 182. Eckholm describes urban sprawl as another environmental stress on the world's food system, "reckless, inadequately measured," and "a myopic activity occurring in both rich and poor countries."

4. Fletcher interview; Zitzmann interview.

5. Little interview; Gray interview.

6. Sampson interview.

7. The descriptions of the group's reasoning come from Little and Fletcher interviews. The commission is described in Sampson, personal notes, 18 January 1977, and "Agricultural Land Resources Review Commission," 19 January 1977, in the personal papers of Neil Sampson.

8. Little, "Case for Retaining Agricultural Land," 3. Little tried to have the Congressional Research Service publish this paper but was turned down because CRS judged the paper to be biased. Little then passed it on to Neil Sampson, who reproduced and circulated copies to interested policymakers. This gave the protection movement an "underground" paper and hastened Little's dissatisfaction with his employers at CRS.

9. Sampson, "Prime Farmlands," 44.

10. Coughlin, "Methods of Protecting Agricultural Land." For an extended analysis of the effectiveness of state and local programs see Coughlin, *Saving the Garden,* or National Agricultural Lands Study, *Protection of Farmland.*

11. Jeffords interview.

12. Ibid.; Gray interview.

13. U.S. Congress, House, Committee on Agriculture, *Agricultural Land Retention Act, Report,* 10. Sampson interview; see also Dunford, "Evolution of Federal Farmland Protection Policy," 133–36.

14. U.S. Congress, House, Committee on Agriculture, *Agricultural Land Retention Act, Report,* 1–6; personal notes, n.d., in the personal papers of Sampson.

15. U.S. Congress, House, Committee on Agriculture, *Agricultural Land Retention Act, Report,* 16. See Callies, "Quiet Revolution Revisited," 135–44. Callies notes that the resurgence of local government planning was often in reaction to the perceived threat of interference from national or regional planning bodies.

16. Sampson interview.

17. Fletcher interview; Fletcher worried most directly about the Jeffords bill

being too weak. In my interviews with them, Little, Sampson, and Gray shared the general impression that the bill was not very strong, yet all of them felt that it was the best that could be hoped for in the political climate of the late 1970s. Finally, of course, even this weak version proved too much. In the context of the coastal act, see Hays, *Beauty, Health, and Permanence,* 167–70.

18. Quoted in Krohe, Jr., "Can Both Corn and Coal Be King in the Midwest?," 38–41.

19. Robert Masterson, Knox County (Illinois) zoning administrator, quoted in U.S. Congress, House, Committee on Interior and Insular Affairs, Subcommittee on Energy and the Environment, *Reclamation Practices,* pt. 2, 20.

20. U.S. Congress, House, Committee on Interior and Insular Affairs, Subcommittee on Energy and the Environment, *Reclamation Practices,* pt. 2, 129.

21. Ibid., pt. 3, 31.

22. Ibid., pt. 2, 131; Ibid., pt. 3, 23–26.

23. U.S. Congress, Senate, Charles Percy, *Congressional Record,* 95th Congress, 1st sess. (21 July 1977), 24347–48; Vietor, *Environmental Politics,* 112–26.

24. Report of the Interagency Task Force on the Issue of a Moratorium or a Ban on Mining in Prime Agricultural Lands, prepared by Office of Management and Budget, Soil Conservation Service, Bureau of Mines, Federal Energy Administration, and Environmental Protection Agency, unpublished, n.d., in the personal papers of Sampson.

25. Esseks, "Nonurban Competition for Farmland," 57–60.

26. U.S. Congress, Senate, Dick Clark, *Congressional Record,* 95th Congress, 1st sess. (26 May 1977), 16861–63.

27. U.S. Congress, House, Committee on Agriculture, Subcommittee on Family Farms, Rural Development, and Special Studies, *Agricultural Land Protection Act of 1979, Hearings,* 21 (hereafter cited as *Agricultural Land Protection Act of 1979*).

28. Ibid., 23. The 1980 comment is from Jeffords, "Vanishing Farmlands," 16–18.

29. *Agricultural Land Protection Act of 1979,* 20; Fletcher interview. Fletcher is quick to add that a stronger bill was politically impossible and that his group did not even get this limited legislation.

30. *Agricultural Land Protection Act of 1979,* 254–56.

31. Ibid., 110.

32. Sampson interview.

33. *Agricultural Land Protection Act of 1979,* 252.

34. Ibid., 204; Bruce Hawley, quoted in Peirce and Hatch, "Preservationists Seek Government Help," 1357–61.

35. This list comes from *Land Use Notes* 10, 8 October 1976. The conference papers were published as *Land Use: Tough Choices in Today's World.*

36. Peterson and Yampolsky, *Urban Development and the Protection of Farmland*; Peterson and McCarthy, "Proposal for an Agricultural Land Preservation Program"; Isberg, "Controlling Growth in the Urban Fringe," 155–61; Miner, "Agricultural Lands Preservation," 52–60.

37. Sampson, "Development on Prime Farmland," 4–6.

38. Quoted in Nesmith, "Urban Sprawl," A4; see also Sampson, "Ethical Dimension of Farmland Protection," 89–98.

39. Clawson, "Preservation of Prime Agricultural Land," 10.

40. Paarlberg, "Scarcity Syndrome," 110–14; Paarlberg, *Farm and Food Policy,* 152.

41. Crosson, Cotner, Anderson, and Boxley interviews.

42. Gardner, "Economics of Agricultural Land Preservation," 1027–36.

43. Quoted in Peirce and Hatch, "Preservationists Seek Government Help," 1357, and in Nesmith, "Urban Sprawl," A4.

44. Bergland, Jeffords, and Cutler interviews; Bob Bergland to James Mills, 31 October 1977, Record Group 16 (hereafter cited as RG), National Archives (hereafter cited as NA).

45. Quoted in *Land Use Notes* 13, 5 August 1977.

46. *Agricultural Land Protection Act of 1979,* 49–62; Jeffords interview.

47. William Haffert to Phillip Alampi, 31 May 1977; Neil Sampson to Peter Sorensen, 6 October 1977, in the personal papers of Sampson.

48. Bergland interview.

49. Howard W. Hjort to Rupert Cutler, n.d., in the personal papers of Sampson.

50. Bergland to Jeffords, 6 October 1977, in the personal papers of Sampson.

51. Jerome Miles to Hjort, n.d., in the personal papers of Sampson.

52. James Webster to Bergland, 10 February 1978, in the personal papers of Sampson.

53. Richard Nolan to Bergland, 19 December 1977, in the personal papers of Sampson.

54. Bergland to Thomas Foley, 11 July 1978, in the personal papers of Sampson.

55. Jeffords, "Dear Colleague" letter, 31 October 1979, in the personal files of Jeffords.

56. U.S. Congress, House, Committee on Agriculture, *Agricultural Land Retention Act, Report,* 1–6.

57. Sampson to Sorensen, 6 October 1977, in the personal papers of Sampson.

58. U.S. Congress, Senate, Warren Magnuson, *Congressional Record,* 95th Congress, 2d sess. (16 March 1978), 7234–39.

59. Gray interview.

60. Cutler interview.

61. Secretary's Memorandum, 30 October 1978, included in the minutes of the USDA Committee on Land Use, in the personal files of Warren Zitzmann.

62. Anthan, "Vanishing Acres," *Des Moines Register,* 8 July 1979, A1, A4.

63. McGovern, "We Must Not Break the Hoop of Life," 12–14.

64. "Long-Range Threats Stalk U.S. Farming."

65. Meyer, "Land Rush," 45–60.

66. Brubaker, "Land—The Far Horizon," 1036–44; Timmons, "Agricultural Land Retention," 6. See also Berry and Plaut, "Retaining Agricultural Activities," 153–78;

67. Peirce and Hatch, "Preservationists Seek Government Help"; U.S. General Accounting Office, *Preserving America's Farmland,* 9.

68. Esseks, "Politics of Farmland Preservation," 199–215; Keene, "Review of Governmental Policies," 119–44; Little, "Farmland Conservancies," 204–11.

69. Sampson interview.

70. U.S. Congress, House, James Jeffords, *Congressional Record,* 96th Congress, 1st sess. (20 March 1979), 5578–82.

71. McClintock, "Global Importance of American Cropland," 26–29; Schiff, "Land and Food," 54–59.

72. U.S. Congress, House, Committee on Agriculture, *Agricultural Land Protection Act, Hearings,* 9–16 (hereafter cited as *Protection Act, Hearings*).

73. Jeffords interview.

74. *Protection Act, Hearings,* 33.

75. U.S. Congress, House, Committee on Agriculture, *Agricultural Land Protection Act, Report,* 22.

76. U.S. Congress, House, Charles Grassley, *Congressional Record,* 96th Congress, 2d sess. (6 February 1980), 2151.

77. *Protection Act, Hearings,* 30.

78. National Association of Conservation Districts, "Conversion of Agricultural Land," unpublished, 6 July 1979, in the personal papers of Sampson.

79. Mel Cotner to Georgiana Francisco, 9 October 1979, RG 16, NA.

80. U.S. Congress, House, Committee on Agriculture, *Agricultural Land Protection Act, Report,* 6.

81. *Protection Act, Hearings,* 37.

82. Ibid., 22, 25.

83. Charles Boothby et al. to Nolan, 30 May 1979, in the personal papers of Sampson; see also Jeffords, "Protecting Farmland," 158–59.

84. *Protection Act, Hearings,* 9.

85. Ibid., 32–33.

86. U.S. Congress, Senate, Select Committee on Small Business, *Availability and Control of Agricultural Land, Hearings,* 96th Congress, 1st sess., 1979.

87. U.S. Congress, House, *Congressional Record,* 6–7 February 1980, 629–33, 690–701.

88. Lyons, "On Capitol Hill," A4.

89. Allbee, "Letters," 243.

90. Jeffords interview.

91. This is consistent with the pattern of support for environmental legislation discerned by historian Samuel P. Hays. See his *Beauty, Health, and Permanence,* 43–52.

92. Anthan, "House Kills Weakened Bill," A1, A10.

93. Frederic Winthrop, Jr., to Jeffords, 26 June 1980, in the personal files of Jeffords.

Chapter Five

1. Bob Daniels to Rupert Cutler and Malcolm Baldwin, 21 February 1978, personal files of Tankersly.

2. Cotner interview.

3. Frank Schnidman to Norman Berg, 21 July 1978, personal files of Tankersly.

4. Frey interview. Other interviews revealed similar sentiments among economists both in and out of the department, notably Cotner, Brewer, and Crosson.

5. Minutes, USDA Committee on Land Use, 30 January 1978, personal files of Tankersly.

6. Mel Cotner to Lynn M. Daft, 2 January 1979, personal files of Tankersly.

7. Bob Bergland to Cutler, 17 August 1978, personal files of Tankersly.

8. Charles Warren to Bergland, 11 October 1978, personal files of Tankersly.

9. Memo, Daft to Stuart Eizenstat, "Study Commission on Agricultural Land Retention," 22 February 1979, White House Central File, Box FG 234, Carter Library; Letter, Neil Sampson to Daft, n.d., White House Central File, NR 4, Carter Library.

10. Bergland and Warren to Jack Watson and Eizenstat, 8 March 1978, personal files of Tankersly.

11. Minutes, USDA Committee on Land Use, 19 December 1978, personal files of Tankersly.

12. Carter, "Environmental Priorities and Programs," 1361, 1368.

13. Memo, Watson and Eizenstat to the President, 30 March 1979, "Comments on Bergland-Warren Memo Regarding Retention of Agricultural Lands," White House Central File, Box FG 123, Carter Library; Memo, Daft to Eizenstat, "Study Commission on Agricultural Land Retention," 22 February 1979, White House Central File, Box FG 234, Carter Library.

14. Boxley and Anderson interviews.

15. Brewer interview.

16. Smythe interview.

17. Fletcher interview.

18. Gray interview.

19. Memo, Eizenstat and Daft to Fran Voorde, 15 October 1979, "Agricultural Lands Study Field Workshops, White House Central File, Box FG 123, Carter Library; Memo, Daft to Eizenstat, 19 November 1979, White House Central Files, Box FG 123, Carter Library.

20. National Agricultural Lands Study, *Where Have All the Farmlands Gone?*

21. Gray and Brewer interviews.

22. Smythe interview.

23. See, for example, Brewer and Boxley, "Potential Supply of Cropland," 93–112.

24. National Agricultural Lands Study, *Final Report,* 14.

25. National Agricultural Lands Study, *Protection of Farmland.*

26. U.S. Congress, Senate, Committee on Agriculture, Nutrition, and Forestry, *Agricultural Land Availability.*

27. Brewer interview.

28. See, for example, "Is the City Heading Your Way?," 36, in which Gray is quoted as follows: "Clearly, it is prime farmland being lost. Such land is now being lost at a consistent rate of 2.9 million acres each year in the U.S." Smythe and Tankersly, in their interviews, expressed this concern that Gray had misconstrued the dimensions of the problem and drawn the exaggerated conclusion that three million acres of prime cropland were being lost each year.

29. Crosson, "Shortage of Agricultural Land?," 8.

30. Tankersly interview.

31. Tankersly and Cotner interviews.

32. Brewer and Boxley, "Agricultural Land," 879.

33. Brown et al., "Assessing Prospects for the Adequacy of Agricultural Land," 283.

34. See, for example, Cook, "Loathing Suburbia," 19–25.

35. Raup, "Agricultural Critique," 267.

36. Fischel, "Urbanization of Agricultural Land," 236–59.

37. Simon, "Farmer and the Mall," 18–20, 40–41; Simon, "Are We Losing Our Farmland?," 62; for Simon's complete approach to resource questions see Simon, *Ultimate Resource.*

38. Brewer, "Changing U.S. Farmland Scene," 3.

39. Brewer and Boxley, "Agricultural Land," 879–87.

40. For a critique that unpacks the conservative values implicit in this view of economics as a neutral science, see Madden, "Beyond Conventional Economics," 221–58.

41. Quoted in Sampson, "Building a Political Commitment to Conservation," 253.

42. Fischel, "Urbanization of Agricultural Land," 257.

43. Stockman, *Triumph of Politics,* 38.

44. Frey, *Expansion of Urban Area,* 1–10; Dunford, *Development and Current Status,* 43–66; Tankersly, "Agricultural Land Conversion—The Issue," draft paper prepared for the 1985 RCA Assessment, in the personal files of Tankersly.

45. U.S. Department of Agriculture, *Second RCA Appraisal,* 18–20.

46. Dovring, Chicoine, and Braden, "Evaluating Land Use Change," 359–61.

47. Raup, "Competition for Land," 41–78.

48. National Agricultural Lands Study, *Final Report,* 56–59.

49. Ibid., 54–55.

50. Boxley, "Competition for Agricultural Land," 112.

51. Batie and Healy, "Future of American Agriculture," 45; McClintock, "Global Significance," 217.

52. National Agricultural Lands Study, *Final Report,* 55.

53. Crosson, "Long-Term Adequacy," 7.

54. Samuelson, "U.S. Farms," 916–19.

55. Cook, "Surplus Madness," 25–28.

56. Soth, "Grain Export Boom," 906.

57. McClintock, "Global Significance of U.S. Cropland," 230–34.

58. Boxley, "Competition for Agricultural Land," 142–48.

59. Tamarkin, "Growth Industry," 90.

60. Crosson, "Future Economic and Environmental Costs," 172–76; Heady, "Adequacy of Agricultural Land," 38–41.

61. Ruttan, "Discussion," 57–61; Ruttan, "Agricultural Research," 117–55.

62. "Vanishing Farm Land," A22; Kneeland, "Urbanization of Rural U.S.," B8; Castle, "Is There a Farmland Crisis?," A23.

63. *National Farmers' Union Washington Newsletter,* 30 January 1981.

64. Bickers, "When Cities Nibble Away at Farmland," 15.

65. "Yesterday's Land Figures," *Farm Bureau News,* 146.

66. "Land Use Planning," *Farm Bureau News,* 31.

67. Quoted in Whyte, "Land and Water Squeeze," 133.

68. Quoted in Cook, "National Agricultural Lands Study," 91.

69. John Block to Jesse Helms, 31 December 1981, Record Group 16 (hereafter cited as RG), National Archives (hereafter cited as NA). See also Whyte, "Land and Water Squeeze," 131–56.

70. Anthan, "HUD Tries to Block Cropland-Saving Order," A1, A9. Minutes of other meetings were made public by George Brown; see U.S. Congress, House, "Cropland Conversion," 97th Congress, 1st sess., *Congressional Record,* Extensions of Remarks, vol. 147, part 23 (8 December 1981), 30048–49, and U.S. Congress, House, "Loss of Cropland to Agriculture," 97th Congress, 1st sess., *Congressional Record,* Extensions of Remarks, vol. 147, part 23 (8 December 1981), 30037–39.

71. Little interview.

72. Jeffords interview.

73. *Farmland Protection Policy Act* (Public Law 97–98), *U.S. Statutes at Large* 95 (1981): 1341–44.

74. U.S. Congress, House, Committee on Agriculture, Subcommittee on Conservation, Credit, and Rural Development, *General Farm Bill of 1981,* 7.

75. Quoted in Sinclair, "Farmers Losing Their Land," A4.

76. Block to Helms, Chairman, Committee on Agriculture, Nutrition, and Forestry, 23 June 1983, Executive Correspondence, USDA.

77. U.S. Department of Agriculture, Soil Conservation Service, "Proposed Rule," *Federal Register* 48 (12 July 1983): 31863–66. For more on LESA, see Wright et al., "LESA," 82–86.

78. Anthan, "Block Orders Release," A1, A9; Anthan, "Jepsen Confronts USDA," A1, A4; for further indications of congressional pressure see Roger Jepsen et al. to Block, 9 April 1984, Executive Correspondence, USDA.

79. Zitzmann, "FPPA Fadeout," 14–15. See also U.S. Department of Agriculture, Soil Conservation Service, "Farmland Protection Policy: Final Rule," *Federal Register* 49 (5 July 1984): 27716–27, and Dunford, *Development and Current Status,* 21–25.

80. Memo, Bob [Gray] to Jim [Jeffords], "Announcement of Final Rule on Farmland Protection Policy Act," n.d., personal files of Jeffords.

81. Bob Bergland quoted in U.S. Congress, House, Committee on Agriculture, Subcommittee on Forests, Family Farms, and Energy, *Structure of Agriculture, Hearings,* 40.

Conclusion

1. See Bonnen, "Observations on the Changing Nature," 309–27; Fite, *American Farmers.*

2. Paarlberg, "Changing Policy Environment," 8.

3. Schwab, "Attraction Is Chemical," 416.

4. Berg, correspondence with the author; Myers, "Conservation at the Crossroads," 10; Cook, "Environmental Era," 362–66.

5. Cook, "Environmental Era," 362.

6. Batie, "Soil Conservation," 116–18.

7. U.S. Department of Agriculture, *Soil, Water, and Related Resources*, 61–64; U.S. Department of Agriculture, *1982 National Resources Inventory*; U.S. General Accounting Office, *Agriculture's Soil Conservation Programs*; National Research Council, Board of Agriculture, *Soil Conservation*, 11, 166.

8. Clark and Haverkamp, *Off-Farm Costs*; see also Nielsen and Lee, *Magnitude and Costs of Groundwater Contamination*; Erwin, "Regulating Water Quality," 65–66; Chesters and Schierow, "Primer on Nonpoint Pollution," 9–13; Duda, "Environmental and Economic Damage," 225–34.

9. Buttel and Swanson, "Soil and Water Conservation," 26–39; Benbrook, Crosson, and Ogg, "Resource Dimensions of Agricultural Policy," 351–75.

10. Jepsen quoted in Galston, *Tough Row to Hoe*, 10, 12; Penn, "Agricultural Structural Issues," 572–76; Guither and Falcrow, *American Farm Crisis*, 77; U.S. General Accounting Office, *Farm Programs*; Rauch, "Farmers' Discord," 2535–39; Luzar, "Natural Resource Management in Agriculture," 563–69.

11. Benbrook, "Integrating Soil Conservation," 160–67; McSweeny and Kramer, "Integration of Farm Programs," 159–73.

12. Grossi, "Politics of Choice," 403.

13. Quoted in Reilly, "Agriculture and Conservation," 14.

14. Larry Gale to Peter Myers, 13 December 1985, Executive Correspondence, USDA.

15. Cook, "Pinch Me," 93–94; Zinn and Carr, "1985 Farm Act," 17–18.

16. John Campbell, USDA Deputy Undersecretary, in U.S. Congress, House, Committee on Agriculture, Subcommittee on Conservation, Credit, and Rural Development, *Formulation of the 1990 Farm Bill*, 3; Ribaudo et al., "CRP," 421–24; Ervin, "Implementing the Conservation Title," 367–70.

17. Grossi, "Implementing CRP," 20–21; Cook, in *Formulation of the 1990 Farm Bill*, 32.

18. Hays, "Political Choice," 124–54; Berg, correspondence with the author, 5 May 1993, confirmed the ongoing interest of the "conservation coalition" in the implementation phase.

19. Ervin and Dicks, "Cropland Diversion," 265–66; Reichelderfer and Boggess, "Government Decision-Making," 1–11; Steiner, *Soil Conservation*, 176; U.S. General Accounting Office, *Conservation Reserve Program*, 2–5.

20. Clark and Johnson, "Implementing the Conservation Title," 29–34; Steiner, *Soil Conservation*, 176; U.S. General Accounting Office, *Conservation Reserve Program*, 2.

21. U.S. Department of Agriculture, Forest Service, *Impacts of the Conservation Reserve Program*; Harris, Habiger, and Carpenter, "Conservation Title," 371–75; Ervin, "Implementing the Conservation Title," 367–70; Dicks, Hyberg, and Hebert, "Implications of Current and Proposed Environmental Policies," 59–60.

22. Clark and Johnson, "Implementing the Conservation Title," 35–36; Mortensen et al., "Analysis of Baseline Characteristics," 141.

23. See the arguments of the National Wildlife Federation and the American Farmland Trust in *Formulation of the 1990 Farm Bill*; Laycock, "History of Grassland Plowing," 3–18; Reichenberger, "CRP," 16–17.

24. Steiner, *Soil Conservation*, 177.

25. U.S. Congress, Senate, Committee on Agriculture, Nutrition, and Forestry, Subcommittee on Nutrition and Investigations, *Soil Conservation Service's Implementation,* 35–40, 102–12; Clark and Johnson, "Implementing the Conservation Title," 40, 41.

26. Steiner, *Soil Conservation,* 178.

27. Zinn, "Conservation in the 1990 Farm Bill," 45–48; Cloud, "Environmentalists, Farmers Square Off," 830.

28. Marty Strange, quoted in U.S. Congress, Senate, Committee on Agriculture, Nutrition, and Forestry, Subcommittee on Nutrition and Investigations, *Soil Conservation Service's Implementation,* 112.

29. Richards, "Global Cropland Conversion," 8.

30. Lester Brown, "Soils and Civilizations," 18–24; Hrabovszky, "Agriculture," 223–28; Eckholm, *Losing Ground,* 25–46, 58–73.

31. Freeman, "Perspectives and Prospects," 5–7; Lester Brown, "Global Competition for Land," 394–97.

32. Shaw, "Climate Change," 286–88; Rosenberg et al., *Policy Options*; Udall, "Nature under Glass," 34–40; U.S. Congress, Senate, Committee on Agriculture, Nutrition, and Forestry, *Potential Impact.*

33. Rosenberg et al., *Policy Options,* 3–4; Adams et al., "Global Climate Change," 219–23; Karl et al., "Greenhouse Effect," 1058–60; Opie, "Drought of 1988," 279–306.

34. Opie, "Drought of 1988," 295.

35. Pimental et al., "World Agriculture," 277–81; National Research Council, *Alternative Agriculture,* 115–16; National Research Council, *Soil Conservation*; Crosson and Stout, *Productivity Effects,* 3; Larsen, Pierce, and Dowdy, "Threat of Soil Erosion," 219–465; Conservation Foundation, *Agriculture and the Environment,* 18.

36. Lester Brown, "Global Competition for Land," 394–95.

37. National Research Council, *Alternative Agriculture,* 50–53, 109–14; Conservation Foundation, *Agriculture and the Environment,* 10; U.S. Department of Agriculture, *Agricultural Resources.*

38. Pimental and Pimental, "Energy and Other Natural Resources," 266–69; Lovins, Lovins, and Bender, "Energy and Agriculture," 68–69; Schusky, *Culture and Agriculture,* 114–19.

39. National Research Council, *Alternative Agriculture,* 40–41.

40. Power and Follert, "Monoculture," 78–86; Altieri, *Agroecology,* 163–71.

41. Pimental et al., "Environmental and Economic Effects," 403; Fowler and Mooney, *Shattering,* 47–49; National Research Council, *Alternative Agriculture,* 120.

42. National Academy of Sciences, *Genetic Vulnerability,* 287; Batie and Healy, "American Agriculture," 26.

43. Conservation Foundation, *Agriculture and the Environment,* 23; U.S. Department of Agriculture, *Agricultural Resources.*

44. Reichelderfer and Hinkle, "Evolution of Pesticide Policy," 155–59; Conservation Foundation, *Agriculture and the Environment,* 25–30; National Research Council, *Alternative Agriculture,* 98–107; Stanfield, "Legalized Poisons," 1062–66.

45. Tiner, *Wetlands of the United States,* 31; Menzel, "Agricultural Management Practices," 305–29.

46. Phipps and Crosson, "Agriculture and the Environment," 10.

47. Lynd, *Knowledge for What?,* especially chap. 6.

48. Ball, "Politics of Social Science," 92; Lynn, Jr., "Introduction," 1.

49. Kirkendall, *Social Scientists,* 195–227.

50. Weiss, "Introduction," 8.

51. Aaron, *Politics and the Professors,* 17.

52. Carol Weiss has written extensively on this point and, in contrast to Aaron, sees social science as having a largely positive influence on policymaking. She refers to this theory as the "enlightenment" model of social science research and suggests a role for social scientists as social critics: "What social science research can do is counteract the mustiness in the corridors of power with critical insights and sharp new perspectives. In its role as critic, social science may provide its most valuable, and valued, contribution. Even if it does not prevail, it offers officials a conceptual language with which to rethink accustomed practice." Weiss, *Social Science Research,* 270; see also Weiss, "Research for Policy's Sake," 521–45.

53. Aaron, *Politics and the Professors,* 159, 156.

54. Ibid., 32.

55. Lampman, "What Does It Do?," 66–82; Haveman, *Poverty Policy,* 163–64.

56. Aaron, *Politics and the Professors,* 98; see also Weiss and Bucuvalas, "Challenge of Research," 213–29.

57. Hadwiger, *Politics of Agricultural Research*; Busch and Lacy, *Science, Agriculture, and the Politics of Research.*

58. Brewer, "Changing U.S. Farmland Scene," 3.

59. Fischel, "Urbanization of Agricultural Land," 258.

60. See, for example, DeGrove, *Land Growth and Politics*; Popper, "Understanding American Land Use," 291–301; Freedgood, "PDR Programs," 329–31; Daniels and Nelson, "Is Oregon's Farmland Preservation Program Working?," 22–31; Peirce, "Land Trusts," 1619; Furuseth, "Public Attitudes," 49–61.

61. Examples include Lockeretz, "Secondary Effects," 205–16; Johnston and Bryant, "Agricultural Adaptation"; Vail, "Suburbanization of the Countryside."

62. Peiser, "Density and Urban Sprawl," 193–204.

63. Sundquist, "Where Shall They Live?," 97.

64. Nietzsche, *Use and Abuse,* 5, 21, 8.

65. Otis L. Graham, "Uses and Misuses of History," 373; for a fuller elaboration of these themes see Graham, Jr., *Losing Time,* especially chap. 11.

66. Hugh Davis Graham, "Stunted Career of Policy History," 19–22.

Bibliography

A Note on Sources

Although I received much cooperation in searching for written documentation for this study, I was disappointed in my search for the archival materials from the National Agricultural Lands Study. As an interagency orphan, the NALS had no logical depository for these records, and, as best as I can reconstruct, they have been lost simply because no one knew what to do with them. I questioned every major participant and looked in several closets and the attic of USDA but was able to find only that the boxes containing these papers were gone. Apparently Bob Gray supervised the cleanup of the NALS materials and had the boxes moved in the trunk of a car to the SCS office in the USDA building. They remained there for a while, shuffled through several closets and the attic, with no one sure of what to do with them. Eventually Bob Gray removed them, at Howard Tankersly's request; he took them to his Maryland home, then disposed of most of the materials. It came as a surprise to all concerned that anyone would actually want to read these materials. While some of the richness of detail and nuance of discourse is irretrievably lost for the historian, other sources, including interviews and personal records, were able to compensate in part for this loss.

Document Collections

Cutler, M. Rupert. Personal papers. Washington, D.C.

Executive Correspondence and Records. Official Secretary's Files. USDA. Washington, D.C.

Jeffords, James. Personal files. Washington, D.C.

Little, Charles. Personal papers. Bethesda, Md.

Office File 1. Franklin D. Roosevelt Library. Hyde Park, N.Y.

Office File 732. Franklin D. Roosevelt Library. Hyde Park, N.Y.

Office File 1017. Franklin D. Roosevelt Library. Hyde Park, N.Y.

Record Group 16. Office of the Secretary of Agriculture. General Correspondence. National Archives. Washington, D.C.

Record Group 83. Bureau of Agricultural Economics. National Archives. Washington, D.C.

Record Group 114. Soil Conservation Service. Historic File. National Archives. Washington, D.C.

Record Group 187. Records of the Land Section. National Resources Planning Board. Washington, D.C.

Sampson, R. Neil. Personal papers. National Association of Conservation Districts. Washington, D.C.

Tankersly, Howard. Records of the Committee on Land Use, USDA. Washington, D.C.

White House Central File. Jimmy Carter Library. Atlanta, Ga.

Zitzmann, Warren. Personal papers. Land Use Staff, Soil Conservation Service, USDA. Washington, D.C.

204   Interviews by Author

Bibliography

Anderson, William D. Economic Research Service, USDA. 20 October 1983, Washington, D.C.

Berg, Norman. Soil Conservation Service, USDA, more recently of the American Farmland Trust. 2 December 1982, additional correspondence on 5 May 1993 and 18 May 1993, Washington, D.C.

Bergland, Robert. Secretary of Agriculture, USDA. 30 January 1984, Washington D.C.

Boxley, Robert F. Economic Research Service, USDA. 19 October 1983, Washington, D.C.

Brewer, Michael. Research Director, National Agricultural Lands Study. 20 October 1983, Washington, D.C.

Cotner, Melvin. Chief, Economic Research Service, USDA. 19 October 1983, Washington, D.C.

Crosson, Pierre. Resources for the Future. 2 December 1982, Washington, D.C.

Cutler, M. Rupert. Assistant Secretary, USDA. 9 April 1985, Washington, D.C.

Fletcher, W. Wendell. Congressional Research Service. 2 December 1982, Washington, D.C.

Frey, Thomas. Economic Research Service, USDA. 19 October 1983, Washington, D.C.

Gray, Robert. Director, National Agricultural Lands Study. 3 December 1982 and 20 October 1983, Washington, D.C.

Jeffords, James. Representative, later Senator from Vermont. 14 June 1989, Washington, D.C.

Little, Charles. Congressional Research Service and American Land Resource Association. January 1983, Bethesda, Md.

Sampson, R. Neil. Soil Conservation Service and National Association of Conservation Districts. 3 December 1982, Washington, D.C.

Smythe, Robert. Council on Environmental Quality. 24 March 1983, Chapel Hill, N.C.

Tankersly, Howard. Land Use Coordinator, Soil Conservation Service. 19 October 1983. Washington, D.C.

Zitzmann, Warren. Land Use Staff, Soil Conservation Service, USDA. 2 December 1982, Washington, D.C.

Government Documents

Advisory Commission on Intergovernmental Relations. *Urban and Rural America: Policies for Future Growth.* Washington: Government Printing Office, 1968.

Barlowe, Raleigh. "Our Future Needs for Nonfarm Lands." In *Yearbook of Agriculture 1958*, 474–79. Washington: Government Printing Office, 1958.

Beale, Calvin L. *The Revival of Population Growth in Non-Metropolitan America.* Washington: USDA, 1975.

Bennett, Hugh H., and W. R. Chapline. *Soil Erosion—A National Menace.* Washington: USDA Circular No. 33, 1928. Reprinted in Wayne D. Rasmussen, ed., *Agricultural History in the United States: A Documentary History.* New York: Random House, 1975.

Bogue, Donald J. *Metropolitan Growth and the Conversion of Land to Nonagricultural Uses.* Washington: USDA, 1956.

Bossleman, Fred, and David Callies. *The Quiet Revolution in Land Use Control.* Washington: Government Printing Office, 1971.

Boxley, Robert F. "The Competition for Agricultural Land to the Year 2000." In *Agricultural Land Availability, Papers on the Supply and Demand for Agricultural Lands in the United States,* 103–86. U.S. Senate. Committee on Agriculture, Nutrition, and Forestry, 1981.

Carter, Jimmy. "Environmental Priorities and Programs, Message to Congress, August 2, 1979." *Public Papers of the Presidents of the United States, 1979,* Book 2. Washington: Government Printing Office, 1980.

Commission on Population Growth and the American Future. *Population Growth and the American Future.* Washington: Government Printing Office, 1972.

Cooper, Thomas P. "Extent and Emergence Character of Problems of Submarginal Land." In *Proceedings of a National Conference on Land Utilization.* Washington: Government Printing Office, 1932.

Cotner, Melvin L. *Land Use Policy and Agriculture: A State and Local Perspective.* Washington: USDA, 1977.

Council on Environmental Quality. *Environmental Quality, 1970.* Washington: Government Printing Office, 1970.

———. *Environmental Quality, 1973.* Washington: Government Printing Office, 1973.

———. *Environmental Quality, 1977.* Washington: Government Printing Office, 1977.

———. *Untaxing Open Space: An Evaluation of the Effectiveness of Differential Assessment of Farms and Open Space.* Washington: Government Printing Office, 1976.

Dideriksen, Raymond, Allen R. Hidlebaugh, and Keith Schmude. *Potential Cropland Study.* Washington: USDA, Soil Conservation Service, 1977.

Dunford, Richard W. *The Development and Current Status of Federal Farmland Retention Policy.* Washington: Library of Congress, Congressional Research Service, 1984.

Durost, Donald D., and Evelyn T. Black. *Changes in Farm Production and Efficiency.* Washington: USDA, Economic Research Service, 1977.

Ely, Richard T. "Adjusting the Tax Burden to the Tax Paying Ability of the Tax Bearer." In *Proceedings of a National Conference on Land Utilization.* Washington: Government Printing Office, 1932.

————. "A National Policy for Land Utilization." In *Report of the National Agricultural Conference,* 112–16. Washington: Government Printing Office, 1922.

Federal Energy Administration and USDA. *Energy and U.S. Agriculture: 1974 Data Base.* Washington: Government Printing Office, 1976.

Final Report. White House Conference on Balanced Growth and Economic Development. Volumes 1 and 2. Washington: Government Printing Office, 1978.

Fletcher, W. Wendell. *Agricultural Land Retention: An Analysis of the Issue, a Survey of Recent and Local Farmland Retention Programs, and a Discussion of Proposed Federal Legislation.* Washington: Congressional Research Service, 1978.

Foster, Ellery A., and Harold A. Vogel. "Cooperative Land Use Planning—A New Development in Democracy." In *Farmers in a Changing World: Yearbook of Agriculture 1940,* 1144–49. Washington: Government Printing Office, 1940.

Freeman, Orville. "The Citizen's Stake in Soil and Water Management." In *Soil, Water, and Suburbia,* 12–19. Washington: Government Printing Office, 1968.

Frey, H. Thomas. *Expansion of Urban Area in the United States: 1960–1980.* Washington: USDA, Economic Research Service, Natural Resource Economics Division, 1983.

————. *Major Uses of Land in the United States: 1974.* Washington: USDA, Economics, Statistics, and Cooperatives Service, 1979.

Frey, H. Thomas, and Robert C. Otte. *Cropland for Today and Tomorrow.* Washington: USDA, Economic Research Service, 1975.

Gaffney, M. Mason. "Urban Expansion—Will It Ever Stop?" In *Yearbook of Agriculture 1958,* 503–23. Washington: Government Printing Office, 1958.

Glick, Philip. "The Soil and the Law." In *Soils and Men: 1938 Yearbook of Agriculture,* 296–318. Washington: Government Printing Office, 1938.

Gray, L. C. "Land-Utilization Problem, Intensified by Depression." In *Yearbook of Agriculture 1932,* 457–78. Washington: Government Printing Office, 1932.

————, et al. "Report of the Committee on Land Utilization." In *1923 Yearbook of Agriculture,* 415–506. Washington: Government Printing Office, 1924.

Hady, Thomas. "Differential Assessment of Open Space and Farmland." In *Agriculture, Rural Development, and the Use of Land,* 83–91. U.S. Congress, Senate, Committee on Agriculture and Forestry, Subcommittee on Rural Development, 93d Congress, 2d sess., 1974.

Helms, Douglas. "The Development of the Land Capability Classification." In *Readings in the History of the Soil Conservation Service,* ed. Douglas Helms, 60–73. Washington: Government Printing Office, 1992.

————. "The Great Plains Conservation Program, 1956–1981." In *Readings in the History of the Soil Conservation Service,* ed. Douglas Helms, 140–57. Washington: Government Printing Office, 1992.

————, ed. *Readings in the History of the Soil Conservation Service.* Washington: Soil Conservation Service, 1992.

Horsfall, James G. "A Fire Brigade Stops a Raging Epidemic." In *That We May Eat: 1975 Yearbook of Agriculture,* 105–15. Washington: Government Printing Office, 1975.

Hyde, Arthur M. "Developing a National Policy of Land Utilization." In *Pro-*

ceedings of a National Conference on Land Utilization, 34–38. Washington: Government Printing Office, 1932.

Johnson, Hugh A. "Planning for the New Land Frontier." In *Yearbook of Agriculture 1958,* 568–83. Washington: Government Printing Office, 1958.

Knight, H. G. "Soil Conservation as a Major Problem of Agricultural Readjustment." In *Proceedings of a National Conference on Land Utilization,* 149–56. Washington: Government Printing Office, 1932.

Ladd, C. E. "New York's Land Utilization Program." In *Proceedings of a National Conference on Land Utilization,* 52–59. Washington: Government Printing Office, 1932.

Laycock, W. A. "History of Grassland Plowing and Grassland Planting on the Great Plains." In *Impacts of the Conservation Reserve Program on the Great Plains,* 3–18. USDA, Forest Service, 1988.

Lee, Linda K. *A Perspective on Cropland Availability.* Washington: Economics, Statistics, and Cooperatives Service of the USDA, 1978.

McClintock, David. "Global Significance of U.S. Cropland." In *Agricultural Land Availability, Papers on the Supply and Demand for Agricultural Lands in the United States,* 217–34. U.S. Senate, Committee on Agriculture, Nutrition, and Forestry, 1981.

McDonald, Angus. *Early American Soil Conservationists.* Washington: USDA Miscellaneous Publication No. 449, 1941.

National Agricultural Lands Study. *Final Report.* Washington: Government Printing Office, 1981.

―――. *The Protection of Farmland: A Reference Guidebook for State and Local Governments.* Washington: Government Printing Office, 1981.

―――. *Where Have All the Farmlands Gone?* Washington: Government Printing Office, 1979.

"National Land-Utilization Program: Summary and Conclusions." In *Proceedings of a National Conference on Land Utilization,* 240–49. Washington: Government Printing Office. 1932.

National Research Council. Board of Agriculture. *Soil Conservation: Assessing the National Resource Inventory Volume 2.* Washington: National Academy Press, 1986.

National Resources Board. *Report on National Planning and Public Works in Relation to Natural Resources and Including Land Use and Water Resources with Findings and Recommendations.* Washington: Government Printing Office, 1934.

―――. *Soil Erosion: A Critical Problem in American Agriculture.* Part 5 of the Supplementary Report of the Land Planning Committee. Washington: Government Printing Office, 1935.

―――. *Supplemental Reports of the Land Planning Committee.* Washington: Government Printing Office, 1936.

National Resources Committee. *The Problems of a Changing Population.* Washington: Government Printing Office, 1938.

―――. *Progress Report—June 15, 1936.* Washington: Government Printing Office, 1936.

————. *Progress Report—December 1938*. Washington: Government Printing Office, 1936.

————. *Progress Report 1939*. Washington: Government Printing Office, 1939.

National Resources Planning Board. *Federal Relations to Local Planning*. Circular No. 14. Washington: Government Printing Office, 1939.

————. *Public Land Acquisition*. Washington: Government Printing Office, 1940.

National Water Commission. *Water Policies for the Future*. Washington: Government Printing Office, 1973.

Nielsen, Elizabeth G., and Linda K. Lee. *The Magnitude and Costs of Groundwater Contamination from Agricultural Chemicals: A National Perspective*. Washington: USDA, Economic Research Service, 1987.

Otte, Robert C. *Farming in the City's Shadow*. Washington: USDA, Economic Research Service, 1974.

President's Materials Policy Commission. *Resources for Freedom*. Washington: Government Printing Office, 1952.

Proceedings of a National Conference on Land Utilization. Washington: Government Printing Office, 1932.

Real Estate Research Corporation. *The Costs of Sprawl*. Washington: Government Printing Office, 1974.

Report of the National Agricultural Conference. Washington: Government Printing Office, 1922.

Rodwin, Lloyd, and Lawrence Susskind. "Land-Use Research Issues Suggested by a National Urban Growth Strategy." In *Environment: A New Focus for Land-Use Planning*. Washington: Government Printing Office for the National Science Foundation, 1973.

Schmude, Keith O. *Development of Nationwide Resources Inventories in the United States*. Washington: Soil Conservation Service, 1988.

Tiner, Ralph W. *Wetlands of the United States: Current Status and Recent Trends*. Washington: Government Printing Office, 1984.

U.S. Bureau of the Census. *Historical Statistics of the United States, Colonial Times to 1970, Bicentennial Edition, Part 2*. Washington: Government Printing Office, 1975.

————. *1978 Census of Agriculture, Irrigation*. Washington: Government Printing Office, 1982.

————. *Statistical Abstract of the United States: 1986*. Washington: Government Printing Office, 1985.

U.S. Congress. House. Committee on Agriculture. *Agricultural Land Protection Act, Hearings*. 96th Congress, 1st sess., 1979.

————. *Agricultural Land Protection Act, Report*. 96th Congress, 1st sess., 1979.

————. *Agricultural Land Retention Act, Report*. 95th Congress, 2d sess., 1978.

————. Subcommittee on Conservation, Credit, and Rural Development. *Formulation of the 1990 Farm Bill (Conservation Title)*. 101st Congress, 1st sess., 1990.

————. *General Farm Bill of 1981, Part 6, Hearings*. 97th Congress, 1st sess., 1981.

U.S. Congress. House. Committee on Agriculture. Subcommittee on Department Operations. *World Population and Food Supply and Demand Situation, Hearings.* 93d Congress, 2d sess., 1974.

————. Subcommittee on Family Farms, Rural Development, and Special Studies. *Agricultural Land Protection Act of 1979, Hearings.* 96th Congress, 1st sess., 1979.

————. Subcommittee on Forests, Family Farms, and Energy. *Structure of Agriculture, Hearings.* 97th Congress, 1st sess., 1981.

U.S. Congress. House. Committee on Banking, Currency, and Housing. Subcommittee on Housing and Community Development. *National Growth and Development, Hearings.* 94th Congress, 1st sess., 1975.

————. Committee on Interior and Insular Affairs. *Land Use and Resource Conservation, Hearings.* 94th Congress, 1st sess., 1975.

————. Subcommittee on Energy and the Environment. *Reclamation Practices and Environmental Problems of Surface Mining, Hearings.* 95th Congress, 1st sess., 1977, parts 1–4.

————. Subcommittee on the Environment. *Land Use Planning Act of 1974, Hearings.* 93d Congress, 2d sess., 1974.

————. *National Land Use Planning, Hearings.* 92d Congress, 1st sess., 1971.

U.S. Congress. House. Select Committee on Hunger. *Population Growth and Hunger.* 98th Congress, 2d sess., 1984.

————. Subcommittee of the Committee on Public Lands. *Hearings.* 74th Congress, 1st sess., 1935.

U.S. Congress. House and Senate. *Congressional Record.* Volumes 123 to 127. 1973 to 1981.

U.S. Congress. Senate. *Report of the Commission on Country Life.* Document No. 705, 60th Congress, 2d sess., 1909.

————. *Report of the National Conservation Commission.* 60th Congress, 2d sess., 1909.

————. Committee on Agriculture and Forestry. Subcommittee on Rural Development. *Agriculture, Rural Development, and the Use of Land.* 93d Congress, 2d sess., 1974.

————. Committee on Agriculture, Nutrition, and Forestry. *Agricultural Land Availability, Papers on the Supply and Demand for Agricultural Lands in the United States.* 97th Congress, 1st sess., 1981.

————. *The Potential Impact of Global Warming on Agriculture.* 100th Congress, 2d sess., 1 December 1988.

————. Subcommittee on Environment, Soil Conservation, and Forestry. *Farmlands Protection Act, Hearings.* 96th Congress, 1st sess., 1979.

————. *Protection and Enhancement of Soil and Water Resources, Hearings.* 95th Congress, 1st sess., 1977.

U.S. Congress. Senate. Committee on Agriculture, Nutrition, and Forestry. Subcommittee on Nutrition and Investigations. *The Soil Conservation Service's Implementation of the Soil Conservation Provisions of the Food Security Act of 1985.* 100th Congress, 2d sess., 1989.

————. Committee on Interior and Insular Affairs. *Land Resource Planning Assistance Act and the Energy Facilities Planning and Development Act, Hearings.* 94th Congress, 1st sess., 1975.

————. *Land Use Policy and Planning Assistance Act, Hearings.* 93d Congress, 1st sess., 1973.

————. *Land Use Policy and Planning Assistance Act, Report.* 93d Congress, 1st sess., 1973.

————. *National Land Use Policy, Hearings.* 92d Congress, 1st sess., 1971.

————. *Stockpile and Accessibility of Strategic and Critical Materials to the United States in Time of War.* Staff Study of the Paley Commission Report. 83d Congress, 2d sess.

U.S. Congress. Senate. Select Committee on Small Business. *The Preservation and Control of Farmland, Hearings.* 96th Congress, 1st sess., 1979.

U.S. Department of Agriculture. *Agricultural Statistics 1985.* Washington: Government Printing Office, 1985.

————. *Agricultural Yearbook 1923.* Washington: Government Printing Office, 1924.

————. *Basic Statistics of the National Inventory of Soil and Water Conservation Needs.* Washington: USDA, 1962.

————. *Basic Statistics—National Inventory of Soil and Water Conservation Needs, 1967.* Washington: USDA, 1971.

————. *Farmers in a Changing World: Yearbook of Agriculture 1940.* Washington: Government Printing Office, 1940.

————. *National Growth and Its Distribution.* Washington: USDA, 1967.

————. *A National Program for Soil and Water Conservation.* Washington: USDA, 1982.

————. *The 1982 National Resources Inventory.* Washington: Soil Conservation Service, 1984.

————. *Perspectives on Prime Lands: Background Papers for a Seminar on the Retention of Prime Lands, July 16–17, 1975.* Washington: Government Printing Office, 1975.

————. *Recommendations on Prime Lands.* Washington: Government Printing Office, 1975.

————. *Soil, Water, and Related Resources in the United States: Status, Conditions, and Trends.* Washington: Government Printing Office, 1981.

————. *Soil and Water Conservation Needs—A National Inventory.* Washington: USDA, 1965.

————. *Soil and Water Resources Conservation Act, 1980 Appraisal, Part 1.* Washington: USDA, 1981.

————. *Soils and Men: 1938 Yearbook of Agriculture.* Washington: USDA, 1938.

————. *That We May Eat: Yearbook of Agriculture 1975.* Washington: USDA, 1975.

————. *A Time to Choose: Summary Report on the Structure of Agriculture.* Washington: USDA, 1981.

————. *Will There Be Enough Food? 1981 Yearbook of Agriculture.* Washington: USDA, 1981.

————. *Yearbook of Agriculture 1932.* Washington: USDA, 1932.

————. *Yearbook of Agriculture 1958.* Washington: USDA, 1958.

————. Economic Research Service. *Farm Real Estate Historical Series Data: 1850–1970.* Washington: Government Printing Office, 1973.

————. Forest Service. *Impacts of the Conservation Reserve Program in the Great Plains.* Washington: Government Printing Office, 1988.

————. Soil Conservation Service. *Basic Statistics: 1977 National Resources Inventory.* Washington: USDA, 1982.

————. "Farmland Protection Policy: Final Rule." *Federal Register* 49 (5 July 1984): 27716–27.

————. "Proposed Rule." *Federal Register* 48 (12 July 1983): 31863–66.

U.S. Department of Agriculture and Department of Housing and Urban Development. *Soil, Water, and Suburbia.* Washington: Government Printing Office, 1968.

U.S. General Accounting Office. *Agriculture's Soil Conservation Programs Miss Full Potential in the Fight against Soil Erosion.* Washington: Government Printing Office, 1983.

————. *Conservation Reserve Program Could Be Less Costly and More Effective.* Washington: General Accounting Office, 1989.

————. *Farm Programs: An Overview of Price Support, Income Support, and Storage Programs.* Washington: General Accounting Office, 1988.

————. *Preserving America's Farmland—A Goal the Federal Government Should Support.* Washington: Government Printing Office, 1977.

————. *To Protect Tomorrow's Food Supply, Soil Conservation Needs Priority Attention.* Washington: Government Printing Office, 1977.

Wehrwein, George S., et al. "The Remedies: Policies for Private Lands." In *Soils and Men: 1938 Yearbook of Agriculture,* 241–45. Washington: Government Printing Office, 1938.

Whyte, William. "The Land and Water Squeeze on Our Food." In *Will There Be Enough Food? 1981 Yearbook of Agriculture,* 131–56. Washington: Government Printing Office, 1981.

Wilson, M. L. "Foreword." In *The Land Utilization Program, 1934–1964: Origins, Development, and Present Status,* i. Washington: USDA, Economic Research Service, 1965.

Wood, Robert C. "Soil, Water, and Suburbia." In *Soil, Water, and Suburbia,* 1–10. Washington: Government Printing Office, 1968.

Wooten, H. H. *The Land Utilization Program, 1934 to 1964: Origins, Development, and Present Status.* Washington: USDA, Economic Research Service, 1965.

Zeimetz, Kathryn, et al. *Dynamics of Land Use in Fast Growth Areas.* Washington: USDA, Economic Research Service, 1976.

Other Sources

Aaron, Henry J. *Politics and the Professors: The Great Society in Perspective.* Washington: Brookings Institution, 1978.

Adams, Richard M., et al. "Global Climate Change and U.S. Agriculture." *Nature* 345 (17 May 1990): 219–23.

Albee, Roger. "Letters." *Journal of Soil and Water Conservation* 37 (September–October 1982): 243.

Albers, J. M. "Progress in County Zoning." *Journal of Land and Public Utility Economics* 16 (November 1940): 393–402.

Albertson, Dean. *Roosevelt's Farmer: Claude R. Wickard in the New Deal.* New York: Columbia University Press, 1961.

Altieri, Miguel A. *Agroecology: The Scientific Basis of Alternative Agriculture.* Boulder: Westview Press, 1987.

Anderson, William D., Gregory C. Gustafson, and Robert F. Boxley. "Perspectives on Agricultural Land Policy." *Journal of Soil and Water Conservation* 30 (January–February 1975): 36–43.

Andrews, Richard N. L., ed. *Land in America: Commodity or Natural Resource?* Lexington, Mass.: D. C. Heath, 1979.

Anthan, George. "Block Orders Release of Farmland Rules." *Des Moines Register,* 23 June 1984, A1, A9.

———. "House Kills Weakened Bill to Help Preserve Farmland." *Des Moines Register,* 8 February 1980, A1, A10.

———. "HUD Tries to Block Cropland-Saving Order." *Des Moines Register,* 22 October 1981, A1, A9.

———. "Jepsen Confronts USDA over Delay in Farmland Act." *Des Moines Register,* 21 June 1981, A1, A4.

———. "Vanishing Acres." *Des Moines Register,* 8–15 July 1979.

Arnold, Peri E. *Making the Managerial Presidency: Comprehensive Reorganization Planning, 1905–1980.* Princeton: Princeton University Press, 1986.

Atkinson, Glen W. "The Effectiveness of Differential Assessment of Agricultural and Open Space Land." *American Journal of Economics and Sociology* 36 (April 1977): 197–204.

Baden, John, ed. *The Vanishing Farmland Crisis: Critical Views of the Movement to Preserve Agricultural Land.* Lawrence: Published for the Political Economy Research Center, Bozeman, Mt., by the University Press of Kansas, 1984.

Baker, O. E. "Changes in Production and Consumption of Our Farm Products and the Trend in Population." *Annals of the American Academy of Political and Social Science* 142 (March 1929): 97–146.

Baldwin, Sidney. *Poverty and Politics: The Rise and Decline of the Farm Security Administration.* Chapel Hill: University of North Carolina Press, 1968.

Ball, Terence. "The Politics of Social Science in Postwar America." In *Recasting America: Culture and Politics in the Age of the Cold War,* ed. Lary May, 76–92. Chicago: University of Chicago Press, 1989.

Balogh, Brian. *Chain Reaction: Expert Debate and Public Participation in American Commercial Nuclear Power.* Cambridge: Cambridge University Press, 1991.

———. "Reorganizing the Organizational Synthesis: Federal-Professional Relations in Modern America." *Studies in American Political Development* 5 (Spring 1991): 119–72.

Barlowe, Raleigh. *Land Resource Economics: The Economics of Real Property.* Englewood Cliffs, N.J.: Prentice Hall, 1972.

Batie, Sandra S. "Soil Conservation in the 1980s: A Historical Perspective." *Agricultural History* 59 (April 1985): 116–18.

Batie, Sandra S., and Robert G. Healy. "The Future of American Agriculture." *Scientific American* 248 (February 1983): 45–53.

———, eds. *The Future of American Agriculture as a Strategic Resource.* Washington: Conservation Foundation, 1980.

Bavel, Cornelius H. M. "Soil and Oil." *Science* 197 (15 July 1977): 3.

Beale, Calvin L. "The Population Turnaround in Rural Small-Town America." In *Rural Policy: Changing Dimensions,* ed. William P. Browne and Don F. Hadwiger, 47–59. Lexington, Mass.: D. C. Heath, 1982.

Bean, Frank D. "The Baby Boom and Its Explanations." *Sociological Quarterly* 24 (Summer 1983): 353–65.

Benbrook, Charles. "Integrating Soil Conservation and Commodity Programs: A Policy Proposal." *Journal of Soil and Water Conservation* 34 (July–August 1979): 160–67.

Benbrook, Charles M., Pierre R. Crosson, and Clayton Ogg. "Resource Dimensions of Agricultural Policy." In *Alternative Agricultural and Food Policies and the 1985 Farm Bill,* ed. Gordon C. Rausser and Kenneth R. Farrell, 351–75. Washington: National Center for Food and Agricultural Policy, Resources for the Future, n.d.

Benedict, Murray R. *Farm Policies of the United States, 1790–1950.* New York: Twentieth Century Fund, 1953.

Bennett, Hugh Hammond. *Soil Conservation.* New York: McGraw Hill, 1939.

Bennett, Hugh Hammond, and W. R. Chapline. "Soil Erosion—A National Menace." Washington: USDA Circular No. 33, 1928. Reprinted in *Agricultural History in the United States: A Documentary History,* vol. 3, ed. Wayne D. Rasmussen. New York: Random House, 1975.

Berg, Norman. "Evolution of Land Use Policy in USDA." In *Farmland, Food, and the Future,* ed. Max Schnepf, 147–63. Ankenny, Iowa: Soil Conservation Society of America, 1979.

———. "Programs to Help People Make Land Use Choices." In *Land Use: Tough Choices in Today's World,* 42–46. Ankenny, Iowa: Soil Conservation Society of America, 1977.

Bergstrom, Georg. *The Hungry Planet: The Modern World at the Edge of Famine.* New York: Macmillan, 1965.

Berry, Brian J. L., and Donald Dahmann. *Population Redistribution in the United States in the 1970s.* Washington: National Academy of Sciences, 1977.

Berry, David, and Thomas Plaut. "Retaining Agricultural Activities under Urban Pressure: A Review of Land Use Conflicts and Policies." *Policy Sciences* 9 (April 1978): 153–178.

Berry, Wendell. *The Unsettling of America: Culture and Agriculture.* San Francisco: Sierra Club Books, 1977.

Bickers, Jack. "When Cities Nibble Away at Farmland." *Progressive Farmer,* August 1981, 15.

Black, John D., ed. "Research in Agricultural Land Utilization." *Social Science Research Council* bulletin no. 2 (June 1931): 3–9.

Bonnen, James T. "Observations on the Changing Nature of National Agricultural Policy Decision Processes, 1946–1976." In *Farmers, Bureaucrats, and*

Middlemen, ed. Trudy Huskamp Peterson, 309–27. Bloomington: Indiana University Press, 1981.

Bookchin, Murray. "Radical Agriculture." In *Radical Agriculture,* ed. Richard Merrill, 3–13. New York: Harper Colophon, 1976.

Borrows, Richard, and Douglas Yanggen. "The Wisconsin Farmland Preservation Program." *Journal of Soil and Water Conservation* 33 (September–October 1978): 209–12.

Bowers, Douglas E. "The Economic Research Service, 1961–1977." *Agricultural History* 64 (Spring 1990): 231–43.

Braeman, John, Robert H. Bremmer, and David Brody, eds. *The New Deal: The National Level.* Columbus: Ohio University Press, 1975.

Brewer, Michael. "The Changing U.S. Farmland Scene." *Population Bulletin* 36 (December 1981): 3–39.

Brewer, Michael, and Robert F. Boxley. "Agricultural Land: Adequacy of Acres, Concepts, and Information." *American Journal of Agricultural Economics* 63 (December 1981): 879–87.

Brink, R. A., J. W. Dunsmore, and G. A. Hill. "Soil Deterioration and the Growing World Demand for Food." *Science* 197 (12 August 1977): 629.

Brink, Wellington. *Big Hugh: The Father of Soil Conservation.* New York: Macmillan, 1951.

Brown, David L. "Agricultural Land Use: A Population Distribution Perspective." In *Farmland, Food, and the Future,* ed. Max Schnepf, 77–88. Ankeny, Iowa: Soil Conservation Society of America, 1979.

Brown, David L., and James J. Zuiches. "Rural-Urban Population Redistribution in the United States at the End of the Twentieth Century." In *The Demography of Rural Life,* ed. David L. Brown, Donald R. Field, and James J. Zuiches, 1–18. University Park, Pa.: Northeast Regional Center for Rural Development, 1993.

Brown, David L., Michael F. Brewer, Robert F. Boxley, and Calvin L. Beale. "Assessing Prospects for the Adequacy of Agricultural Land in the United States." *International Regional Science Review* 7, no. 3 (1982): 273–84.

Brown, Lester. *By Bread Alone.* New York: Praeger, 1974.

———. "The Global Competition for Land." *Journal of Soil and Water Conservation* 46 (November–December 1991): 394–97.

———. "Soils and Civilizations." *Audubon,* January 1982, 18–24.

———. *The Twenty-Ninth Day.* New York: W. W. Norton, 1978.

———. "Vanishing Croplands." *Environment* 20 (December 1978): 6–35.

Brubaker, Sterling. "Land—The Far Horizon." *American Journal of Agricultural Economics* 59 (December 1977): 1036–44.

Bryant, William R., and Howard E. Conklin. "New Farmland Preservation Programs in New York." *Journal of the American Institute of Planners* 41 (November 1975): 390–96.

Burner, David. *Herbert Hoover: A Public Life.* New York: Knopf, 1979.

Busch, Lawrence, and William B. Lacy. *Science, Agriculture, and the Politics of Research.* Boulder: Westview Press, 1983.

Buttel, Frederick R. *Environment, Energy and Society.* Belmont, California: Belmont Publishing Co., 1982.

Buttel, Frederick R., and Louis E. Swanson. "Soil and Water Conservation: A Farm Structural and Public Policy Context." In *Conserving Soil: Insights from Socioeconomic Research,* ed. Stephen B. Lovejoy and Ted L. Napier, 26–39. Ankenny, Iowa: Soil Conservation Society of America, 1986.

Callies, David L. "The Quiet Revolution Revisited." *Journal of the American Planning Association* 46 (April 1980): 135–44.

Carson, Rachel. *Silent Spring.* Boston: Houghton Mifflin, 1962.

Carter, Harold O., and Warren E. Johnston. "Structure, Organization, and Control of American Agriculture." *American Journal of Agricultural Economics* 60 (December 1978): 738–48.

Carter, Luther. "Land Use Law (I): Congress on the Verge of a Modest Beginning." *Science* 182 (16 November 1973): 691–97.

―――. "Soil Erosion—The Problem Persists Despite the Billions Spent on It." *Science* 195 (22 April 1977): 409–11.

Castle, Emery N. "Is There a Farmland Crisis?" *Christian Science Monitor,* 31 August 1981, A23.

Chase, Stuart. "The New Patriotism." *The Land* 1 (Summer 1941): 181–85.

Chesters, Gordon, and Linda-Jo Schierow. "A Primer on Nonpoint Pollution." *Journal of Soil and Water Conservation* 49 (January–February 1985): 9–13.

Christgau, Victor. "Adjustment for Production in Agriculture." *Journal of Farm Economics* 13 (January 1931): 1–8.

Clark, Edwin H., and Jennifer Haverkamp. *The Off-Farm Costs of Soil Erosion.* Washington: Conservation Foundation, 1985.

Clark, Janice M. "Agricultural Zoning in Black Hawk County, Iowa." In *Land Use: Tough Choices in Today's World,* 149–54. Ankenny, Iowa: Soil Conservation Society of America, 1977.

Clark, Richard T., and James B. Johnson. "Implementing the Conservation Title of the 1985 Food Security Act: Conservation or Politics?" In *Implementing the Conservation Title of the Food Security Act of 1985,* ed. Ted L. Napier. Ankenny, Iowa: Soil and Water Conservation Society, 1990.

Clawson, Marion. *New Deal Planning: The Natural Resources Planning Board.* Baltimore: Johns Hopkins University Press for Resources for the Future, 1984.

―――. "Preservation of Prime Agricultural Land." *Environmental Comment,* January 1978, 10.

―――. *Suburban Land Use Conversion in the United States: An Economic and Governmental Process.* Baltimore: Johns Hopkins University Press for Resources for the Future, 1971.

Clawson, Marion, Burnell R. Held, and Charles H. Stoddard. *Land for the Future.* Baltimore: Johns Hopkins University Press for Resources for the Future, 1960.

Cloud, David S. "Environmentalists, Farmers Square Off on Farm Bill." *Congressional Quarterly Weekly Report* 48 (17 March 1990): 830.

Cochrane, Willard W. *The Development of American Agriculture: A Historical Analysis.* Minneapolis: University of Minnesota Press, 1979.

―――. *The World Food Problem: A Guardedly Optimistic View.* New York: Thomas Y. Crowell Co., 1969.

Cochrane, Willard W., and Mary E. Ryan. *American Farm Policy, 1948–1973.* Minneapolis: University of Minnesota Press, 1976.

Cole, William E., and Hugh Price Crowe. *Recent Trends in Rural Planning.* New York: Prentice Hall, 1937.

Collins, Richard C. "Agricultural Land Preservation in a Land Use Planning Perspective." *Journal of Soil and Water Conservation* 31 (September–October 1976): 182–89.

Commission on Country Life. *Report of the Commission on Country Life.* New York: Sturgis and Walton, 1917.

Commoner, Barry. *The Poverty of Power: Energy and Economic Crisis.* New York: Knopf, 1976.

Conard, Rebecca Ann. *The Conservation of Local Autonomy: California's Agricultural Land Policies, 1900–1966.* Ph.D. diss., University of California at Santa Barbara, 1984.

Conkin, Paul. *FDR and the Origins of the Welfare State.* New York: Thomas Y. Crowell Co., 1967.

Conservation Foundation. *Agriculture and the Environment in a Changing World Economy.* Washington: Conservation Foundation, 1986.

"Conservatives at Court." *Public Opinion,* February–March 1981.

Cook, Kenneth A. "The Environmental Era in U.S. Agricultural Policy." *Journal of Soil and Water Conservation* 44 (September–October 1989): 362–66.

———. "Got Those GAO Blues Again." *Journal of Soil and Water Conservation* 38 (July–August 1983): 346–50.

———. "Loathing Suburbia." *American Land Forum Magazine* 4 (Summer 1983): 19–25.

———. "The National Agricultural Lands Study Goes Out with a Bang." *Journal of Soil and Water Conservation* 36 (April 1981): 91–93.

———. "Pinch Me, I Must Be Dreaming." *Journal of Soil and Water Conservation* 41 (March–April 1986): 93–94.

———. "RCA: No Federalism in New Federalism." *Journal of Soil and Water Conservation* 37 (July–August 1982): 213–14.

———. "Surplus Madness." *Journal of Soil and Water Conservation* 38 (January–February 1983): 25–28.

Corrigan, Richard. "Environment Report/Interior Department Finesses HUD in Scramble over Land Use Program." *National Journal* 3 (20 March 1971): 597–607.

———. "Methods of Protecting Agricultural Land." In *Protecting Agricultural Lands: Workshop Papers.* Unpublished, in the personal papers of Charles Little.

Coughlin, Robert E., et al. *Saving the Garden: The Preservation of Farmland and Other Environmentally Sensitive Land.* Philadelphia: Regional Science Research Institute, 1977.

Craven, Avery O. *Soil Exhaustion as a Factor in the Agricultural History of Virginia and Maryland, 1606–1860.* Urbana: University of Illinois Press, 1925.

Critchlow, Donald T., and Ellis Hawley, eds. *Federal Social Policy: The Historical Dimension.* University Park: Pennsylvania State University Press, 1988.

Crosson, Pierre R., ed. *The Cropland Crisis: Myth or Reality?*. Baltimore: Johns Hopkins University Press for Resources for the Future, 1982.

————. "Demands for Food and Fiber." In *Land Use: Tough Choices in Today's World,* 49–61. Ankenny, Iowa: Soil Conservation Society of America, 1977.

————. "Future Environmental and Economic Costs of Agricultural Land." In *The Cropland Crisis: Myth or Reality?,* ed. Pierre R. Crosson, 165–91. Baltimore: Johns Hopkins University Press for Resources for the Future, 1982.

————. "The Long-Term Adequacy of Agricultural Land in the United States." In *The Cropland Crisis: Myth or Reality?,* ed. Pierre R. Crosson, 1–22. Baltimore: Johns Hopkins University Press for Resources for the Future, 1982.

————. "A Shortage of Agricultural Land?" *Resources,* March 1982, 8.

Crosson, Pierre R., and Sterling Brubaker. *Resource and Environmental Effects of U.S. Agriculture.* Washington: Resources for the Future, 1982.

Dahlberg, Kenneth A. *Beyond the Green Revolution: The Ecology and Politics of Global Agricultural Development.* New York: Plenum Press, 1979.

————, ed. *New Directions for Agriculture and Agricultural Research.* Totowa, N.J.: Rowman and Allanheld, 1986.

Danbom, David. *The Resisted Revolution.* Ames: Iowa State University Press, 1979.

Danhof, Clarence. *Change in Agriculture: The Northern United States, 1820–1870.* Cambridge: Harvard University Press, 1969.

Daniels, Thomas L., and Arthur C. Nelson. "Is Oregon's Farmland Preservation Program Working?" *Journal of the American Planning Association* 52 (Winter 1986): 22–31.

Davis, Lance E., et al. *American Economic Growth: An Economist's History of the United States.* New York: Harper and Row, 1972.

DeGrove, John. *Land Growth and Politics.* Washington: American Planning Association, 1984.

Delafons, John. *Land-Use Controls in the United States.* Cambridge: MIT Press, 1962.

Demkovich, Linda E. "The Perils of Petaluma—Keeping a Lid on Growth." *National Journal* 8 (1 May 1976): 588–96.

DeVoto, Bernard. *The Easy Chair.* Boston: Houghton Mifflin, 1955.

Devring, Folke, David L. Chicoine, and John B. Braden. "Evaluating Land Use Change in Illinois." *Journal of Soil and Water Conservation* 37 (November–December 1982): 359–61.

Dewhurst, J. Frederick, and Associates. *America's Needs and Resources.* New York: Twentieth Century Fund, 1947.

Dicks, Michael R., Bengt Hyberg, and Thomas Hebert. "Implications of Current and Proposed Environmental Policies for America's Rural Economies." In *Implementing the Conservation Title of the Food Security Act of 1985,* ed. Ted L. Napier, 51–66. Ankenny, Iowa: Soil and Water Conservation Society, 1990.

Dideriksen, Raymond I., and R. Neil Sampson. "Important Farmlands: A National View." *Journal of Soil and Water Conservation* 31 (September–October 1976): 195–97.

Doering, Otto C. III. "Energy Dependence and the Future of American Agriculture." In *The Future of American Agriculture as a Strategic Resource,* ed. Sandra S. Batie and Robert G. Healy, 165–99. Washington: Conservation Foundation, 1980.

Doherty, J. C. "Public and Private Issues in Nonmetropolitan Government." In *Growth and Change in Rural America,* ed. Glenn V. Fuguitt, Paul R. Ross, and J. C. Doherty, 51–101. Washington: Urban Land Institute, 1979.

Downie, Leonard, Jr. "A Move to Save What Is Left." *Nation* 217 (17 December 1973): 649–52.

Doyle, Jack. *Altered Harvest.* New York: Viking, 1985.

Duda, Alfred M. "Environmental and Economic Damage Caused by Sediment from Agricultural Nonpoint Sources." *Water Resources Bulletin* 21 (February 1985): 225–34.

Dunford, Richard W. "The Evolution of Federal Farmland Protection Policy." *Journal of Soil and Water Conservation* 37 (May–June 1982): 133–36.

———. "Saving Farms and Farmland: The King County Program." *Journal of Soil and Water Conservation* 36 (January–February 1981): 19–21.

Easterlin, Richard. "The American Baby Boom in Historical Perspective." *American Economic Review* 51 (December 1961): 869–911.

Ebeling, Walter. *The Fruited Plain: The Story of American Agriculture.* Berkeley: University of California Press, 1979.

Eckholm, Erik. *Losing Ground: Environmental Stress and World Food Prospects.* New York: W. W. Norton, 1976.

Eden, Robert, ed. *The New Deal and Its Legacy.* New York: Greenwood Press, 1989.

Ehrlich, Paul R. *The Population Bomb.* New York: Ballantine Books, 1968.

Ehrlich, Paul R., Anne H. Ehrlich, and John P. Holdren. *Ecoscience: Population, Resources, Environment.* San Francisco: W. H. Freeman, 1970, 1977.

Eisenhower, Milton. "Earth and the Human Burden." *The Land* 7 (Summer 1948): 183–89.

Elliot, F. F. "Discussion." *Journal of Farm Economics* 21 (February 1939): 85–88.

Ellsworth, Clayton S. "Theodore Roosevelt's Country Life Commission." *Agricultural History* 34 (October 1960): 155–72.

Ely, Richard T. *The Foundation of National Prosperity: Studies in the Conservation of Permanent National Resources.* New York: Macmillan, 1917.

Ensminger, Douglas. "The Community in County Planning." *Land Policy Review* 3 (March–April 1940): 44–51.

Ervin, Christine A. "Implementing the Conservation Title." *Journal of Soil and Water Conservation* 44 (September–October 1989): 367–70.

Ervin, David E., and Michael R. Dicks. "Cropland Diversion for Conservation and Environmental Improvement: An Economic Welfare Analysis." *Land Economics* 64 (August 1988): 255–70.

Erwin, Will. "Regulating Water Quality: A Farmer's Perspective." *Journal of Soil and Water Conservation* 43 (January–February 1988): 65–66.

Esseks, J. Dixon. "Nonurban Competition for Farmland." In *Farmland, Food, and the Future,* ed. Max Schnepf, 49–66. Ankenny, Iowa: Soil Conservation Society of America, 1979.

————. "The Politics of Farmland Preservation." In *The New Politics of Food,* ed. Don F. Hadwiger and William P. Browne, 199–215. Lexington, Mass.: D. C. Heath, 1978.

Evan, Peter B., Dietrich Rueschemeyer, and Theda Skocpol, eds. *Bringing the State Back In.* Cambridge: Cambridge University Press, 1985.

Fausold, Martin L. *The Presidency of Herbert C. Hoover.* Lawrence: University Press of Kansas, 1985.

Fellmeth, Robert C. *The Politics of Land.* New York: Grossman, 1973.

Fischel, William A. "The Urbanization of Agricultural Land: A Review of the National Agricultural Lands Study." *Land Economics* 58 (May 1982): 236–59.

Fitchen, Janet M. *Endangered Spaces, Enduring Places: Change, Identity, and Survival in Rural America.* Boulder: Westview Press, 1991.

Fite, Gilbert. *American Farmers: The New Minority.* Bloomington: Indiana University Press, 1981.

Fleming, Donald. "History of the New Conservation Movement." *Perspectives in American History* 6 (1972): 7–91.

Fletcher, W. Wendell, and Charles E. Little. *The American Cropland Crisis.* Bethesda, Md.: American Land Forum, 1982.

Fowler, Cary, and Pat Mooney. *Shattering: Food, Politics, and the Loss of Genetic Diversity.* Tucson: University of Arizona Press, 1990.

Fox, Stephen. *John Muir and His Legacy.* Boston: Little, Brown, 1981.

Frederick, Kenneth. "Irrigation and the Adequacy of Agricultural Land." In *The Cropland Crisis: Myth or Reality?,* ed. Pierre R. Crosson, 117–59. Baltimore: Johns Hopkins University Press for Resources for the Future, 1982.

————. "Water and the West." In *The Future of American Agriculture as a Strategic Resource,* ed. Sandra S. Batie and Robert G. Healy. Washington: Conservation Foundation, 1980.

Freedgood, Julia. "PDR Programs Take Root in the Northeast." *Journal of Soil and Water Conservation* 46 (September–October 1991): 329–31.

Freeman, Orville L. "Perspectives and Prospects." *Agricultural History* 66 (Spring 1992): 3–11.

Fuguitt, Glenn V., Paul R. Ross, and J. C. Doherty. *Growth and Change in Rural America.* Washington: Urban Land Institute, 1979.

Furuseth, Owen. "Public Attitudes Toward Local Farmland Protection Programs." *Growth and Change* 18 (Summer 1987): 49–61.

Galambos, Louis, ed. *The New American State: Bureaucracies and Policies since World War II.* Baltimore: Johns Hopkins University Press, 1987.

Galston, William A. *A Tough Row to Hoe: The 1985 Farm Bill and Beyond.* Lanham, Md.: Lanham Press, by the Roosevelt Center for American Policy Studies, 1985.

Gardner, B. Delworth. "The Economics of Agricultural Land Preservation." *American Journal of Agricultural Economics* 59 (December 1977): 1027–36.

Gates, Paul W. "Comments." *Agricultural History* 37 (October 1973): 214–15.

————. "An Overview of American Land Policy." *Agricultural History* 50 (January 1976): 217–29.

Gever, John, Robert Kaufman, David Skole, and Charles Vorosmarty. *Beyond Oil: The Threat to Food and Fuel in the Coming Decades.* Cambridge, Mass.: Ballinger Publishing Co., 1986.

Gilbert, Robert Lind. *Land Economics and Natural Resource Conservation: The Effort to Build a More Permanent American Agriculture, 1915–1933.* M.A. thesis, University of North Carolina at Chapel Hill, 1988.

Goto, Junko. *Soil and Water Conservation Programs in Action: The Vernon County Wisconsin Experience.* M.S. thesis, University of Wisconsin–Madison, 1981.

Grant, Kenneth E. "Land Use: Past and Present." In *National Land Use Policy: Objectives, Components, Implementation,* 13–22. Ankenny, Iowa: Soil Conservation Society of America, 1973.

Graham, Otis L., Jr. *Losing Time: The Industrial Policy Debate.* Cambridge: Harvard University Press, 1992.

———. "National Growth Report." *Center Magazine* 10 (January–February 1977): 68–76.

———. *Toward a Planned Society.* New York: Oxford University Press, 1976.

———. "The White House Conference on Economic Growth." *Center Magazine* 11 (July–August 1978): 52–59.

Gray, L. C. "National Land Use Policies in Retrospect and Prospect." *Journal of Farm Economics* 13 (April 1931): 231–45.

Green, Donald. *Land of the Underground Rain.* Austin: University of Texas Press, 1973.

Grossi, Ralph. "Implementing CRP: A Conservation Organization View." *Journal of Soil and Water Conservation* 43 (January–February 1988): 20–22.

———. "The Politics of Choice." *Journal of Soil and Water Conservation* 46 (November–December 1991): 401–6.

Guither, Harold D., and Harold G. Falcrow. *The American Farm Crisis.* Ann Arbor, Mich.: Pierian Press, 1988.

Gustafson, Gregory C., and L. T. Wallace. "Differential Assessment as Land Use Policy: The California Case." *Journal of the American Institute of Planners* 41 (November 1975): 379–89.

Guttenberg, Albert Z. "The Land Utilization Movement of the 1920s." *Agricultural History* 50 (July 1976): 477–90.

Hadwiger, Don F. *The Politics of Agricultural Research.* Lincoln: University of Nebraska Press, 1982.

Hadwiger, Don F., and William P. Browne. *The New Politics of Food.* Lexington, Mass.: Lexington Books, 1978.

———. *Rural Policy: Changing Dimensions.* Lexington, Mass.: D. C. Heath, 1982.

Halcrow, Harold G., Earl O. Heady, and Melvin L. Cotner. *Soil Conservation Policies, Institutions, and Incentives.* Ankenny, Iowa: Soil Conservation Society of America, 1982.

Hamilton, David E. *From New Day to New Deal: American Farm Policy from Hoover to Roosevelt, 1928–1933.* Chapel Hill: University of North Carolina Press, 1991.

Hansen, David E., and Seymour I. Schwartz. "Prime Land Conservation: The

California Land Conservation Act." *Journal of Soil and Water Conservation* 31 (October–November 1976): 198–203.

Hardin, Charles Meyer. *The Politics of Agriculture: Soil Conservation and the Struggle for Power in Rural America.* Glencoe, Ill.: Free Press, 1952.

Hargreaves, Mary W. M. "Land-Use Planning in Response to Drought: The Experience of the Thirties." *Agricultural History* 50 (July 1976): 561–82.

Harlan, Jack R. "Crop Monoculture and the Future of American Agriculture." In *The Future of American Agriculture as a Strategic Resource,* ed. Sandra S. Batie and Robert G. Healy, 225–50. Washington: Conservation Foundation, 1980.

Harris, B. L., J. N. Habiger, and Z. L. Carpenter. "The Conservation Title: Concerns and Recommendations from the Great Plains." *Journal of Soil and Water Conservation* 44 (September–October 1989): 371–75.

Hart, John Fraser. "Urban Encroachment on Rural Areas." *Geographic Review* 66 (January 1976): 1–17.

Haveman, Robert H. *Poverty Policy and Poverty Research: The Great Society and the Social Sciences.* Madison: University of Wisconsin Press, 1987.

Hawley, Ellis W. "The New Deal State and the Anti-Bureaucratic Tradition." In *The New Deal and Its Legacy,* ed. Robert Eden, 77–93. New York: Greenwood Press, 1989.

———. "Social Policy and the Liberal State in Twentieth-Century America." In *Federal Social Policy: The Historical Dimension,* ed. Donald T. Critchlow and Ellis W. Hawley, 117–39. University Park: Pennsylvania State University Press, 1988.

Hays, Samuel P. *Beauty, Health, and Permanence: Environmental Politics in the United States, 1855–1985.* Cambridge: Cambridge University Press, 1987.

———. *Conservation and the Gospel of Efficiency.* Cambridge: Harvard University Press, 1959.

———. "Political Choice in Regulatory Administration." In *Regulation in Perspective: Historical Essays,* ed. Thomas K. McCraw, 124–54. Cambridge: Harvard University Press, 1981.

———. "The Politics of Environmental Administration." In *The New American State: Bureaucracies and Policies since World War II,* ed. Louis Galambos, 21–53. Baltimore: Johns Hopkins University Press, 1987.

Heady, Earl O. "The Adequacy of Agricultural Land: A Demand-Supply Perspective." In *The Cropland Crisis: Myth or Reality?,* ed. Pierre R. Crosson, 23–56. Baltimore: Johns Hopkins University Press for Resources for the Future, 1982.

Healy, Robert G. *Competition for Land in the American South: Agriculture, Human Settlement, and the Environment.* Washington: Conservation Foundation, 1985.

———. "Rural Land: Private Choices, Public Interests." *Conservation Foundation Letter,* August 1977.

Healy, Robert G., and James L. Short. *The Market for Rural Land: Trends, Issues, Policies.* Washington: Conservation Foundation, 1981.

Healy, Robert G., and John S. Rosenberg. *Land Use and the States.* 2d ed. Baltimore: Johns Hopkins University Press for Resources for the Future, 1979.

Held, R. Burnell, and Marion Clawson. *Soil Conservation in Perspective.* Baltimore: Johns Hopkins University Press for Resources for the Future, 1965.

Hightower, Jim. *Eat Your Heart Out: Food Profiteering in America.* New York: Crown Press, 1975.

———. *Hard Tomatoes, Hard Times.* Washington: Agribusiness Accountability Project, 1972.

Hill, James J. *Highways of Progress.* New York: Doubleday, Page, and Co., 1910.

Hoskins, T. H. "New England Agriculture." *Popular Science Monthly* 38 (March 1891): 700.

House, Peter W., and Edward R. Williams. *Planning and Conservation: The Emergence of a Frugal Society.* New York: Praeger, 1977.

Hrabovszky, Janos R. "Agriculture: The Land Base." In *The Global Possible,* ed. Robert Repetto, 223–28. New Haven: Yale University Press, 1985.

Increasing Understanding of Public Froblems and Policies 1988. Oak Brook, Ill.: Farm Foundation, 1988.

Isberg, Gunnar. "Controlling Growth in the Urban Fringe." *Journal of Soil and Water Conservation* 28 (July–August 1973): 155–61.

"Is the City Heading Your Way?" *Progressive Farmer,* February 1981, 36.

Jacks, G. V., and R. O. Whyte. *Vanishing Lands: A World Survey of Soil Erosion.* New York: Doubleday, Doran, and Co., 1939.

Jackson, Kenneth T. *The Crabgrass Frontier: The Suburbanization of the United States.* New York: Oxford University Press, 1985.

Jackson, Wes, Wendell Berry, and Bruce Colman, eds. *Meeting the Expectations of the Land: Essays in Sustainable Agriculture and Stewardship.* San Francisco: North Point Press, 1984.

Jarrett, Henry, ed. *Perspectives on Conservation.* Baltimore: Johns Hopkins University Press for Resources for the Future, 1958.

Jeffords, James M. "Protecting Farmland: Minimizing the Federal Role." *Journal of Soil and Water Conservation* 34 (March–April 1979): 158–59.

———. "Vanishing Farmlands: Do We Need a Crisis?" *EPA Journal* 6 (July–August 1980): 16–18.

Jeske, Walter E. *Economics, Ethics, Ecology: Roots of Productive Conservation.* Ankenny, Iowa: Soil Conservation Society of America, 1981.

Johnston, Thomas R., and Christopher R. Bryant. "Agricultural Adaptation: The Prospects for Sustaining Agriculture near Cities." In *Sustaining Agriculture near Cities,* ed. William Lockeretz, 21. Ankenny, Iowa: Soil and Water Conservation Society, 1987.

Joint Committee on Bases of Sound Land Policy. *What about the Year 2000?* Federated Societies on Planning and Parks, 1929.

Karl, Barry D. *The Uneasy State: The United States from 1915 to 1945.* Chicago: University of Chicago Press, 1983.

Karl, Thomas R., et al. "The Greenhouse Effect in Central North America: If Not Now, When?" *Science* 251 (1 March 1991): 1058–60.

Keene, John C. "A Review of Governmental Policies and Techniques for Keeping Farmers Farming." *Natural Resources Journal* 19 (January 1979): 119–44.

Kirkendall, Richard. "L. C. Gray and the Supply of Agricultural Land." *Agricultural History* 37 (October 1963): 206–14.

———. "The New Deal and Agriculture." In *The New Deal: The National Level,* ed. John Braeman, Robert H. Bremmer, and David Brody, 83–110. Columbus: Ohio State University Press, 1975.

———. "The Second Secretary Wallace." *Agricultural History* 64 (Spring 1990): 199–206.

———. *Social Scientists in the Age of Roosevelt.* Columbia: University of Missouri Press, 1966.

Klein, John V. N. "Preserving Farmland on Long Island." *Environmental Comment,* January 1978, 11–13.

Kneeland, Douglas. "Urbanization of Rural U.S. Called Peril to Farmland." *New York Times,* 16 June 1981, B8.

Kramer, Carol S., ed. *The Political Economy of U.S. Agriculture: Challenges for the 1990s.* Washington: Resources for the Future, 1989.

Krohe, James, Jr. "Can Both Corn and Coal Be King in the Midwest?" *Planning* 44 (April–May 1978): 38–41.

Kuhl, Arthur D. "The 1957 Conservation Needs Inventory: A Historical Aspect of Soil Survey." *Soil Survey Horizons* 30 (Winter 1989): 84–88.

Lampman, Robert J. "What Does It Do for the Poor?: A New Test for National Policy." *Public Interest* 34 (Winter 1974): 66–82.

Land Use: Tough Choices in Today's World. Ankenny, Iowa: Soil Conservation Society of America, 1977.

Land Use Notes. Ed. Warren Zitzmann. Published by the Land Use Staff, Soil Conservation Service, 1977–1982.

"Land Use Planning." *Farm Bureau News,* 26 January 1981, 31.

Lappe, Frances Moore, and Joseph Collins. *Food First: Beyond the Myth of Scarcity.* Boston: Houghton Mifflin, 1977.

Lapping, Mark. "Agricultural Land Retention Strategies: Some Underpinnings." *Journal of Soil and Water Conservation* 34 (May–June 1979): 124–27.

Leopold, Aldo. *Sand County Almanac.* New York: Oxford University Press, 1949.

Leuchtenburg, William E. "The Pertinence of Political History: Reflections on the Significance of the State in America." *Journal of American History* 73 (December 1986): 585–600.

Lewis, John D., and Ewart Lewis. "The Farmer Helps to Plan." *New Republic,* 20 October 1941, 504–5.

Lint, Henry C. "Buildings or Farms?" *Soil Conservation Magazine* 16 (September 1950): 42–43.

Little, Charles. "The Case for Retaining Agricultural Land." In *Protecting Agricultural Lands: Workshop Papers.* Unpublished, in the personal papers of Charles Little.

———. "Farmland Conservancies: A Middleground Approach to Agricultural Land Preservation." *Journal of Soil and Water Conservation* 35 (September–October 1980): 204–11.

———. "Land and Food: The Preservation of U.S. Farmland." *American Land Forum Report* 1 (Spring 1979): 1–64.

————. "Toward a Land Resource Policy Agenda." *American Land Forum Magazine* 4 (Summer 1983): 19.

Lockeretz, William. "Secondary Effects on Midwestern Agriculture of Metropolitan Development and Decreases in Farmland." *Land Economics* 65 (August 1989): 205–16.

————, ed. *Sustaining Agriculture near Cities.* Ankenny, Iowa: Soil and Water Conservation Society, 1987.

"Long-Range Threats Stalk U.S. Farming." *Conservation Foundation Newsletter,* August 1980.

Lord, Russell. *Behold Our Land.* Boston: Houghton Mifflin, 1938.

————. *The Care of the Earth.* New York: Mentor Books, 1962.

————. "Proceedings." *The Land* 1 (Winter 1941): 14–23.

————. *The Wallaces of Iowa.* Boston: Houghton Mifflin, 1947.

Lovejoy, Stephen B., and Ted L. Napier, eds. *Conserving Soil: Insights from the Socionomic Research.* Ankenny, Iowa: Soil Conservation Society of America, 1986.

Lovins, Amory B., L. Hunter Lovins, and Marty Bender. "Energy and Agriculture." In *Meeting the Expectations of the Land,* ed. Wes Jackson, Wendell Berry, and Bruce Colman, 68–86. San Francisco: North Point Press, 1984.

Lowenthal, David. *George Perkins Marsh: Versatile Vermonter.* New York: Columbia University Press, 1958.

Luzar, Jane E. "Natural Resource Management in Agriculture: An Institutional Analysis of the 1985 Farm Bill." *Journal of Economic Issues* 22 (June 1988): 563–69.

Lyday, Noreen. *The Law of the Land.* Washington: Urban Land Institute, 1976.

Lynd, Robert S. *Knowledge for What?: The Place of Social Science in American Culture.* Princeton: Princeton University Press, 1939.

Lynn, Laurence, ed. *Knowledge and Policy: The Uncertain Connection.* Washington: National Academy of Sciences, 1978.

Lyons, Richard L. "On Capitol Hill." *Washington Post,* 8 February 1980, A4.

McAllister, Donald M., ed. *Environment: A New Focus for Land-Use Planning.* Washington: Government Printing Office for the National Science Foundation, 1973.

McClintock, David. "The Global Importance of American Cropland." *EPA Journal* 7 (April 1981): 26–29.

McCraw, Thomas K., ed. *Regulation in Perspective: Historical Essays.* Cambridge: Harvard University Press, 1981.

McEvedy, Colin, and Richard Jones. *Atlas of World Population History.* New York: Facts on File, 1979.

MacFadyen, Tevere J. *Gaining Ground: The Renewal of America's Small Farms.* New York: Holt, Rinehart, and Winston, 1984.

McGovern, George. "We Must Not Break the Hoop of Life." *EPA Journal* 6 (July–August 1980): 12–14.

McKeown, Thomas. *The Modern Rise of Population.* New York: Academic Press, 1976.

McNamara, Robert S. "Time Bomb or Myth: The Population Problem." *Foreign Affairs* 62 (Summer 1984): 1107–31.

McSweeny, William T., and Randall A. Kramer. "The Integration of Farm Programs for Achieving Soil Conservation and Nonpoint Pollution Control Objectives." *Land Economics* 62 (May 1986): 159–73.

Madden, Patrick. "Beyond Conventional Economics—An Examination of the Values Implicit in the Neoclassical Paradigm as Applied to the Evaluation of Agricultural Research." In *New Directions for Agriculture and Agricultural Research,* ed. Kenneth A. Dahlberg, 221–58. Ottawa, N.J.: Rowman and Allanheld, 1986.

Magee, Thomas. "Overworked Soils." *Overland Monthly* 1 (October 1868): 327–33.

Magida, Arthur J. "Environment Report/Land Use Legislation Again Gets Udall-Jackson Priority." *National Journal* 7 (8 March 1975): 367–69.

Marsh, George Perkins. *Man and Nature.* New York: Charles Scribner, 1864. Reprint, Cambridge: Harvard University Press, 1965.

Martin, Albro. *James J. Hill and the Opening of the Northwest.* New York: Oxford University Press, 1976.

May, Lary, ed. *Recasting America: Culture and Politics in the Age of the Cold War.* Chicago: University of Chicago Press, 1989.

Meadows, Donella H., et al. *The Limits to Growth.* New York: Universe Books, 1972.

Menzel, Bruce W. "Agricultural Management Practices and the Integrity of Instream Biological Habitat." In *Agricultural Management and Water Quality,* ed. Frank W. Schaller and George W. Bailey, 305–29. Ames: Iowa State University Press, 1983.

Merrill, Richard, ed. *Radical Agriculture.* New York: Harper and Row, 1976.

Meyer, Peter. "Land Rush." *Harper's* 258 (January 1979): 45–60.

Meyers, Peter C. "Conservation at the Crossroads." *Journal of Soil and Water Conservation* 44 (September–October 1989): 10–13.

Miner, Dallas D. "Agricultural Lands Preservation: A Growing Trend in Open Space Planning." In *Management and Control of Growth,* vol. 3, ed. Randall W. Scott, David J. Brower, and Dallas D. Miner, 52–60. Washington: Urban Land Institute, 1975.

———. "Agricultural Retention: An Emerging Issue." *Environmental Comment,* May 1975, 1.

Moon, Henry Edward, Jr. *The Loss of Farmland: The Process of Urbanization in Alabama's Black Belt.* M.S. thesis, University of Alabama, 1984.

Morgan, Robert J. *Governing Soil Conservation: Thirty Years of the New Decentralization.* Baltimore: Johns Hopkins University Press for Resources for the Future, 1965.

Morrison, P. A., and J. P. Wheeler. "Rural Renaissance in America?: The Revival of Population Growth in Remote Areas." *Population Bulletin* 32 (1976): 1–26.

Mortensen, Timothy, et al. "An Analysis of Baseline Characteristics and Economic Impacts of the Conservation Reserve Program in North Dakota." In *Implementing the Conservation Reserve Title of the Food Security Act of 1985,* ed. Ted L. Napier. Ankenny, Iowa: Soil and Water Conservation Society, 1990.

Moynihan, Daniel P. "Toward a National Urban Policy." *Public Interest* 17 (Fall 1969): 3–20.

Muller, Peter O. *Contemporary Suburban America.* Englewood Cliffs, N.J.: Prentice Hall, 1981.

Napier, Ted, ed. *Implementing the Conservation Title of the Food Security Act of 1985.* Ankenny, Iowa: Soil and Water Conservation Society, 1990.

National Academy of Sciences. *Genetic Vulnerability of Major Crops.* Washington: National Academy of Sciences, 1972.

"National Agricultural Lands Study: An Interview with Bob Gray." *Journal of Soil and Water Conservation* 36 (March–April 1981): 62–68.

National Land Use Policy: Objectives, Components, Implementation. Ankenny, Iowa: Soil Conservation Society of America, 1973.

National Research Council. *Alternative Agriculture.* Washington: National Academy Press, 1989.

———. *Soil Conservation: Assessing the National Resources Inventory.* Washington: National Academy Press, 1986.

Nesmith, Jeff. "Urban Sprawl Is Threatening to Destroy Vital U.S. Natural Resource—Farmland." *Atlanta Constitution,* 22 July 1979, A4.

"New American Land Rush." *Time* 102 (1 October 1973): 83–99.

Nietzsche, Friedrich. *The Use and Abuse of History.* New York: Liberal Arts Press, 1949.

Nolan, Thomas B. "The Inexhaustible Resource of Technology." In *Perspectives on Conservation,* ed. Henry Jarrett, 49–66. Baltimore: Johns Hopkins University Press for Resources for the Future, 1958.

Noone, James A. "Resources Report/Senate, House Differ on Approaches to Reform of Nation's Land-Use Laws." *National Journal* 4 (22 July 1972): 1192–1201.

Odum, Howard T. *Environment, Power, and Society.* New York: John Wiley and Sons, 1971.

Opie, John. "The Drought of 1988, The Global Warming Experiment, and Its Challenge to Irrigation in the Old Dust Bowl Region." *Agricultural History* 66 (Spring 1992): 279–306.

———. *The Law of the Land: Two Hundred Years of American Farmland Policy.* Lincoln: University of Nebraska Press, 1987.

Ordway, Samuel H. *Resources and the American Dream.* New York: Ronald Press, 1953.

Osborn, Fairfield. *Our Plundered Planet.* Boston: Little, Brown, 1948.

Owen, A. L. Riesch. *Conservation under FDR.* New York: Praeger, 1983.

Paarlberg, Don. "The Changing Policy Environment for the 1990 Farm Bill." *Journal of Soil and Water Conservation* 45 (January–February 1990): 8.

———. *Farm and Food Policy: Issues of the 1980s.* Lincoln: University of Nebraska Press, 1980.

———. "The Scarcity Syndrome." *American Journal of Agricultural Economics* 64 (February 1982): 110–14.

Paddock, William, and Paul Paddock. *Famine 1975.* Boston: Little, Brown, 1967.

Parker, William N. "Agriculture." In *American Economic Growth: An Economist's*

History of the United States, ed. Lance E. Davis et al., 371–89. New York: Harper and Row, 1972.

Pease, James R., and Philip L. Jackson. "Farmland Preservation in Oregon." *Journal of Soil and Water Conservation* 34 (November–December 1979): 256–59.

Peirce, Neal R. "Land Trusts Keeping Bulldozers at Bay." *National Journal* 22 (30 June 1990): 1619.

Peirce, Neal R., and George M. Hatch. "Preservationists Seek Government Help as Farmland Gives Way to Developers." *National Journal* 12 (16 August 1980): 1357–61.

Peiser, Richard B. "Density and Urban Sprawl." *Land Economics* 65 (August 1989): 193–204.

Penn, J. B. "Agricultural Structural Issues and Policy Alternatives for the 1980s." *American Journal of Agricultural Economics* 66 (December 1984): 572–76.

Perelman, Michael. *Farming for Profit in a Hungry World.* New York: Allan Held, 1979.

Perkins, John H. "The Rockefeller Foundation and the Green Revolution, 1941–1956." *Agriculture and Human Values* 7 (Summer–Fall 1990): 6–18.

Peterson, Craig A., and Claire McCarthy. "A Proposal for an Agricultural Land Preservation Program." *Land Use Law and Zoning Digest* 29, no. 8 (1977): 4–8.

Peterson, George E., and Harvey Yampolsky. *Urban Development and the Protection of Farmland.* Washington: Urban Institute, 1975.

Peterson, Trudy Huskamp, ed. *Farmers, Bureaucrats, and Middlemen.* Washington: Howard University Press, 1980.

Phipps, Tim T., and Pierre R. Crosson. "Agriculture and the Environment: An Overview." In *Agriculture and the Environment,* ed. Tim T. Phipps, Pierre R. Crosson, and Kent A. Price, 3–30. Washington: Resources for the Future, 1986.

Phipps, Tim T., Pierre R. Crosson, and Kent A. Price, eds. *Agriculture and the Environment.* Washington: Resources for the Future, 1986.

Pimental, David, et al. "Environmental and Economic Effects of Reducing Pesticide Use." *Bioscience* 41 (June 1991): 403.

———. "Food Production and the Energy Crisis." *Science* 182 (2 November 1973): 446.

———. "Land Degradation: Effects on Food and Energy Resources." *Science* 194 (October 1976): 149–55.

———. "World Agriculture and Soil Erosion." *Bioscience* 37 (April 1987): 277–81.

Pimental, David, and Marcia Pimental. *Food, Energy, and Society.* New York: John Wiley and Sons, 1979.

Pimental, David, and Susan Pimental. "Energy and Other Natural Resources Used by Agriculture and Society." In *New Directions for Agriculture and Agricultural Research,* ed. Kenneth A. Dahlberg. Ottowa, N.J.: Roman and Allanheld, 1986.

Pisani, Donald J. "Forests and Conservation, 1865–1890." *Journal of American History* 72 (September 1985): 340–59.

Platt, Rutherford H., and George Macinko, eds. *Beyond the Urban Fringe: Land Use Issues in Nonmetropolitan America.* Minneapolis: University of Minnesota Press, 1983.

Plotkin, Sidney. *Keep Out: The Struggle for Land Use Control.* Berkeley: University of California Press, 1987.

————. "Policy Fragmentation and Capitalist Reform: The Defeat of National Land Use Policy." *Politics and Society* 9 (1980): 409–45.

Popper, Frank J. *The Politics of Land-Use Reform.* Madison: University of Wisconsin Press, 1981.

————. "Understanding American Land Use Regulation since 1970." *Journal of the American Planning Association* 54 (Summer 1988): 291–301.

"Population Horror Stories." *The Other Side,* January–February 1985, 6.

Portney, Paul R., ed. *Current Issues in National Policy.* Washington: Resources for the Future, 1982.

Powell, John Wesley. *Report on the Lands of the Arid Region of the United States.* Washington: United States Geographical and Geological Survey, 2d ed., 1879. Reprint, Cambridge: Harvard University Press, 1962.

Power, J. F., and R. F. Follert. "Monoculture." *Scientific American* 256 (March 1987): 78–86.

Presto, John A. "Shrinking Farmlands: Sprawl of Cities Stirs Fears that Agriculture Will Run Out of Space." *Wall Street Journal,* 20 July 1971, A1.

Rasmussen, Wayne D., ed. *Agricultural History in the United States: A Documentary History.* New York: Random House, 1975.

————. "History of Soil Conservation, Institutions, and Incentives." In *Soil Conservation Policies, Institutions, and Incentives,* ed. Harold G. Halcrow, Earl O. Heady, and Melvin L. Cotner, 3–18. Ankeny, Iowa: Soil Conservation Society of America, 1982.

Rauch, Jonathan. "Farmers' Discord over Government Role Produces a Farm Bill That Pleases Few." *National Journal* 17 (9 November 1985): 2535–39.

Raup, Philip M. "An Agricultural Critique of the National Agricultural Lands Study." *Land Economics* 58 (May 1982): 250–73.

————. "Competition for Land and the Future of American Agriculture." In *The Future of American Agriculture as a Strategic Resource,* ed. Sandra S. Batie and Robert G. Healy, 41–78. Washington: Conservation Foundation, 1980.

————. "Urban Threats to Rural Lands." *Journal of the American Institute of Planners* 41 (November 1975): 371–78.

————. "What Is Prime Land?" *Journal of Soil and Water Conservation* 31 (September–October 1976): 180–81.

Rausser, Gordon C., and Kenneth R. Ferrell, eds. *Alternative Agricultural and Food Policies and the 1985 Farm Bill.* Washington: Resources for the Future, n.d.

Redfield, Sarah. *Vanishing Farmland: A Legal Solution for the States.* Lexington, Mass.: D. C. Heath, 1984.

Reichelderfer, Katherine, and Maureen Kuwano Hinkle. "The Evolution of Pesticide Policy." In *The Political Economy of U.S. Agriculture: Challenges for the 1990s,* ed. Carol S. Kramer, 147–72. Washington: Resources for the Future, 1989.

Reichelderfer, Katherine, and William G. Boggess. "Government Decision-Making and Decision Performance." *American Journal of Agricultural Economics* 70 (January 1988): 1–11.

Reichenberger, Larry. "CRP: Looking Ahead to Year Eleven." *Farm Journal* (January 1988): 16–17.

Reilly, William K. "Agriculture and Conservation: A New Alliance." *Journal of Soil and Water Conservation* 42 (January–February 1987): 14–16.

———, ed. *The Use of Land: A Citizens' Policy Guide to Urban Growth.* New York: Thomas Y. Crowell Co., 1973.

Repetto, Robert, ed. *The Global Possible: Resources, Development, and the New Century.* New Haven: Yale University Press, 1985.

Report of the Mid-Century Conference on Resources for the Future. *A Nation Looks at Its Resources.* Resources for the Future, 1954.

Resource Constrained Economies: The North American Dilemma. Ankenny, Iowa: Soil Conservation Society of America, 1979.

Ribaudo, Marc, et al. "CRP: What Economic Benefits?" *Journal of Soil and Water Conservation* 44 (September–October 1989): 421–24.

Richards, John. "Global Cropland Conversion." *Environment* 26 (November 1984): 5–12.

Robbins, Roy. *Our Landed Heritage: The Public Domain, 1776–1970.* 2d ed., rev. Lincoln: University of Nebraska Press, 1976.

Roosevelt, Franklin D. *The Genesis of the New Deal, 1928–1932,* vol. 1 of *The Public Papers and Addresses of Franklin D. Roosevelt,* comp. Samuel I. Rosenman. New York: Random House, 1938.

Rosenberg, Norman J., et al. *Policy Options for Adaptation to Climate Change.* Washington: Resources for the Future, 1989.

Rosenman, Samuel I., comp. *The Public Papers and Addresses of Franklin D. Roosevelt,* vol. 1. New York: Random House, 1938.

Rowe, Peter G. *Making a Middle Landscape.* Cambridge: MIT Press, 1991.

Rowley, William D. *M. L. Wilson and the Campaign for Domestic Allotment.* Lincoln: University of Nebraska Press, 1970.

Russell, Louise B. *The Baby Boom Generation and the Economy.* Washington: Brookings Institution, 1982.

Ruttan, Vernon W. "Agricultural Research and the Future of American Agriculture." In *The Future of American Agriculture as a Strategic Resource,* ed. Sandra S. Batie and Robert G. Healy, 117–55. Washington: Conservation Foundation, 1980.

———. "Discussion." In *The Cropland Crisis: Myth or Reality?,* ed. Pierre R. Crosson, 57–61. Baltimore: Johns Hopkins University Press for Resources for the Future, 1982.

Saloutos, Theodore. *The American Farmer and the New Deal.* Ames: Iowa State University Press, 1984.

———. "Land Policy and Its Relation to Agricultural Production and Distribution, 1862 to 1933." *Journal of Economic History* 22 (December 1962): 445–60.

Sampson, R. Neil. "Building a Political Commitment to Conservation." *Journal of Soil and Water Conservation* 37 (September–October 1982): 252–54.

———. "Development of Prime Farmland." *Environmental Comment,* January 1978, 4–6.

———. "The Ethical Dimension of Farmland Protection." In *Farmland, Food, and the Future,* ed. Max Schnepf, 89–98. Ankenny, Iowa: Soil Conservation Society of America, 1979.

———. *Farmland or Wasteland: A Time to Choose.* Emmaus, Pa.: Rodale Press, 1981.

———. *For the Love of Land.* League City, Tex.: National Association of Conservation Districts, 1985.

———. "Prime Farmlands: The Situation." In *Protecting Agricultural Lands: Workshop Papers.* Unpublished, in the personal papers of Charles Little.

Samuelson, Robert J. "U.S. Farms—More Acres, More Exports and Less Federal Aid on the Horizon." *National Journal* 13 (23 May 1981): 916–19.

Schaller, Frank W., and George W. Bailey, eds. *Agricultural Management and Water Quality.* Ames: Iowa State University Press, 1983.

Schapsmeier, Edward L., and Frederick H. Schapsmeier. *Henry A. Wallace of Iowa: The Agrarian Years, 1910–1940.* Ames: Iowa State University Press, 1968.

Schiff, Stanley D. "Land and Food: Dilemmas in Protecting the Resource Base." *Journal of Soil and Water Conservation* 34 (March–April 1979): 54–59.

———. "Saving Farmland: The Maryland Program." *Journal of Soil and Water Conservation* 34 (September–October 1979): 204–7.

Schlesinger, Arthur M., Jr. *Robert Kennedy and His Times.* Boston: Houghton Mifflin, 1978.

Schnepf, Max, ed. *Farmland, Food and the Future.* Ankenny, Iowa: Soil Conservation Society of America, 1979.

Schultz, Theodore W. "The Declining Importance of Agricultural Land." *Economic Journal* 61 (December 1951): 725–40.

Schumacher, E. F. *Small Is Beautiful: Economics as if People Mattered.* New York: Harper and Row, 1973.

Schwab, Jim. "The Attraction Is Chemical." *Nation* 249 (16 October 1989): 415–20.

Scott, Randall W., David J. Brower, and Dallas D. Miner. *Management and Control of Growth.* Washington: Urban Land Institute, 1975.

Sears, Paul B. *Deserts on the March.* 1935. Reprint, Norman: University of Oklahoma Press, 1959.

Shaw, Robert H. "Climate Change and the Future of American Agriculture." In *The Future of American Agriculture as a Strategic Resource,* ed. Sandra S. Batie and Robert G. Healy, 272–98. Washington: Conservation Foundation, 1980.

Shepard, Ward. *Food or Famine: The Challenge of Erosion.* New York: Macmillan, 1945.

Shover, John L. *First Majority, Last Minority: The Transformation of Rural Life in America.* Dekalb: Northern Illinois University Press, 1976.

Simon, Julian L. "Are We Losing Our Farmland?" *Public Interest* 67 (Spring 1982): 49–62.

———. "The Farmer and the Mall: Are American Farmlands Disappearing?" *American Spectator,* August 1982, 18–20, 40–41.

———. *The Ultimate Resource.* Princeton: Princeton University Press, 1981.

Sims, D. Harper. *The Soil Conservation Service.* New York: Praeger, 1970.

Sinclair, Ward. "Farmers Losing Their Land and Livelihoods to Urban Growth." *Washington Post,* 4 November 1982, A4.

Skocpol, Theda. "Bringing the State Back In: Strategies of Analysis in Current Research." In *Bringing the State Back In,* ed. Peter B. Evans, Dietrich Rueschemeyer, and Theda Skocpol, 3–37. Cambridge: Cambridge University Press, 1985.

Skowenrek, Stephen. *Building a New American State: The Expansion of National Administrative Capacities, 1877–1920.* Cambridge: Cambridge University Press, 1982.

"Soil Erosion Could Be Eliminated by 1995." *Earth Science* 43 (Summer 1990): 8–9.

Soth, Lauren. "The Grain Export Boom: Should It Be Tamed?" *Foreign Affairs* 59 (Spring 1981): 8895–8912.

Soule, George. "Planning for Agriculture." *New Republic,* 7 October 1931, 204–6.

Stegner, Wallace. *Beyond the Hundredth Meridian.* Boston: Houghton-Mifflin, 1954.

———. *The Uneasy Chair: A Biography of Bernard DeVoto.* New York: Doubleday, 1974.

Steiner, Frederick R. *Soil Conservation in the United States.* Baltimore: Johns Hopkins University Press, 1990.

Steinhart, John S., and Carol E. Steinhart. "Energy Use in the U.S. Food System." *Science* 184 (19 November 1974): 307–15.

Stilgoe, John R. *Borderland: Origins of the American Suburb.* New Haven: Yale University Press, 1988.

Stockman, David A. *The Triumph of Politics: How the Reagan Revolution Failed.* New York: Harper and Row, 1986.

Strong, John L. "Cotton Experiments in California." *Overland Monthly* 6 (April 1871): 633.

Sullivan, Joseph P. "Agricultural Districts: The New York Experience in Farmland Preservation." In *Land Use: Tough Choices in Today's World,* 122–30. Ankenny, Iowa: Soil Conservation Society of America, 1977.

Sundquist, James. "Where Shall They Live?" *Public Interest* 18 (Winter 1970): 97.

Supalla, Raymond J. "Land Use Planning: An Institutional Overview." *American Journal of Agricultural Economics* 58 (December 1976): 895–901.

Swain, Donald C. *Federal Conservation Policy, 1921–1933.* Berkeley: University of California Press, 1963.

Sweezy, Alan. "The Economic Explanation of Fertility Changes in the United States." *Population Studies* 25 (July 1971): 255–68.

Tamarkin, Bob. "The Growth Industry." *Forbes,* 2 March 1981, 90–94.

Taylor, Henry C., and Anne Dewees Taylor. *The Story of Agricultural Economics in the United States, 1840–1932.* Ames: Iowa State University Press, 1952.

"TDR: What's Happening Now." *Practicing Planner* 7 (March 1977): 10–14.

Timmons, John. "Agricultural Land Retention and Conversion Issues: An Introduction." In *Farmland, Food, and the Future,* ed. Max Schnepf, 1–12. Ankenny, Iowa: Soil Conservation Society of America, 1979.

Tolley, Howard. *The Farmer Citizen at War.* New York: Macmillan, 1943.

Trimble, Stanley W. "Perspectives on the History of Soil Erosion Control in the Eastern United States." *Agricultural History* 59 (April 1985): 162–80.

Tugwell, Franklin. *The Energy Crisis and the American Economy.* Stanford: Stanford University Press, 1988.

Tugwell, R. G. "Farm Relief and Permanent Agriculture." *The Annals of the American Academy of Political and Social Science* 142 (March 1929): 271–82.

———. "The Place of Government in a National Land Program." *Journal of Farm Economics* 16 (January 1934): 55–69.

Turner, Frederick Jackson. *The Frontier in American History.* New York: Holt, Rinehart, and Winston, 1920.

Vail, David. "Suburbanization of the Countryside and the Revitalization of Small Farms." In *Sustaining Agriculture near Cities,* ed. William Lockeretz, 23–36. Ankenny, Iowa: Soil and Water Conservation Society, 1987.

"Vanishing Farm Land." *Washington Post,* 5 August 1981, A22.

Vasey, Daniel E. *An Ecological History of Agriculture: 10,000 B.C.–10,000 A.D.* Ames: Iowa State University Press, 1992.

Vaughn, Stephen, ed. *The Vital Past.* Athens: University of Georgia Press, 1985.

Vietor, Richard H. K. *Environmental Politics and the Coal Coalition.* College Station: Texas A & M University Press, 1980.

Vining, Daniel R., Jr. "The Future of American Agriculture." *Journal of the American Planning Association* 48 (Winter 1982): 112–16.

Vining, Daniel R., Thomas Plaut, and Kenneth Bierri. "Urban Encroachment on Prime Agricultural Land in the United States." *International Regional Science Review* 2, no. 2 (1977): 143–56.

Vogt, William. *Road to Survival.* New York: William Sloan Associates, 1948.

Wall, Robert L. "California's Agricultural Land Preservation Program." In *Land Use: Tough Choices in Today's World,* 131–34. Ankenny, Iowa: Soil Conservation Society of America, 1977.

Wallace, Henry A. "The Challenge to Science." In *Democracy Reborn,* ed. Russell Lord, 47–52. New York: Reynal and Hitchcock, 1944.

———. "Country Matters." *The Land* 4 (Autumn 1945): 392.

———. *Democracy Reborn,* ed. Russell Lord. New York: Reynal and Hitchcock, 1944.

Warken, Philip W. *A History of the National Resources Planning Board, 1933–1943.* Ph.D. diss., Ohio State University, 1969.

Warnock, John H. *The Politics of Hunger.* London: Methuen, 1987.

Wehrwein, George S. "Discussion." *Journal of Farm Economics* 17 (February 1935): 50–54.

———. "Public Control of Land Use in the United States." *Journal of Farm Economics* 21 (February 1939): 74–85.

Weiss, Carol H. "Research for Policy's Sake: The Enlightenment Function of Social Research." *Policy Analysis* 3 (Fall 1977): 521–45.

—. *Social Science Research and Decision-Making.* New York: Columbia University Press, 1980.

—, ed. *Using Social Research in Public Policy Making.* Lexington, Mass.: D. C. Heath, 1977.

Weiss, Carol H., and Michael J. Bucuvalas. "The Challenge of Research to Decision Making." In *Using Social Research in Public Policy Making,* ed. Carol H. Weiss, 213–29. Lexington, Mass.: D. C. Heath, 1977.

Whyte, William H. *The Last Landscape.* Garden City, N.Y.: Doubleday, 1968.

Wiley, H. W. "The Conservation of the Fertility of the Soil." In *Report of the National Conservation Commission, with Accompanying Papers,* vol. 3, 269–300. Reprint, New York: Arno Press, 1972.

Williams, Melville C., and Harold L. Price. "Law of the Land: 1939." *Land Policy Review* (July–August 1939): 32–33.

Wilson, M. L. "Agricultural Conservation—An Aspect of Land Utilization." *Journal of Farm Economics* 19 (February 1937): 3–12.

—. "Facets of County Planning." *Land Policy Review* 2 (January–February 1939): 1–7.

—. "A Land Use Program for the Federal Government." *Journal of Farm Economics* 15 (April 1933): 217–35.

—. "The Report on Land of the National Resources Board." *Journal of Farm Economics* 17 (February 1935): 39–50.

Wolf, Peter. *Land in America: Its Value, Use, and Control.* New York: Pantheon Books, 1981.

Wood, William W. "Prime Lands—Definition and Policy Problems." *American Journal of Agricultural Economics* 58 (December 1976): 909–13.

Woodruff, Archibald M., ed. *The Farm and the City: Rivals or Allies?* Englewood Cliffs, N.J.: Prentice Hall, 1980.

Worster, Donald. "A Sense of Soil: Agricultural Conservation and American Culture." *Agricultural and Human Values* 2 (Fall 1985): 28–35.

Wyant, William. *Westward in Eden: The Public Lands and the Conservation Movement.* Berkeley: University of California Press, 1982.

"Yesterday's Land Figures Could Lead to Hardships for Tomorrow's Farmers." *Farm Bureau News,* 10 August 1981, 146.

Youngbert, Garth. "The Alternative Agriculture Movement." In *The New Politics of Food,* ed. Don F. Hadwiger and W. P. Browne, 227–46. Lexington, Mass.: D. C. Heath, 1979.

Zinn, Jeffrey A. "Conservation in the 1990 Farm Bill: The Revolution Continues." *Journal of Soil and Water Conservation* 46 (January–February 1991): 45–48.

Zinn, Jeffrey A., and A. Barry Carr. "The 1985 Farm Act: Hitting a Moving Target." *Forum for Applied Research and Public Policy* 3 (Summer 1988): 17–18.

Zitzmann, Warren. "FPPA Fadeout." *American Land Forum Magazine* 5 (Spring 1985): 14–15.

Index

236

Index

Date Due